NEW IDEAS FROM DEAD CEOs

ALSO BY TODD BUCHHOLZ

New Ideas from Dead Economists
From Here to Economy
Market Shock
Bringing the Jobs Home

FICTION
The Castro Gene

NEW
IDEAS
FROM
DEAD
CEOs

**Lasting Lessons from
the Corner Office**

Todd Buchholz

Collins

An Imprint of HarperCollins*Publishers*

HarperCollins books may be purchased for educational, business,
or sales promotional use. For information, please write:
Special Markets Department, HarperCollins Publishers,
10 East 53rd Street, New York, NY 10022.

FIRST EDITION

Designed by Ellen Cipriano

Printed on acid-free paper

Library of Congress Cataloging-in-Publication Data
Buchholz, Todd G.
New ideas from dead CEOs : lasting lessons from the corner office / Todd Buchholz.
p.   cm.
Includes index.
Contents: A.P. Giannini : Bank of America, the gladiator of banking — Thomas
Watson, Sr. and Jr. : IBM, a tale of two Watsons — Mary Kay Ash and Estee Lauder :
the most beautiful balance sheets — Mary Kay Ash — Estee Lauder, even the rich
like freebies — David Sarnoff : the road to 30 Rock — Ray Kroc, McDonalds king
of the road — Akio Morita : Sony, the sound of the people — Walt Disney : Disney,
the imagination machine — Sam Walton : Wal-Mart, a penny saved is a billion earned.
ISBN: 978-0-06-119762-8
ISBN-10: 0-06-119762-9
1. Chief executive officers—United States—Biography.   2. Businesspeople—
United States—History—20th century.   3. Entrepreneurship—United States—
Case studies.   4. Success in business—United States—Case studies.   I. Title.
HC102.5.A2B77 2007
338.092'273—dc22   2007060866

07   08   09   10   11   DIX/RRD   10   9   8   7   6   5   4   3   2   1

To the millions of men and women who wake up to the blare of an alarm, hug their children tight, and then go off to make CEOs look good

Contents

Introduction

Late-Night Obsessions

It is midnight during a blistering August night in New York City, 1949: Estée Lauder stands in front of a stove in a backroom kitchen with no air-conditioning, scalding her hands while stirring, struggling to get a pot of cream to congeal into a valuable cosmetic. A few blocks uptown, Thomas Watson Jr. collapses onto his bed, only to be summoned by his domineering father, who complains that the punch card machines are jamming up, and customers are dumping IBM. In Princeton, New Jersey, the prince of broadcasting, David Sarnoff, rolls up his sleeves and carries midnight coffee to his RCA scientists, who are battling to beat CBS in the race to create color television. In Tokyo, Akio Morita is crawling on his hands and knees, brushing magnetized goo onto a tape, using the bristles of a badger's belly. All this in one night. All this brought us television, DVDs, computers, and a youthful complexion.

Nobody accomplishes great things alone. Each year on the anniversary of his father's death, Thomas Watson Jr. would follow a ritual. He would sit at home quietly, take stock of IBM's latest accomplishments, and say aloud, "That's another year I've made it alone." Not really. Thomas Jr. was building on the obsession of his father. And we as consumers do the same.

These days it is common to hear about a rich businessman who began by "tinkering in his garage." I do not believe it. The marketplace is too fierce for tinkerers, too unforgiving for dilettantes. That businessman either lied about the tinkering or is lying about his bank account. Tennessee Williams was wrong. We do not depend on the kindness of strangers. *We are free riders on the obsessions of others.*

Today, our headlines blare about corporate theft, overcompensation, and underperformance. Before CEOs were known for bullying and cheating, they were known for pushing their companies to the pinnacle through their intellect, creativity, and judgment. The CEOs featured in this book were not candidates for sainthood. Many of them knew "God" only as a prefix to "damn it." But they were devoted to their businesses, not just to their egos, personal bank accounts, and yachts. Amadeo P. Giannini, who brought banking to the dockworkers in San Francisco and to people across the world through the Bank of America, swore that he would never become a millionaire. He once came perilously close and immediately wrote a charitable check for $509,000.

Are you CEO material? First, a simple test. Then a more complex test. If you had a newspaper route as a kid and turned it into a business by hiring others to help, you might be a CEO inside. If you simply tossed the papers from your Schwinn as a solitary chore and then ran off to school, you're probably a worker bee. Sam Walton made $4,000 a year with his paper route—at a time when that could buy a brand-new Schwinn and a couple of Cadillacs, too. Not that Sam would spring for a shiny brand-name set of wheels. That is part of it, too. The great CEOs understood that they were working for tomorrow. They often had to scrimp. Mary Kay Ash saved the first dollar she made selling pots and pans. Last year I visited Mary Kay's office in Dallas, which is still preserved like a pink room at Versailles. But the Renoir is a fake. Yes, Mary Kay bought a gold-plated toilet seat, but she did so to motivate her future sales executives, not to glorify her personal movements.

What is my more complex test for a great, visionary CEO? I have concluded that the subjects of this book were united by falling into the "upper tail" of three separate bell-curve distributions: First, passion or drive. Second, talent. Third, luck. All three are necessary. The bankruptcy courts are filled with brilliant, talented people who were just not willing to sweat past midnight or just not lucky enough to meet the right partner. Likewise, I am sure there are fortunate, hard-driving people experimenting in their garages, but without a clue as to what they are doing. There are no stupid people in this book—though if I someday decide to write *New Ideas from Dead Politicians,* there may be room.

This book blends the lives and the business challenges of the featured CEOs in order to expose their strengths and the circumstances they had to overcome. Luck seems like an odd subject for a book about business lessons. I am not talking about the good fortune of winning a Las Vegas jackpot. I am discussing the circumstances, good and bad, that slap us across the face or push us forward like the tailwinds on a cross-country flight. In 1906, David Sarnoff strode into the lobby of a downtown office building and knocked on the wrong door. Bad luck? The "right" door might have led him to a career writing obituaries for the *New York Herald*. By knocking on the "wrong" door, Sarnoff met Guglielmo Marconi and led America into the age of radio and television.

We do not get to choose our parents, our century, or the legal system we do business in. Six-year-old Amadeo Giannini watched a laborer shoot his father to death at the family farm. Walt Disney wept as his first cartoon success was ripped from his hands because of a contract he did not understand. Nine-year-old David Sarnoff showed up on the docks from Russia without knowing any English, after a childhood of utter isolation. The CEOs here navigated a century marked by two world wars, the Great Depression, and a globalized economy that shredded dependable business traditions. We will see how they coped and how they led.

In this book, I am not trying merely to summarize biographies. I have chosen these CEOs by deploying several criteria. First, they had to be innovators, not just outstanding managers. *It is better to make yourself obsolete than to wait and let your competitors do it for you.* These CEOs did not wait. They pushed hard. Second, the CEOs had to be interesting to me. I am sure there is a wonderful CEO who led the charge to turn dung into red bricks, but we can leave him for a sequel. The CEOs discussed in this book teach us about the forces that made the twentieth century so uplifting in its technology and brutal in its politics. Thomas Watson Jr. piloted military missions over dangerous skies. Mary Kay Ash figured out how to empower women when most businesspeople imagined them only sitting at home, worrying how to rid their husband's shirts of that stubborn "ring around the collar." Third, and most important, I chose to focus on CEOs who teach us lessons that we can apply today, either as managers or as investors, trying to figure out which companies may be worthy of our portfolios. Therefore, you will encounter Dell, Krispy Kreme, AOL–Time Warner, and Airbus, companies that emerged long after these CEOs had passed from the scene. Ray Kroc from McDonald's would have saved Krispy Kreme from its meltdown. Sam Walton would have applauded Carnival Cruise Lines. We will see why.

As you plunge forward, you may notice a social theme that also unites these outstanding CEOs. They believed in progress, in a century that would give more freedom and more choices to more people. They were convinced that the huddled masses would indeed breathe free. They would bet on the people. Giannini lent to those who looked torn and tattered. J. P. Morgan would have sneered. Kroc contended that a working man could launch a successful franchise. Disney imagined a park that would invite the lowliest laborer to spend time with his children. Mary Kay insisted that working-class women could have skin as soft as any Hollywood starlet's. The CEOs in this book placed the right bet. They bet on progress and that a rising tide would lift all boats. In this book, the century literally starts on a boat, with David Sarnoff crushed into steerage along with hundreds of desperate souls. By the end of the century, Ted Arison from Carnival Cruise Lines built luxury cruise ships to carry the children and grandchildren of those immigrants on tropical vacations.

Of course, each of these CEOs failed at some point. Faced with bankruptcy and defections, they could have succumb to psychological depression or the siren call of politicians offering class warfare. They each heard nos, the tsk-tsks of friends, and a schadenfreude chorus scoffing at their failure. But they pushed on, energized by passion, ego, money, and the promise of glory. You cannot build a successful business or economy on the kindness of strangers. These CEOs relied on more dependable, more human drives. Drives that took them on fascinating rides.

Come find out.

NEW IDEAS FROM DEAD CEOs

1

A. P. Giannini: Bank of America

The Gladiator of Banking

He was a big man, but he was terrified. At 5:18 a.m., his wooden house shook and bucked like an insane bronco, tossing his pregnant wife out of bed. She clung to him; he was over six feet two, with massive shoulders and a chin they could have used on Mount Rushmore. But even he could not hold on as the floor beneath their feet turned to waves of sloshing sand and soil. Amadeo and Clorinda Giannini looked up at the writhing ceiling and then tore across the hallway to the bedrooms of their seven children, throwing their bodies over them, as continual jolts battered the walls for twenty-eight of the longest seconds of their lives. For their son Mario, a hemophiliac, a splintered post could be fatal.

And then silence. The walls shimmied but finally rested as the small children shrieked. They were among the lucky ones, for their house was in San Mateo, seventeen miles from the epicenter of the San Francisco earthquake on April 18, 1906. We still do not know exactly how many died—more than three thousand for sure—in the tightly packed city, where gas lines ripped open and the relentless flames tossed penniless wharf dwellers into the streets alongside the moneyed dowagers of Nob Hill. The fleeing and looting would soon begin. Amid the chaos and lawlessness, any sane person would fear for his life and his pocketbook.

Amadeo Peter, known as A.P., knew what he had to do next. He had to open his bank to the public. He had to defy the blocked roads, the roaming thugs, the jealous competitors. On this day when San Francisco turned into a flaming crucible, the postman stayed home. Herodotus's ancient promise about "Neither snow nor rain nor heat nor gloom of night" did not cover seismic eruptions. But the thirty-five-year-old A.P. held himself to a higher standard. He launched himself on a grueling trip just to cross the seventeen miles to his bank. The trains were jammed with mobs. Fearing damaged tracks, the engineers slowed the pace to a crawl. A.P. jumped off. He could thumb a ride or even walk faster, despite his lumbering gait. Five hours later, he trudged into the heart of the city, a city he could barely recognize through black smoke, pluming flames, and an endless series of explosions as firefighters dynamited buildings, hoping to rob the fires of kindling wood.

Was he insane? Hungry for power? For glory? Or just blindly devoted to the "little guy" who would need cash in a moment of despair? Not even A.P. himself knew, but by the time he reached his bank, he realized he had made a terrible mistake. Despite his size, his determination, and his fame, not even he could protect the bank's bags of silver and gold from the marauding gangs.

This chapter tells the story of a man who could stare into the eyes of ruthless outlaws, yet still trust his fellow man. A. P. Giannini invented modern banking because he, not the Morgans of New York, the Rothschilds of London, nor the Riggs of Washington, realized that small-business owners, family men, and yes, even housewives could be entrusted with money. Before A.P. came to San Francisco, banks were only for rich people, and the bars on the teller cages kept everyone in their cells. A.P. took a hacksaw to the bars and liberated the American economy from the past. Most countries around the world are still learning his lessons.

THE EARLY YEARS

Before there was a Bank of America, there was a Bank of Italy, and before there was a Bank of Italy, there was a young Italian couple running the Swiss Hotel in San Jose, California. A.P.'s father, Luigi, was the son of a vineyard owner in Genoa, and his mother, a very young beauty named Virginia from the walled city of Lucca in Tuscany. In 1871, after making money on the bustling hotel, Luigi bought a forty-acre orchard that could make his relatives in the old country envious with its bright red strawberries and cherries. A.P. was born in 1870 and quickly learned to help with farmwork and to play games with friends in the fields.

The Gianninis provided just one story of the thousands of Italian immigrant tales that were created at the turn of the century in Northern California. *The Most Happy Fella,* a 1956 Broadway hit, with songs such as "Abbondanza" ("Abundance") and "She Gonna Come Home Wit' Me," featured Italian American orchard hands of this era. The number of Italians soared in the 1890s, and by the 1930s, second- and third-generation Italians made up one-fifth of the population, which included a youngster named Giuseppe Paolo DiMaggio, who in the streets of San Francisco would learn to hit a curveball as well as anyone ever would. While San Francisco bulged with gold rush speculators in the 1850s, by 1870 there was only one way to make money in the Bay Area: hard work. People rode the new transcontinental railroad not with sieves, seeking a glimmer of gold specks, but with shovels and rakes. The money was in the land, but you had to coax it out using a strong back. Between 1870 and 1890, the number of farms in the United States jumped by nearly 80 percent, to 4.5 million, as did the value of farm property.

Even as a boy A.P. witnessed the rich harvests and saw wagons and crates loaded onto steamers and trains bound for New York, Boston, and abroad. Though A.P. attended school in a one-room schoolhouse in Alviso, he did not grow up in some isolated rural outpost. He attended school with French, German, Armenian, and Greek children. Not even his teachers could pronounce his Italian name correctly, so they called him "Amador Jenning." A.P. lived on the edge of a new globalized world. All he lacked was the patience to watch it go by.

He grew up faster than he should have. On August 13, 1876, young A.P. was standing in front of his house when his father drove up in a horse-drawn wagon filled with produce. Suddenly, a field worker popped up, infuriated with Luigi. It was a money dispute. A dollar bill was in question. As A.P. stood by, the laborer reached down to his waistband aimed a gun, and fired a murderous shot at Luigi. Luigi died quickly.

A.P.'s twenty-two-year-old mother was made of strong stuff. Of course Virginia mourned, but soon after Luigi's death, she threw all her energy and her shrewd mind into vital tasks: keeping the orchard going and her three children fed. She did not shirk and, with A.P. alongside, would manage the fields and ride with the crops on a boat to the market in San Francisco. Along the way, she would meet a young man named Lorenzo Scatena, who would drive her produce to an agriculture dealer in the city. They married in 1880, though it was hardly an even trade. She showed up at the altar owning a teeming orchard; he showed up with a horse. A caring man, Lorenzo moved to the Giannini orchard and proved to be a wonderful stepfather for A.P. and his brothers, who forever called him "Pop." Though Lorenzo had charm to spare, Virginia quickly found out why he drove a truck. Lorenzo simply did not have the green thumb needed to produce bumper crops in the Santa Clara Valley.

Virginia was too ambitious to preside over a farm that was not living up to its potential. She gazed up at the mansions of Nob Hill and figured that the Giannini-Scatena clan was clever enough to climb up that slope. She organized the family to move to the big city when A.P. was twelve. It was probably the smartest and the most frustrating decision she would ever make.

A.P. was a math whiz at school, though he cringed when called "teacher's pet." But school could not keep him in his seat. He did not suffer from attention deficit disorder. He simply heard the call of the docks, the merchants haggling, and the ships' horns blaring. He needed to be in the mix, like Pop Scatena, who got a job with Galli and Company brokering fruits and vegetables. The produce business was a nighttime affair. When the exhausted day workers slept, the merchants would rifle through crates of apples and artichokes, assessing their quality and bargaining on price: "How many ya got? What's your freight? Someone gettin' a vig?" It was clatter, it was boisterous, and it was macho. To A.P., it was Verdi.

When ambitious Virginia prodded Pop to demand a raise, Galli said no. So Pop quit, and the next day, he launched L. Scatena & Company. In his first month, he cleared $1,500 in profits, not a bad raise from the $250 the Gallis paid him. Pop had a secret weapon, of course: A.P., who shadowed him through the night.

Pop did not mind his quick-witted stepson by his side. "We left home at midnight; 1:00 a.m. was a late hour—often too late—to show up on the docks," Scatena recalled.[1] When dawn broke and all the tomatoes and artichokes had been crated away, Pop Scatena counted the profits and met his accountant, a crusty Irishman named Tim Delay. Delay noticed right away that A.P. was a triple threat: he worked hard, loved the brokering business, and could keep an eye on a balance sheet. The kid had a future. After an early breakfast, A.P. would hurry to beat the school bell. This dual life would not last long. At age fifteen, against his mother's advice, he chose to work full-time for Pop. To placate her and sharpen his analytical skills, he took a three-month accounting course at a local business school. He breezed through it in six weeks and hardly missed a moment on the docks.

At fifteen A.P. had piercing, hooded eyes, thick black hair, and a muscular body that had passed six feet in height. He towered over most Italian men, who stood on average just five feet four inches.[2] His size came in handy on occasion when a left hook to the chin of an unscrupulous competitor helped to seal a deal on fresh cantaloupe. With his powerful build, confident manner, and farm-raised expertise in crops, A.P. made a devastating impression among the brokers, shippers, and buyers on the docks. Like the rare politician who actually likes kissing babies, A.P. loved schmoozing, haggling, and jostling with the myriad ethnic characters who made up the produce trade. Pop's business involved brokering, buying, and speculating on future crops. At first Pop and A.P. traveled together up and down the Sacramento River, bidding for the best produce. Eventually the young teen would make the trips alone. He would do anything for a deal. Once he spotted a competitor riding a buggy to make an offer to a farmer. Seeing a shortcut, A.P. stripped off his clothes and swam across a swampy pond while holding his clothes above water in order to beat the buggy rider to the farmer's house.[3]

During one season, A.P. sensed that peaches would be in short supply. He bought up as many as he could, well before the price doubled. "It was a big gamble but I guessed right. I made $50,000 for the Scatena firm with the deal."[4] One of his admirers, a competitor named George Webster, observed, "I've seen men go against him, after having rehearsed themselves [to] buy beans . . . at three cents a pound under his price; but before the story ever stumbled from their lips, they would be signing their names to an order at his figure." [5] When A.P. hit age twenty-one, Pop granted him half the firm of L. Scatena & Company, which flourished, bringing in hundreds of thousands of dollars each year.

When A.P. was not wading through muck, speculating on peach crops, or hoisting crates onto carriages, he cleaned up quite nicely. Like the Stephen Sondheim character who says this "bum'll be Beau Brummell," A.P. would stroll on New Year's Day adorned with a top hat, gloves, and a gold-tipped walking stick. At twenty-one, he ran into a young woman named Clorinda Cuneo, daughter of one of the wealthiest Italian immigrants in the city. That she wore an engagement ring from a fiancé in Europe made little difference to A.P., who wooed her and won. The poor guy in the old country did not stand a chance. Soon, the children started coming; meanwhile, the money kept flowing into A.P. and Pop's bulging pockets. Following his father-in-law's lead, A.P. put the money in real estate. After about fifteen years with Pop, A.P. decided to "retire" from the fruits-and-vegetable business. He was just thirty-one but now felt too restless to manage a mature business like L. Scatena & Company. Pop bought him out for $100,000, and A.P. had already socked away $300,000 more. In today's dollars, this would be a hefty $9.6 million nest egg.

INTO THE BREACH WITH BANKING

Retire at thirty-one? Hardly. A.P. was just looking for a new challenge. He found it in real estate, investing, and then in banking. Before A.P. retired from L. Scatena & Company, he and Pop were already drifting toward banking, as farmers began asking for advances to help pay for seeds, tools, and labor as they planted the next season's crops. Instead of asking for interest on the loans, the Scatena company paid a lower price at harvesttime. Because Pop and A.P. were keen judges of character and farming skills, they could provide credit without jeopardizing their own profit-and-loss statements.

A.P.'s real entry into banking came when his father-in-law, Joseph Cuneo, died in 1902, at age ninety-two. (A.P.'s daughter Claire would also live to ninety-two, having been the first woman to serve on the boards of Bank of America and Sears Roebuck.) Joseph was a sharp investor, but not much of a detail man, as it turned out: he left eleven children but no will. He did pencil in one important item; for executor of his assets, he wrote, "A.P. Giannini." Aside from his real estate work, Cuneo had also served on the board of a local bank, the Columbus Savings & Loan Society.

Eager to serve, A.P. took Cuneo's former seat at the boardroom table. He had ideas, networking contacts, and advertising slogans ready to share with the bank managers in order to expand the bank. But this was not the wharf, where the sharpest elbow and the loudest voice reigned. Even though the Columbus S&L was run by Italian immigrants, it had all the vigor of J. P. Morgan's last cigar. In New York, Morgan had set the standard for banks. He had been a stodgy young man who grew up to be a stodgy old man and could hardly use the word "competition" without first uttering the adjective "ruinous." [6] Mimicking the Morgan banks, the Columbus S&L wanted very little to do with lending to people. Oh, developers, yes! Successful moguls, step right in! But the ma-and-pa owner of a deli? Or a hat shop? What was the point? They were either shiftless or too poor to pay back a loan. A.P. bristled at the tone and irritated his fellow board members. He had new ideas, and he could not be stopped. How could he put his new ideas into practice?

He charged into the office of a diminutive but spirited friend named James J. Fagan, who served as vice president of the American National Bank. He made Fagan, obviously an Irishman, into an honorary paisan and said, "Giacomo, I'm going to start a bank. Tell me how to do it!"

Fagan blinked and warned A.P. that San Francisco already had more than enough banks. But A.P. was not listening; he was ready to launch a totally new kind of bank.

NEW IDEAS FROM A. P. GIANNINI

From Rabble to Riches

A.P. was no fool. He realized that his best chance of success was not to challenge the big banks for their best customers. Instead he would go after the customers they sneered at. The haughty Columbus bank lent money to the mighty White Star shipping line, the people who would launch the *Titanic*. A.P. would gladly lend money to the makers of little lifeboats and dinghies.

Perhaps the best way to think about A.P.'s revolutionary idea is to consider that A.P.'s biggest fan in Hollywood turned out to be the director Frank Capra. Capra, a Sicilian immigrant, would later direct two films that recalled A.P. The first, *American Madness* (1932), starred Walter Huston as a folksy banker who fights off a bank run and loans money on the basis of character. The second, and far more famous, was the Christmas classic *It's a Wonderful Life,* in which Jimmy Stewart's character, Peter Bailey, argues with a nasty monopolist banker named Potter.

The crotchety and bitter Potter believes that Bailey's flexible loan policies would only produce "a discontented, lazy rabble instead of a thrifty working class."

In response, Peter Bailey delivers an inspired paean to Potter's "rabble," the working people: "They do most of the working and paying and living and dying in this community. Well, is it too much to have them work and pay and live and die in a couple of decent rooms and a bath? Anyway, my father didn't think so. People were human beings to him but to you, a warped, frustrated old man, they're cattle. Well, in my book, he died a much richer man than you'll ever be."[7]

To A. P. Giannini, lending to the little people was not charity. It was damn good business. He was willing to ride the wave of America's wealth building and had the striking insight to see that small businesses might be just as creditworthy as big businesses. If you visit Manhattan today, you can search in vain for the trophy signs that used to mark the Pan Am Building and RCA Building. Those were dominant names that sparked the interest of traditional banks, which were absolutely delighted to cozy up to them. But those names have vanished. Now stroll over to Seventh Avenue, and you can still see the neon lights marking the Carnegie Deli, a landmark since 1937. Giannini realized that a multimillion-dollar behemoth might not have the staying power of a good pastrami sandwich.

Years later A.P. testified before Congress and explained, "The little fellow is the best customer that a bank can have. . . . He starts in with you and stays to the end. Whereas the big fellow is only with you so long as he can get something out of you." And so in 1904, A.P. recruited Giacomo Fagan and opened up the Bank of Italy. The Bank of Italy not only aimed at a different kind of customer, but also revolutionized the economics of banking and the economy itself. The Morgan model spurned deposits. If you ambled into the lobby of a Morgan bank and asked to open an account or take out a loan, the bankers would have looked at you as if you had just asked to lunch with Napoleon. The banks were like private clubs. Yes, they held deposits in their vaults, but merely to provide a convenience for wealthy people who could no longer fit their excessive savings under their mattresses. Unlike banks today, those deposits were not immediately lent out to others. In 1900, if the Morgan Bank had $500 million in deposits, it would basically keep $500 million in its vaults. Today the Federal Reserve Board requires banks to keep just 10 percent readily on hand. The remaining 90 percent can be lent out, so it multiplies through the economy, allowing the economy to expand.[8]

Around the time A.P. established the Bank of Italy, Jews, Italians, Greeks, and other immigrant groups on the East Coast were forming community finance groups. Often called "burial societies" (because part of the goal of many of their members was to save enough money for a proper burial), the groups would create a pool of savings to lend to new arrivals and new entrepreneurs. New entrepreneurs would be obligated to plow some profits back into the pool to aid the next wave. Even in the 1980s and 1990s, this model financed many of the Korean grocers in New York City.

Spread the Word and Fling Open the Doors

If A.P. aimed at a new set of customers, how would he get them? Columbus and Morgan got their clients in the parlors and country clubs, where all the borrowers knew precisely which fork to use when. A.P. knew the answer: back to the docks! He would bring the bank to the people by trolling the wharf for clients, by advertising, and by offering the best rates in town. From the perspective of traditional banks, this was an outrageous assault on good taste and possibly a crime. Newspaper advertising? Traditional bankers did not believe that the hoi polloi could read. In the first few weeks, plumbers, teamsters, and tomato packers wandered into the Bank of Italy. They had no idea what to do, until A.P. and his small team taught them about deposit slips and interest rates. While tradesmen could never be taken seriously by old-line bank managers, there was another reason they felt welcome at the Bank of Italy. A.P. promulgated a rule that the Bank of Italy would not keep "banker's hours." How could a welder get to a bank that was open only between 9 a.m. and 5 p.m.? A.P. kept the bank open evenings and often on Sundays. An abomination!

Even today, I cannot understand why so many businesses refuse to cater to their customers and maintain flexible hours. Have you ever tried to shop at a car dealer on a weekend? They are almost never open on Sundays, and even on Saturdays, the sales staff may be limited. How many people can afford to leave their desks on, say, a Tuesday morning to test-drive a Pontiac? Unfortunately for General Motors, few bother on any day. Imagine: 7-Eleven's founders chose their name in 1927 because they were bragging about how hard they worked: "By God, we're up before anybody else and won't go to sleep until everyone is tucked into bed at 11 p.m." Now, I drive past a 7-Eleven at 6:30 in the morning and honk my horn: "Get up you lazy layabouts." The truth, of course, is that 7-Eleven is now open around the clock to please its customers. Unfortunately, many other companies still do not understand the message A.P. Giannini sent back in 1904.

Though the Bank of Italy's early advertisements did not have the slick appeal of today's jingles and flashes of color, A.P. used print advertising to spell out clearly the bank's philosophy:

> The Bank of Italy has been, from its inception and is now, ready and anxious to make loans to people owning, or intending to build, their own homes—to the smaller mortgage borrowers who need $1000 or less.
>
> The Bank of Italy has built up its present reputation, its present enormous resources, largely by catering to the small depositor—the wage earner, the producer, the small business man, the man who owns a small home or a piece of improved property, the man who is the bone and sinew of . . . California's progress."[9]

Traditional banks despised the advertisements for two reasons. First, they believed that advertising cheapened the image of their profession.

Back in A.P.'s day, the outfield fences of ballparks were painted with signs advertising, for example, Gem razor blades ("Avoid 5 O'Clock Shadow"), Lifebuoy soap ("The Red Sox Use It!"), and Vimms vitamins ("Get that Vimms Feeling!"). Honus Wagner was the first celebrity endorser, autographing a Louisville Slugger in 1905. But a bank was not a bar of soap, especially since professional bankers looked down on the public as the great unwashed. Banks also opposed advertising for a second, and more biting reason: advertising drove down prices and profits! Once the Bank of Italy started offering a 3.5 percent return to savers, the big banks felt pressure to pony up, too. Likewise, when A.P.'s bank charged just 6 percent for a mortgage, how could other San Francisco banks get away with heftier fees? They could not.

A classic economic study shows that eyeglasses cost far less in states that permit optometrists to advertise.[10] Have you noticed how the cost of laser eye surgery has plummeted in the past decade? Have you also noticed all the radio and billboard ads promoting expert ophthalmologic surgeons? As annoying as the ads may be, there is a connection between more information and more value for the consumer. Today's industry of quick-lube auto shops would have been impossible if auto dealerships could have prevented their advertising. We should be intensely suspicious of industries that forbid advertising. Think how much money lawyers made selling boilerplate wills when they were insulated from comparison shopping. Similarly, you can thank A. P. Giannini in part when you pay $8 to trade stock rather than handing your brokerage house a huge cut.[11]

Although A.P. was unleashing a revolution, in the early days, he could afford only a few key people. He lured away from the Columbus bank a hand-smooching smoothie named Armando Pedrini to charm the ladies and backslap the men. Pedrini was like everybody's favorite maître d', only instead of rolling over an antipasto cart, he rolled over interest-bearing savings accounts. While A.P. could not afford to hire a large staff, he did make a strategic decision about the bank's ownership: he sold shares widely and resisted any concentration of shares. Of the three thousand bank shares issued, no one could own more than one hundred. No exceptions, not even for A.P. himself. Within a year, the Bank of Italy surpassed $1 million in assets. The Columbus people noticed and were furious. They had been sure that A.P.'s little folly would flounder, but they had to wait six years, until 1910, to see a mortgage foreclosure on the books of the Bank of Italy.[12] But Columbus executives burned for another reason. A.P. always knew how to tweak his competitors. He launched his Bank of Italy at the corner of Columbus Street and Washington Street—in a building that rented space to Columbus! The Columbus people erupted with anger, sued, and lost. When Columbus paid the rent, it had to make out the check to its former director and new rival, A.P. Giannini and the Bank of Italy. After a few months of this humiliation, Columbus packed its bags of gold and marched to a building across the street.

A.P. had another reason to locate the bank at this corner location. It was just one block from the city jail, and A.P. figured that policemen would routinely be patrolling the area. This was no joke. In the early days of banking, a solid vault or safe was a rare thing. Many banks had been created in the nineteenth century simply because a general-store merchant happened to have a good safe, and customers began to ask whether they could keep their valuables in it. When A.P. opened the Bank of Italy, he could not afford a highly reliable safe. He called the bank's strongbox a "cracker box without a top."[13] To offset such a flimsy security system, A.P.'s friend Giacomo Fagan (who at the time served as head cashier at the Crocker National Bank and would later jump ship to the Bank of Italy) arranged for A.P. to keep valuables at the well-established Crocker. Every morning a buggy carrying bags of gold and silver would track across town from the impenetrable Crocker safe to the cracker box and reverse the trip every evening.

Price and Pride

A.P.'s Bank of Italy was not the only game in town for small-time borrowers. Even though established brands like Columbus and the Crocker bank turned down men looking to borrow $100, there was an alternative: the loan sharks. The Bank of Italy quickly quashed the loan sharks by lending at comparatively low rates, around 6 percent, instead of the typical 20 percent per month. In cities such as San Francisco, one-fifth of families were subject to loan sharks and the bloody mitts of their enforcers.[14] In the 1920s, Bertolt Brecht came along and told us of a certain businessman named Macheath, nicknamed "Mack the Knife": "When that shark bites, with his teeth, dear/Scarlet billows start to spread."

During the early years, the Bank of Italy earned a nice spread between what it paid lenders and what it charged borrowers, roughly 3 percent. Today Citigroup and JPMorgan would be delighted to get that spread. Back in 1904, though, the forerunners of those institutions mocked A.P., who laughed all the way to his own bank.

Who's Worthy of a Loan?

A.P. asserted an intriguing economic concept while servicing the "little man." Conventional bankers warned that offering low interest rates would attract marginal borrowers, the bad credit risks. By charging high rates, banks were weeding out the deadbeats. A.P. took the opposite view. First of all, he believed that low interest rates would also attract good credit risks. Everyone likes a bargain, after all. Even today, I am astounded at how many affluent friends of mine brag about the bargains they nab at Costco. Second, and more intriguing, he observed that people who searched for bargains—in this case, low borrowing rates—were demonstrating their intelligence and industriousness. In terms used by modern economists, they were signaling their creditworthiness by responding to better terms. *Searching for better terms was a form of sweat equity.* A.P. argued that "the man who will fight for cheaper interest rates is the one we want to loan money to."[15] For over forty years the Northeast-based clothier Sy Syms has sold discounted designer wear to bargain hunters, festooning the following slogan on his stores: "An educated consumer is our best customer." The nattily attired A. P. Giannini beat Sy to the punch by sixty years.

Before we go any further, I should note that for all A.P.'s talk of "the little fellow" and the "man who is the bone and sinew" of the economy, A.P. doffed his hat to women and children. The minutes from the first board meeting of the Bank of Italy show that of the first eleven large loans approved, at least three went to women. Later, A.P. opened a women's department and again launched a complete advertising campaign: "Meet me at the women's banking department!"[16] Even aside from having a women's department, the Bank of Italy hardly looked like other banks. A.P. believed in "open-office architecture" ninety years before Silicon Valley whiz kids started hurtling down office hallways on skateboards. He took down the intimidating teller cages and pushed his office to the middle of the floor. No executives would be hiding in cushy offices behind some grand mural.

A.P. and his people knocked on doors in every ethnic neighborhood in the city. He later required that every staffer speak at least two different languages. From the Sicilian sardine hauler to the Mexican strawberry picker to the timber worker in Oregon, A.P. wanted to sign up customers. When he heard about a tremendous salmon run up north, he sent a man to Alaska to sign up the lucky fishermen. Many years later, during World War II, A.P. actually set up banks in Japanese internment camps. His success brought great pride to the Italian community, of course. One man told the *San Francisco Examiner*, "I was a dago. Now I am an American."[17]

A.P.'s bank representatives even invaded the school system, signing up forty thousand children, offering them savings accounts and literally collecting the nickels and dimes each week. The administrative costs were huge, and the bank made no money on the accounts. Nonetheless, the children developed good savings habits. This tradition continues in many communities and is an effective tool for developing allegiances, too. When I first arrived as an economics graduate student at Cambridge University, I was surprised that my classmates were always talking about whether their bank manager would let them go on vacation or buy a television. I didn't know my bank manager—why did they? I quickly learned that my friends were routinely permitted to write overdrafts, unlike my experience back home. But the managers at Barclays let them. Why? Because Barclays was slugging it out in a hotly competitive match with NatWest and wanted to make long-lasting friends among twentysomethings. Seventy years before, A.P. boasted that 60 percent of the children in his school account program stayed on the Bank of Italy books.

What's Worthy of a Loan?

If you asked the Columbus, Crocker, or Morgan bank what constituted collateral, you would hear about gold bricks or a solid stone building.

Once again, A.P. took a wider view. He once said, "The West hasn't even started yet," and he fervently believed that the twentieth-century economy would no longer be tied to the gilded age or the stone age of "hard assets." He was right. What has been the value of Coca-Cola's formula? Or the iPod's sleek style? Or George Lucas's imagination and the *Star Wars* franchise? Each is worth billions, yet none is made of gold or rock. Quite simply, A.P. was willing to consider nearly anything as collateral. Again, given the development of the modern economy, his timing was exquisite. He lent on cows, clothing, automobiles, apricot crops, and even motion pictures. He did not do this naively. He directed the Bank of Italy, and later Bank of America, to become an expert in these areas. When the bank was building an automobile financing group or an agricultural arm, it hired seasoned professionals who could actually give advice to the auto dealer or farmer looking for the loan. Other banks refused to get involved with livestock lending. A.P.'s bank lobbied the Borden Milk Company for business and figured out how to lend to dairymen in exchange for the future value of the milk. They limited the loans to $30 per cow, but that was enough to turn the dairymen into loyal customers. In later years, the bank held an enormous portfolio of refrigerator loans to ma-and-pa homeowners.

With his brother Attilio, a medical doctor who frequently argued with A.P., the Bank of Italy later began financing upstarts in Hollywood. Upstarts with names like Charlie Chaplin, Samuel Goldwyn, and Cecil B. DeMille—the voice of God in *The Ten Commandments*. From *Wuthering Heights* to *King Kong* to *Mutiny on the Bounty*, A.P.'s bank underwrote some of the most brilliant (and on occasion some of the tackiest) stuff ever to come out on film. In the 1930s, when Walt Disney was struggling to pay for *Snow White*, Disney acted out the whole show for the Gianninis and ultimately won over the bankers. The film raked in $8 million, and Disney quickly paid a tidy sum to the bank. A.P.'s insight was not about distinguishing brilliance from schlock. *His insight was to recognize the collateral value of the film negative.* When most Hollywood professionals were tossing old negatives into the dustbin, A.P. wanted to retrieve them. How prescient! The invention of cable television, the VCR, and later the DVD demonstrated that the real value of studios would come from their old film libraries. When Ted Turner bought MGM from Kirk Kerkorian in

1986, he was paying for the catalog, not the sound stages, costumes, and microphones. Today, Michael Jackson's ownership of the $500 million Beatles' music catalog is about the only thing that keeps him from the poorhouse. That and crafty lawyers.

Back to the Earthquake: The Size of the Safe Matters

In the style of old movie reels, we started this chapter with a cliffhanger. It was 1906, and A.P. fought his way into the erupting, flaming disaster of the San Francisco earthquake. When he arrived, he realized that he and his beloved bank were in desperate shape. Soon after the earthquake, but before the fires and looting began, Armando Pedrini had bravely ridden a horse-drawn buggy to the Crocker National Bank to withdraw the Bank of Italy's gold and silver, worth $80,000, from Crocker's immense and impregnable steel vaults. This was the entire hard asset base of the bank. The Crocker people could not understand Pedrini's bravado; they had bolted their doors shut and were staying closed on this horrible day. But Pedrini thought differently. Call it machismo. Call it brave. Call it stupid. But when A.P. arrived, he realized that amid fires and a "cracker box" safe, his bank's valuables would be subjected to dynamite explosions, toppling buildings, and worst of all, vandals and thieves. Nearly thirty thousand buildings would be crumbling about them. A.P. had just dodged bricks and cement blocks. All he and Pedrini had was a flimsy six-shooter that seemed better suited for a kids' game of cowboys and Indians.

A.P. barked his orders, instructing two men to go to Scatena's warehouse and come back with two fruit trucks—and to stack crates of fruits and vegetables on top. What was he doing? They needed guns, not oranges and bananas. As the mystified men left on their dangerous mission, A.P. and a few others began piling up bank records and some fixtures on the sidewalk. When the fruit trucks returned, pulled by frightened horses, A.P. stealthily dragged out the bags of gold and silver and stuffed them at the bottom of the trucks. Then he ordered the men to pile high all of the fruit and vegetables. The hard assets of the young Bank of Italy were now hidden under oranges, tomatoes, and bananas at the bottom of a truck with the name "L. Scatena & Co. Fruits and Vegetables." A.P. leaped onto a truck and cracked the whip, and the well-concealed, mobile bank began a treacherous trek out of town. Amid the chaos, the wagons bumped against fleeing San Franciscans, and when night fell, A.P. could hardly believe that the bags of gold and silver had not simply spilled into the streets: "We didn't have any guards. All the police and soldiers were fighting the fire. . . . I saw would-be robbers on every street corner."[18]

A.P. directed the trucks to his house in San Mateo. He hid the $80,000 under the fireplace, just in case unwanted guests showed up. He slept in front of the fireplace. He had rescued the life savings of many people. It was the right decision. The Bank of Italy's building later collapsed, and the Crocker National Bank was rubble, though its fireproof vaults stood erect in the smoldering mess. It took weeks for the steel to cool enough to be opened.

But now what? What would A.P. do with the assets that, he later said, smelled like orange juice for weeks after the earthquake? Three days after the earthquake, on Saturday, April 21, San Francisco's bankers met to discuss their next move. Most seemed paralyzed, some because they did not have the fortitude, others because their banks were still burning or their vaults were simply too hot to touch. Many agreed that their banks could not reopen until the fall. But the city's economy desperately needed cash and would spiral downward to barbarism without it.

A.P. was never a man to take orders. Let others baa like sheep following the consensus. He announced that he would open his bank the next day, on a Sunday! You can imagine the outrage. A Sunday? You can imagine the disdain of the other bankers: Your bank is gone, Giannini. Are you blind or insane?

The next day A. P. Giannini wrote himself into the history of banking. He posted a letter to his depositors and declared that the bank holiday was over. He planted $10,000 at the bottom of a buggy and rode it from San Mateo to the wharf at the end of Washington Street. At the wharf, he and some key employees rolled two large wooden barrels and stood them up about six feet apart from each other. They hoisted a heavy plank and dropped it on the barrels. The Bank of Italy was a plank by the wharf. But it was open and the only game in town. He did not need a marble lobby to reopen his bank. Now, this was thinking outside the box!

Soon the lines formed, and, of course, the $10,000 in funds would be overwhelmed. But like the Jimmy Stewart character in *It's a Wonderful Life,* Giannini coaxed his weary customers into accepting smaller loans, so that he could literally spread the wealth:"Could you get by with half?" he'd ask gently but firmly.

His enthusiasm helped launch an economic revival. With his guidance the Italian North Beach neighborhoods recovered more quickly than others. His people scoured the destroyed neighborhoods, asking the refugees to deposit any extra cash so he could multiply it into a recovery. He knew that the city needed lumber, so he pressed cash into the hands of sea captains, urging them to go north to Oregon and Washington State and return with lumber. By December 1906, all the banks had reopened, but the Bank of Italy was the only one that had doubled its assets and multiplied its goodwill and reputation a thousandfold.

Unpardonable Sin

A.P.'s plank on the wharf was a stunning example of leadership. But to conventional bankers, his wooden plank was something else: a branch. They believed that banks should stay in one place, not expand throughout a city, a state, or, heaven forfend, the whole country. This is hard for us to imagine today, when we can withdraw cash from ATM machines in Nepal. But the California League of Independent Bankers (CLIB) called branch banking "the menace of the hour," "economically wrong, monopolistic in nature, and un-American in principle." [19] This "wicked" system had already taken hold in Canada. In 1908, A.P. attended a Denver meeting of the American Bankers Association. A little-known university president named Woodrow Wilson delivered a speech that elicited moans. Wilson asserted that banks were the most jealously regarded and least liked instrument of business in the country . . . remote from the people [who] regard them . . . as . . . hostile power." He argued that branch banking would open up more opportunities for local shop owners and farmers who were currently beholden to just a few local banks. The attitude of "plain men" would be "changed utterly within a generation," he added.

A.P. knew that California was the perfect launchpad. Small, local banks simply could not handle the seasonal demands of farmers. With so many different harvests and plantings at different times of year, dispersed branches made a great deal of sense. Why shouldn't the owner of an orange grove in Escondido, California, be able to borrow from a big bank in San Francisco? By borrowing from a big bank, the orange grove owner could get the brain power and agricultural know-how of a larger entity. Finally, A.P. realized that by operating branches throughout the state, a city bank would have an even more diversified portfolio, and therefore, be less risky. Hadn't the earthquake proved the adage about having your eggs in one basket? A.P. concluded that there was only one clear reason to oppose branch banking: local banks were afraid of the competition.

A.P. started to move forward, despite the anger he aroused in the profession. He visited Canada and observed the branches of Montreal- and Toronto-based banks. Though he admired the system, he pledged that his branches would have a local flavor, rather than looking like they were taking orders from central command. The manager of a rural branch should be from that town, not an alien who just rode in on the train from back east. Further, the new branch should sell ownership shares to people in the community, so they would have a stake in the success.

A.P. began his revolution with a branch in San Jose—his birthplace—in the middle of the Santa Clara Valley's agricultural belt. He knew the land; he knew the people. He was not going to go on a foolhardy spree, erecting buildings all over the state. Instead, he planned to purchase existing banks that needed more capital to expand. Officers at San Jose's Commercial and Savings Bank, one of the state's oldest, had actually traveled to San Francisco to ask for A.P.'s help. Taking over an existing bank was cheaper than building a new one; in addition, it allowed the Bank of Italy to draw on local management experience. A.P.'s deputy James Bacigalupi explained to Congress that the Bank of Italy would acquire "a staff, an advisory board, and local stockholders who were interested in the locality and familiar with local people, values, and conditions."[20]

After taking over the San Jose bank, A.P. spent years examining the dynamics and the viability of branch banking. Finally, he felt confident enough to make a run for statewide banking. As A.P. visited other regions, the venom started flowing, and latent bigotry turned overtly poisonous.

A headline in a Los Angeles newspaper screamed, "Park Bank Taken Over by Italians." A well-known preacher began referring to the Bank of Italy as the "Pope's bank," and roughly five hundred members of the CLIB took a vow never to "sell out to Giannini." The Bank of Italy was called an "octopus," and by the 1920s, A.P. was compared to Mussolini (despite A.P.'s wonderfully wavy hairline).

What was the economic result of the Bank of Italy's massive expansion, as it spread across the state, amassing by the 1920s more depositors than any other bank in the United States? Did branch banking smash the communities and drive out or under the farmers or shopkeepers? Hardly. The Bank of Italy, which in the late 1920s dropped its obviously ethnic name and replaced it with the more patriotic "Bank of America," offered lower loan rates than smaller banks of the Santa Clara Valley. The other banks were forced to lower their rates, thus, putting more money into the hands of the "little fellow." Giannini reported that he had reduced loan rates in small towns to 7 percent, slashing prevailing rates by anywhere from 2 to 5 percentage points.[21] In the days before branch banking, small-town monopolistic financiers wielded extraordinary power, à la Frank Capra's character Mr. Potter. Now no banker would have the economic incentive to be as nasty as Potter. But *It's a Wonderful Life* also shows how risky small-town life was without competition, without consumer choice, and without the free flow of credit. After A.P. took the state by storm, anyone like Mr. Potter would be bankrupt in minutes, for no one would need to borrow a dime from his locked vault.

Before A.P. came along, people bought their homes with cold cash. If a family did not have enough cash, they might be able to borrow some money for a few years, but then an enormous balloon payment would come due, including all of the principal and interest. The repo men would quickly rush in. This kind of cash economy still exists in many less-developed countries. A few years ago I traveled to Crete, where I saw hundreds of half-built concrete foundations. Why were they all abandoned? I asked my guide. "Oh, they're not abandoned. They build a little bit each year, if they have the money. When the cash runs out, they wait." And the concrete sits waiting for the next cash infusion.

A.P. realized that housing was uniquely suited to attract credit. Why?

First, a house is a fixed asset. Barring extraordinary guile, it cannot be moved, stolen, or erased. If the owner runs from his debt, he cannot take his three-bedroom Victorian with him. Second, a house can be redeployed, that is, the bank can sell it to someone else in need of three bedrooms and a bath. In contrast, if the manufacturer of, say, garden hoses abandons his factory, it is tougher to find a new owner.

A.P.'s bank certainly put its money where its advertising was. During the 1920s, Bank of America spread into the tiniest hamlets, unlike its competitors who preferred urban commerce. The bank placed fifty-three branches in towns with fewer than a thousand people. How many branches had the bank's three biggest competitors (Security Trust, American Bank, and California Bank) placed in small towns? Just twelve in total for the three competitors.[22]

During the 1920s, almost half of California's banks were absorbed by other banks. A brutal test of A.P.'s branch system came in 1929 with the Great Depression. This was almost as fiery a time as the great earthquake of '06. Careful statistical evidence shows that if Bank of America "established a branch in a California town, it increased the odds that the other banks survived the Great Depression." In the Depression era, a bank that proved it could compete against Bank of America had an expected survival time one and half times longer than a bank that had not faced off against A.P.[23] How so? By invading small towns, A.P. forced existing banks to shake up their operations and become more efficient. Sure, some competitors failed, but the survivors had the right stuff to squeeze through the Great Depression. States like California (and countries like Canada), which approved branch banking, had lower failure rates than states that protected the status quo.[24] When the Depression hit, banks realized that A.P. Giannini was the sharpest, most lethal sparring partner they had ever faced—but those that survived appreciated the harsh training he put them through.

Now, make no mistake, the Depression and stock market crash pummeled Bank of America, and A.P. worried about the enormous swings in the value of his enterprise and the impact on investors and borrowers. Later, John Steinbeck, in *The Grapes of Wrath*, would denounce "monster" bankers who would foreclose on vulnerable farmers. But Bank of America, relative to its competitors, foreclosed on fewer farmers, and did so more reluctantly, than any of the traditional banks A.P. picked fights with.

Going Over the Heads of the Bosses

One more historic business challenge demonstrates A.P.'s connection with common people. In 1928 and 1929, A.P. was suffering from extended bouts of pleurisy, a painful and sometimes fatal inflammation of the lining of the lung. He was hospitalized in Rome while a particular ruthless set of negotiations was taking place in New York and San Francisco between his officers and J. P. Morgan Jr. With his health imperiled and the stock market gyrating violently, A.P. agreed to allow a highly respected Wall Street financier, Elisha Walker, to lead Transamerica, a new holding company for the Bank of Italy and Bank of America. The company would have $1 billion in assets. But as the Depression deepened, Walker began making decisions that A.P. deemed cowardly and stupid. The chief executive cut dividends and reined in credit. A.P. spent thousands of dollars sending cables across the Atlantic, trying to persuade Walker, while in New York A.P.'s son Mario, now Transamerica's president, protested in person. A.P. was proud of Mario, who had overcome the psychological trauma of his hemophilia and climbed his way up the ranks of Bank of America, after graduating from law school at the University of California, Berkeley.

In the corporate trauma room, though, Walker ignored the protests of father and son Giannini. He announced that the holding company's book value had plunged from nearly $50 per share in 1929 to just $14.50. By 1931, Walker was actually discussing completely liquidating A.P.'s empire, a fire sale. Transamerica's share price plunged to just $2, from a high of $67.

A fire sale? For a company that A.P. had created from the fires of 1906? Impossible. In 1931, A.P. was almost hopelessly bed-bound and partially paralyzed with polyneuritis in an Austrian clinic. But this humiliating business adversity somehow recharged his stricken body. Upon reading the infuriating cables from his son Mario, A.P. pulled himself out of bed and formed his battle plan. He replied to Mario's cable: "There's no compromise with right or principle. . . . No sir, never my boy. Dad." [25] Then, wanting to keep the element of surprise, he secretly sailed via Vancouver to San Francisco, where he reconnoitered with Mario. The old bull was charging into battle.

Now sixty-one, with his posture stooped, his hair graying, and his jowls sagging, A.P. could hardly win the fight by unleashing the left hook that had served him well on the docks of his youth. Nor could he persuade the Transamerica board, which had now been stacked against him by Wall Streeters who were paralyzed by the Depression and disdainful of this radical Californian upstart. No, he would take his fight to the people, the little shareholders unloading crates on the wharf along North Beach, packing lettuce in the valley, and opening up the general store in a dusty town. A.P. had always fought for dispersing shares widely. Now he would strike Walker and Transamerica's board with a proxy fight. He would try to win over the bank's two hundred thousand shareholders. Today we are used to seeing proxy fights, as corporate managers hire publicists and advertisers to explain why, for example, Hewlett-Packard should merge with Compaq or why Carl Icahn thought that the Time Warner board should be dumped. But in 1931, this was rare and certainly not the way gentlemen bankers played.

A.P. began a barnstorming campaign up and down the California coast, kissing babies, shaking hands, and shaking fists at the Wall Street rascals. He explained that while he took a salary of $1 per year, Walker had paid himself $100,000. Hell, Babe Ruth made only $80,000, and Ruth had a much better year than Elisha Walker. Each time A.P. heard the train whistle sound, another youthful surge of energy traveled through his old body.

When they counted the votes, A.P. had collected over 60 percent of the shares, and Walker and the House of Morgan had been shattered by A.P.'s unorthodox but passionate fighting style.

Of course, taking back control did not stop the bleeding right away, since the bank was losing roughly $3 million in deposits per day. But A.P. dragged his office chair into the middle of the San Francisco lobby and got to work. He had to cut salaries, but he avoided the thousands of layoffs everyone expected. Then he sent his "boys and girls" back into the streets, just as he had done in 1906, scouring for deposits and vowing to keep them safe. A. P. Giannini had returned, and by Christmas 1932, deposits were flowing into the bank, and he declared that dividends were back. He instructed his 410 branch managers to seek out new borrowers and help rescue the California economy. He needed a symbol of his commitment to the Golden State. A civil engineer named Joseph Strauss had an idea for a construction project. The government had approved the project, but no one had the money to back it. In 1932, A.P. and Bank of America bought the entire $6 million bond issue for the humble project. Today the whole world knows it as the Golden Gate Bridge.

And Ever After

In modern times, A.P.'s lessons still ring true. Back during the vicious 1992 riots in Los Angeles, a Korean American banker named Benjamin Hong paced up and down his house just a few blocks from the fires and the beatings. He was sickened and worried as his customers saw marauders torch and loot their stores. He pulled a biography of A. P. Giannini from his bookshelf and turned to the section on the earthquake. Inspired by the example, Hong instructed his branch managers to offer existing customers $100,000 without collateral. According to *Business Week,* fifty customers accepted the offer and not one defaulted.[26]

Today A.P.'s beloved California illustrates many telling examples of his principles. Just as A.P. saw the fields of Santa Clara yielding avocados, tomatoes, and immigrant bank clients, so do Asian bankers today. Over twenty Asian American banks serve Southern California. A handful that began in Los Angeles's Chinatown or Koreatown have grown into multibillion-dollar institutions. They don't start with glitzy offices designed by Frank Gehry. One small specialty bank in Anaheim that loans to the Indian owners of local motels is sandwiched between a Hooters and a half-mile-wide blacktop parking lot.[27] These banks have their eyes on customers that other banks ignore or cannot communicate with.

East West Bancorp, now a huge success, figured out that Chinese immigrants who just stepped off the boat might not have three years of

IRS-approved tax returns. Bank president Dominic Ng told his staff that "if they have a 30 percent down-payment, I do not care where the money is coming from—if they borrow from their sister and brother."[28] Where others saw recklessness, Ng saw an entrepreneurial volcano. If you go to the bank's Web site, you will see a button that quickly changes the site into Chinese characters, allowing depositors and borrowers seamlessly to pay bills and transfer money online in Chinese languages. It also teamed up with SBC to provide customers with discounted high-speed Internet access. Just as A. P. Giannini trolled the wharf, these banks, inspired by his example, seek out clients everywhere in every language.

Wall Street banks gave up arguing with A.P. many, many years ago. JPMorgan Chase has been on a publicity rampage in Manhattan, pasting ads on everything from taxi doors to coffee cups. New York is now a battleground for the House of Morgan, Bank of America, and Commerce Bancorp. In 2006, Morgan created a new gimmick: ATM machines were spitting out tickets to the U.S. Open Tennis championship. Here's to the twenty-first century: the snobbiest of old banks offers the common man admission to one of the snobbiest old sports.

A. P. Giannini's real genius was in seeing the possibility of the common man in America. Before Giannini, banking was not for the common man—but what was? Certainly not symphonic music or literature. Aaron Copland's "Fanfare for the Common Man" showed up in 1942. Arthur Miller's famous essay "Tragedy and the Common Man" arrived in the *New York Times* in 1949, along with *Death of a Salesman*. Years before Copland and Miller, Giannini saw that the guy on the wharf could live just as triumphantly, and just as tragically, as a European duke or Wall Street trader.

When A.P. died in 1949 at age seventy-nine, he left Bank of America as the biggest bank in the world. Mario ran the bank until his death three years later. A.P. did not leave a personal fortune to the Giannini family. Many people were surprised, but back in 1924, A.P. had told a reporter that he would leave a modest estate. "It won't be a million." Twenty years later he reported that he was "in danger" of becoming a millionaire. He had to stop this nefarious development! He donated $509,000 to Bank of America–Giannini Foundation to provide education scholarships for his employees and to fund medical research. When he died, there was just $489,000 left in his estate. A tidy sum for most, but a pittance compared to the fortunes he made for others.

To his last days, A.P. warned his officers to stick to their shared principles. In *The Grapes of Wrath,* Tom Joad says, "I'll be there in the dark—I'll be everywhere. Wherever you look—wherever there's a fight, so hungry people can eat, I'll be there." A.P. had battled earthquakes, fires, vandals, monopolists, and racists. At his retirement, he spoke to his directors in a deep voice that resonated through the boardroom: "If I ever hear that any of you are trying to play the big man's game and forgetting the small man, I'll be back here fighting."

2

Thomas Watson Sr. and Jr.: IBM

A Tale of Two Watsons

Let us start with a Freudian word-association test. I say, "IBM." You say, "White shirts, dark suits, square jaws, straitlaced, and sober." Indeed, Thomas J. Watson Sr. and his son Thomas Jr. molded the most straitlaced, most competitive sales force in history.

But even they could come untied under the pressure. Early in his career, Tom Sr. was sentenced to a year in jail for illegally undermining his competitors. Even as he broke the law, Tom Sr. was lecturing sales reps under a sign reading "Do Right." One day Tom Jr. was thrown out of school for dumping a bottle of extracted skunk juice into the building's heating vents, stinking up every classroom. At age twelve the boy sat slumped on the curb in front of his house, sobbing, "I can't do it. I can't go to work at IBM." At that point in his life, nobody had asked.

The two Watsons built IBM into a powerhouse but nearly beat each other to a pulp in the process. Tom Jr. called their arguments "savage, primal, and unstoppable." He said, "It amazes me that two people could torture each other to the degree Dad and I did and not call it quits."[1] And yet when Dad died and Tom Jr. had to face the office alone, he said that he was the most frightened man in America. To the outside world, IBM was the very face of efficiency, grace, and rectitude. But behind the slick, perfectly straight horizontal lines of the big blue IBM logo were towering waves of passion, hatred, and warfare. Tom Sr. acted like an egomaniacal narcissist; his son, a dyslexic depressive.

Sigmund Freud visited the United States only once in his lifetime. It is a good thing that he did not drop in on the Watson house, or he would have left America a very confused man.

This chapter is not about psychoanalysis (though it could be). It is about the lessons we can learn from the Watsons, who realized that America's economy in the twentieth century was not based just on sheer mass, but on digesting bits of information. Before the Watsons came along, accountants wore green eyeshades and were relegated to the back rooms, where they simply counted coins and shuffled bills. The Watsons taught the world that numbers could be, well, cool. Their salesmen showed companies how to dive into data, looking for new correlations and new opportunities to save money or boost customer sales. Today, any twelve-year-old willing to put down his iPod for a moment can correlate telephone area codes, incomes, and purchases. In the pre-Watson era, those would have been three separate stacks of numbers locked in file drawers on opposite sides of the room. Just as electron microscopes allowed biologists to understand and manipulate animal cells, IBM allowed firms to understand and manipulate data. The Watsons revolutionized more than data. They taught us how to build sales forces, how to hang on to wavering customers, and, most dramatically, how to "bet the company" on one big gamble. The two Watsons could be visionaries, teetotalers, hustlers, and bruisers. All at once. All in one family.

TOM SR.: THE EARLY YEARS

Tom Sr. had little in common with Walt Disney, except for this: as young men, they both liked to practice their signatures. Watson scrawled his signature on village monuments and did not consider it graffiti. Both men knew their future careers depended on their own drive and what folks used to call "moxie" (named after a nineteenth-century cure-all drink that would perk up every part of your body). Certainly, neither Watson nor Disney could depend on a trust-fund check. Elias Disney, a no-nonsense Protestant, struggled to raise crops in Missouri, while Watson's father, a brawny and darkly bearded timberman of Scots descent, wandered through New York State trying to support his five children. "My father was never meant to be a rich man," Tom Sr. surmised, while also declaring, "I was absolutely sure that I was a smarter man than my father."[2] In fact, Tom's father's timber work brought in enough money to feed the family and to live on High Street in a little town called Painted Post. Tom Sr.'s harsh and gratuitous comments suggest that the Watson family was plagued with intergenerational rivalry long before Tom Jr. came on the scene to sob curbside.

The little town of Painted Post is named after a piece of carved wood, and though today it has only about two thousand residents, it sits along the great glassblowing belt of New York, a few miles from Corning and within the county of Steuben. Perhaps young Tom Sr. thought his father had missed out by focusing on an "old economy" product like timber, instead of a "new economy" product like glass, which was creating millions of dollars of wealth for such nearby families as the Houghtons (Corning). The Houghton family included a congressman and later a modestly successful actress named Katharine Houghton Hepburn.

Though Tom Sr. grew into a legendary salesman, he was not a born charmer. He was shy, quick-tempered, and loath to play with other children. A smart boy, he had little interest in the heavy lifting, sweaty life of his father. He certainly looked the part, with a granite jaw, strong arms, and six feet two inches of height. But Tom chopped enough trees to know that he somehow needed to make a career without an ax in his hand. After finishing high school, Tom immediately enrolled in a school of commerce in nearby Elmira. For his first job, he traded in lumber for rump roast, earning $6 per week at a Painted Post butcher shop. He did not do much slicing, but mostly acted as a bookkeeper. While good with numbers, Tom was not good about sitting in one place and watching the same customers stroll in and out of the door each day. A butcher's helper merely takes orders. It's a passive job once the butcher finishes taking his aggression out on the steer. Tom needed some action. He wanted to sell the customers on something new. If a customer asked for a pound of chuck, why not try to talk her into a pound and a half of rib eye? Tom quit the butcher shop and began work as an assistant to a "music man" who traveled from farm to farm, peddling pianos and organs. Now Tom was earning double his butcher shop salary. But that was not enough for him. He asked for a raise, and his boss turned him down while asking whether Tom wanted to buy the whole business. What Tom really wanted, and could not get, was a compensation package based on commissions. He learned a lesson that would not leave him: Reward your salesmen by dangling big carrots in front of them. It will not make them feel like donkeys; it will make them feel like winners.

Tom looked around and decided there were just not enough carrots hanging in Painted Post. He trekked across the state to Buffalo, where the Erie Canal linked America's emerging industrial belt to New York. Tom did not have a job lined up, family to stay with, and much more than a few coins in his pocket. He slept on a pile of sponges in a drugstore basement. He owned just one suit, and when he could afford to get it pressed, he would stand in the back of the tailor shop in his long johns waiting for the job to be done.[3] He was a hick in the big city and would soon meet some very interesting and shady characters. He briefly sold sewing machines—a revolutionary industry at the time, which liberated women and drove down the price of clothing. Unfortunately, he lost that job after celebrating a big sale with too many drinks at a saloon. Tom staggered through the doors to find that while he was toasting his success, thieves had stolen his horse, buggy, and samples. His boss was not impressed and fired him. (Stung by his bitter experience in the saloon and still aching from his time sleeping on sponges, Tom later forbade his IBM staff from drinking. Tom did not reveal his youthful indiscretion to his employees, and IBMers would spend years wondering why the old man was such a stickler for sobriety.) He struggled to find another job, but the U.S. economy was tumbling into the depression of 1893. Raging storms followed by droughts had pummeled American farmers in the early 1890s, even as wheat prices tumbled. Meanwhile, railroad magnates slowed down the expansion of new tracks crisscrossing the country, and the jobless rate topped 10 percent.

By this point, Tom was vulnerable to the city slickers, and a two-timing, fast-talking, card-shuffling character named C. B. Barron arrived on the scene to separate Tom from his last coin. Barron could and did peddle just about anything. He convinced Tom to join him selling shares in a Buffalo building and loan operation. The plan seemed to work well, and soon each of them received sizable commissions. Pledging his commission, Tom invested in a butcher shop, for he still fondly remembered something about the finances of tenderloin. But Barron was not content merely to con the rubes who bought the suspect bank shares. He also swindled Tom, stealing the commissions and effectively leaving Tom standing on the side of the road next to a side of beef that he could not afford.

Besides an occasional meat loaf dinner, only one good thing came from Tom's butcher shop debacle. Tom had bought a cash register for the butcher shop. Cash registers had been very controversial just a few years before. Some people looked at cash registers with hatred. Now, what kind of paranoid person could possibly hate a cash register? Sales clerks. To them, the cash register was an insult to their intelligence and their honesty, akin to asking them to work while wearing handcuffs. Not only did Tom's butcher shop have a cash register, but also the shiny machine was manufactured by the powerful National Cash Register Company. A machine made by NCR, nicknamed the "Cash," aroused even more passion. To the critics of cash registers, the Cash was like a financial terrorist gumming up the gears of commerce and threatening their jobs. Clerks threatened to tar and feather approaching salesmen. They ripped up mailings from the Cash, and when the Cash caught on, the clever clerks ripped up any letter postmarked from Dayton, Ohio, home of the Cash.[4] Why was the Cash, a company that bent shiny metal and built bells to go *ding-ding,* so awe-inspiring?

The answer comes with the story of the legendary John Patterson, NCR's founder, who was extraordinarily resourceful, successful, clever, and, frankly, loony. Here was a man who can be credited with inventing the science of salesmanship. While other salesmen relied on charm, smarm, and blarney to inveigle cloudy-headed customers, Patterson designed punctilious sales protocols. He built a school for his sales team and forced them to memorize manuals and perform skits in front of scenery depicting barbershops, dress shops, and drugstores. A sales pitch should leave nothing to chance or charm. Know your product and know precisely how to show it off. Just as today clocks and watches are set in store windows at ten minutes after ten to best display their shapely hands, Patterson insisted that his sales team carry exactly $7.16 in a specially designed purse. Apparently this was the precise sum needed to best demonstrate the cash register's change mechanism.[5]

It was all very rational. All except Patterson himself. Here was a man who would set desks on fire or chop them in half with an ax and who embarked on bizarre food fasts to cleanse his system, as he chased after eating fads. (On this latter point, he might have been a hundred years ahead of his time.) Patterson would fire loyal employees who were showing too much success and therefore could somehow threaten him. Meanwhile, he put a London gymnast on the board of directors because the gymnast would help Patterson's personal exercise regimen. According to one witness, Patterson was quite a sight as he lectured salesmen, crushing red chalk in his hands, rubbing it in a frenzy over his hands and hair, "throwing his arms up, looking like a tousled but well-tailored Comanche" while shouting at the top of his lungs.[6]

A LASTING LESSON

For all of Patterson's eccentricities, one thing is clear: the Cash had a great product and a finely tuned sales force that numbered in the hundreds. After Tom's butcher shop went bankrupt in 1895, he parlayed his empty cash register into a job selling Cash machines in Buffalo. This was, no joke, the big time. Tom was in a big city, finally, selling for a company with a national reputation. No more get-rich-quick schemes or trying to peddle pianos door to door. No more lessons of how to sell from a huckster. He quickly realized that he needed a master teacher. After he failed to sign up any customers in his first few weeks with the Cash, he tried to placate his boss by claiming there was "good business in sight." The head man in Buffalo, John J. Range, pounced on the young man's blarney and slugged him with a sarcastic verbal barrage that in today's world would have triggered some kind of EEOC lawsuit. "In sight?" Range asked. "How far away is it? Can I see it?" he demanded, while accusing Watson of laziness. "Don't you ever waste my time."[7] With Tom quivering and all but looking for the next canal boat back to Corning, Range suddenly turned and did something no one had ever done for young Tom Watson: he offered to take Tom under his wing and mentor him.

Range hopped on the wagon with Tom, and together they put the NCR sales formula to work. "If we fall down, we'll fall down together," Range assured Tom.[8]

The memory of Range's rapid and almost violent about-face, first mocking and then mending, stayed with Tom throughout his career. Now, perhaps Range was just another example of a harried salesman plagued with bipolar disorder. More likely, though, Range was deliberately trying to whip Tom into fighting shape, much as a Marine drill sergeant breaks down a recruit before building him up again. Cold-calling in a hostile climate was hard work that required tough men.

Sharing a wagon with Range, equipped with the best advice and the finest product in the business, Tom started to ring the register, so to speak. Range taught him a lasting lesson that Tom spent his career passing down to thousands of IBM salesmen: Put yourself in your customer's shoes. Tom turned this into a literal commandment, demanding that his salesmen dress like their customers, generally in suits and white shirts. Today psychologists tell salesmen they can create empathy with customers by actually mimicking their gestures. If a customer steeples his hands, you should mirror the gesture. Range's point was more profound than mimicry. He directed Tom not to try to convince a reluctant customer that he needed an NCR cash register. That tack would immediately trigger alarms and put them in an adversarial relationship, especially in an era when snake oil salesmen were roaming the plains. Instead, Tom should engage in conversation, offer some helpful hints on business, and elicit from the customer what his real needs were. "Remember," Range said, "don't do all the talking."

A very wise and hard-nosed salesman once explained the sales game to me. This man traveled the country inducing multibillion-dollar pension plans to invest in funds he represented. "Todd," he said with a cynical gleam in his eye, "this is the sales racket: I tell the prospect what I've got, and then I shut up. I wait, and I wait. I don't quiver or get nervous and shift my weight. Just wait. Whoever speaks next is the sucker."

Tom was not as battle-scarred as my friend, but he learned to shut up. After maintaining his silence and creating a friendly relationship by offering some advice, Tom could later return to the prospect and gently nudge him toward a purchase. With Range's guidance, Tom started selling so many units that he needed more than a cash register to keep his weekly earnings, which often topped $100, equal to about $2,400 today.

FIND A HOOK

Tom's success in posing as a trusted friend of a prospect later inspired him to create *Think* magazine for IBM. *Think* was a general-interest magazine filled with current-affairs articles and editorials by leading thinkers of the day. It did not blare IBM's name on the cover or on every page. But if an IBM salesman found his prospect shoving him toward the door, the salesman could reach into his briefcase and say, "Mr. Jones, I can see that you're not very interested, and these machines don't fit everywhere. But while I'm here, let me give you a magazine that may interest you. This one, for instance, has speeches by Franklin Roosevelt and Tom Dewey. . . . If you like, you can have a subscription free. Just let me know, and I will get you on the list."[9] In the 1940s, the subscription list for *Think* grew to about 100,000, though IBM had just 3,500 customers. Who were the other 96,500 recipients? They were Tom's future customer list, as well as all the ministers, rabbis, teachers, and Rotarians who could say nice things about IBM to their congregants and colleagues. Today my mailbox is stuffed with free magazines and newsletters from stock brokers, realtors, and travel agents. Costco sends a handsome magazine each month that includes interesting articles among the advertisements. Tom Watson Sr. inspired this flood of mailbox stuffers, but he did so with more class and less conniving than that broker who is promising to triple my money if I invest in emu meat. (Sorry, but I like birds to be smaller than me.)

INTO THE LEGAL BREACH

Tom's rigorous devotion to selling NCR cash registers caught the attention of the bigwigs in Dayton, Ohio. They were paying out huge commissions to Tom, about 35 percent of his sales revenues. Patterson did not begrudge paying Tom big commissions. But he did resent one new development: competition from sellers of secondhand NCR machines. NCR machines were remarkably sturdy and apparently indestructible. The only loose screw at NCR was in Patterson's head. The sturdy machines led to a secondary market as merchants realized they could save money by buying a used NCR. Patterson's own machines were cannibalizing his new sales revenues. As any self-respecting autocrat would think, Patterson figured that since NCR had built the secondhand machines, by God, he had the right to destroy the secondary market. But how could he do it without leaving obvious fingerprints? He needed a secret agent. By 1903 Patterson and the senior executives at NCR had heard about young Tom, especially rumors that he had sabotaged cash registers made by NCR competitors. They concocted a plan for Tom.

It started in New York City, down the street from a secondhand shop on Fourteenth Street owned by a man named Fred Brainin. Tom hung a shingle that said "Watson's Cash Register and Second Hand Exchange." Note that he left out the word "National." It was not a careless slip. He even introduced himself to Brainin as a friendly small-business owner. Heck, New York is full of streets where similar businesses flourish right next door: the wedding gown district, the plant district, the music district, etc. A woman in Levi's can enter Manhattan, jog down just three streets, and quickly exit the city wearing a white lace veil, cradling a rhododendron, and playing the saxophone. Brainin probably figured there was room for a used-cash-register district. But Tom and the Dayton crew had no interest in a district. When Brainin would offer a used NCR machine for $15, Watson would mark down an identical item to $14. When Brainin peered into Watson's shop and saw the $14 sign, he would mark his to $13. Watson would scratch out $14 and slash the price to $10. Money was no object to Tom: he was getting the machines free. Unlike Brainin, Tom did not have a stock boy to pay or a creditor to pay off. Poor Brainin needed to make a profit. Poor Brainin was the prey in a vicious predatory pricing scheme. Once Tom had trounced Brainin, he moved on to other streets in other cities, leaving a string of corporate corpses behind.

He got caught, along with Patterson, Range, and other senior NCR managers. In 1912, after nearly ten years of domination, federal authorities indicted them for flagrantly violating the Sherman Antitrust Act and committing acts of commercial piracy, bribery, and libel. They were fined thousands of dollars and sentenced to a year in jail. Tom was shocked, angry, and defiant. When he marked down the price of cash registers, weren't consumers benefiting from the bargains? Shouldn't the antitrust laws recognize that his aggressive pricing made it possible for more people to afford cash registers? These arguments did not persuade. But Tom refused to recant. Tom Jr.'s autobiography features a remarkable photograph of Tom Sr. rallying NCR salesmen in 1913, the year the federal court convicted him. At the bottom of his handwritten notes resting on the easel, he wrote in large letters, "Do right."

The NCR conviction signaled the death of unbridled power for Patterson and other autocrats. Shortly before his death, J. P. Morgan remarked that American business must be done with "glass pockets." [10] (Of course, if Morgan had hung around for another hundred years, he would have seen the deep and dark pockets of Enron, Global Crossing, and WorldCom.)

I should add here that modern economists do not necessarily see predatory pricing as a virulent scourge. It seldom works effectively for the predator beyond the short term. Let us say that NCR's scheme drove Brainin to bankruptcy. During that predatory phase, cash register buyers did in fact get the benefit of lower prices. Now, say, Brainin shutters his door, allowing NCR to jack up the prices of secondhand registers to greedily high levels. What would happen? Somebody else would jump into the field and open up a store to take advantage of the high prices and high profits on secondhand machines. As long as the "barriers to entry" (the costs and trouble of setting up a business in a given field) are not terribly high, predators have trouble holding on to their monopoly profits. When it comes to secondhand goods, the barriers are awfully low. Any college student can post a sign on a lawn or online to sell his used books. Poor neighborhoods have pawnshops, and rich neighborhoods have "garage sales," though they tend to call them "estate sales" in order not to sully their high-class status. Apparently, rich people would prefer shoppers to think that old Aunt Harriet dropped dead, rather than that she finally cleaned out her basement.

During the trial and sentencing period, Tom's professional life was in turmoil, but his personal life improved when he found a bride, a petite but strong Dayton debutante named Jeanette Kittredge. Her father headed a company that made railroad cars. Tom later bragged that convincing Jean to marry him was the toughest and most important sale of his life. She got pregnant at the same time that Tom's career at NCR imploded.

Patterson's and Tom's reputations were, ironically, saved by a flood. In March 1913, Ohio faced the biggest natural disaster in its history, as the Great Miami River exploded through levees, drowning Dayton in nearly twenty feet of fetid water. Gas mains ruptured, and fires broke out, while firefighters tried to rescue citizens from the rapids that suddenly formed. Hundreds of people died, and the streets were littered with the carcasses of horses.[11] As the waters poured into the city, Patterson urged his fellow citizens to find sanctuary in the NCR plant, which was constructed on high ground. NCR had actually begun building boats before the levees broke, as they had witnessed the floods ravage Indiana and in neighboring communities. Thousands took refuge under NCR's roofs, and the company aided them with blankets, bread, and hymns. Though Tom was in New York, he jumped into action, quickly arranging for railroad trains to rush westward with supplies. In the frenzy of relief operations, Tom worked himself to exhaustion that required hospitalization.

When the waters subsided, Patterson and Tom had revived their reputations and achieved heroic status. Soon after, though, Patterson fired Tom. Tom insisted that the firing had little to do with the Sherman Antitrust Act and more to do with Patterson's ego. Patterson, who could selflessly risk his life and fortune to help others in a flood, did not care to share the stage with another.

But Tom never spoke ill of Patterson, who, true to mercurial form, paid Tom an enormous $50,000 severance, equal to $1 million today. Though Tom had trouble finding work right away, this lump sum easily fed the family. Besides, if Patterson had not axed Tom, Tom would not have had the chance to invent IBM.

A NEW START

Who would want to hire a convicted felon waiting to be locked up behind bars? I cannot imagine Enron CEO Jeffrey Skilling received many job offers while wearing stripes (although Martha Stewart did nab a reality television show while in the pokey). In fact, one man did not mind meeting with a convicted felon—an international explorer, financier, and bon vivant named Charles Flint. Flint shows up around the world like Zelig in the Woody Allen movie. There he is, with wavy hair and fluffy muttonchops, in Manaus, Brazil, installing electric streetlights and streetcars. Then in Nicaragua as consul general, in St. Petersburg buying arms for the czar in the Russo-Japanese war, and in Chicago creating American Chicle, the maker of Chiclets and Dentyne chewing gums. By the time Flint met Watson, he had already met enough millionaires, potentates, and scoundrels that he was not shaken by Tom Watson's impending jail sentence. For his business machinations among oligopolists, Chicago newspapers had already dubbed Flint the "father of trusts."

Flint had bolted together three different companies that all had something to do with measuring things. Under the acronym CTR, he had jammed together the Computing Scale Company, which made butcher scales; the Tabulating Machine Company, which manufactured an electric device to record census data on punch cards; and the International Time Recording Company, which made time clocks for workers to punch into at the beginning and end of each work shift. Although these three companies were devoted to empowering customers to run a more rational business, CTR itself was a rickety shell that owed bondholders millions of dollars beyond its capacity to pay. Flint wanted to hire Tom as general manager so that Tom could straighten the rickety mess into a sturdy structure and inspire his four hundred demoralized salesmen.

With a jail sentence and fine hanging over his head, Tom found it tough to inspire CTR's board of directors, who asked Flint, "What are you trying to do? Ruin this business? Who is going to run this business while he serves his term in jail?"[12] As board directors so often do, however, they relented and let Flint hire Tom. And did Flint ever! Tom negotiated a salary equivalent to over half a million dollars today. Tom applied his experience as a salesman to demand a hefty commission, equal to a percentage of the company's profits. This was the most financially savvy deal Tom ever made. Under this formula, which gave him 5 percent of the profits, he eventually became the highest-paid man in America. You might recall the famous anecdote of Babe Ruth earning $80,000 in 1931. When a reporter asked him whether he felt guilty earning more than President Herbert Hoover, the Babe answered, "Why not? I had a better year." By the 1930s, Tom had earned the title the "Thousand-Dollar-a-Day-Man" as he took home several times the Babe's salary. Of course, if the Babe, like Tom, had laid off beer and whiskey, he might have hit even more home runs and outearned even Tom.

Shortly after Tom arrived at CTR, good news came out of the federal courts: they overturned his conviction. Though his acquittal had more to do with technicalities and rules of evidence, it cleansed his record and allowed Flint to promote him to president of CTR. Now, without the fear of jail and the resentment of the board of directors, he could start moving CTR beyond its current state, known as a place for cigar-chomping guys hawking meat grinders. IBM was just a few dreams and a few steps away.

FROM MEAT GRINDERS TO IBM

Tom Watson had a hunch that he turned into a billion-dollar company. The hunch was this: the twentieth century would be the first "measured century."[13] How much does it cost? How long will it take? How much does it weigh? Now, these were questions people had asked since Noah asked God how big to make his ark (three hundred cubits, as it turned out). But Watson realized that in this new century, numbers would be kept, stored, retrieved, and recalculated, all in an effort to make businesses more efficient. He knew that his tabulating machines had saved the Census Bureau millions of dollars and several years in compiling the 1890 reports. Tom conjectured that old numbers could be as important as new numbers, as businesses charted their growth, their costs, and their return on investment. When I was in second grade, the kids in my neighborhood bought baseball cards on Opening Day. We spent the summer trading them and trying to collect a card for each of the players. (We also spent the rest of the summer trying not to break our teeth on the flat, hard gum that accompanied the cards. Other than glass, no other substance shattered when it fell to the floor.) In October, after the World Series, we did what is now the unthinkable: we threw away the cards! Who needed old baseball cards? Wait till next year for a new batch, we foolishly thought. Before Tom Watson, most businessmen thought of their own company data in this same reckless way. But Tom figured that those figures would come in handy as businesses grew bigger, faster, and more flexible. CTR would be king of the numbers. To wear the crown, though, CTR would need to find some ways to link the *C*, the *T*, and the *R*. Today it is a cliché to talk about synergies, but no such cliché existed a hundred years ago.

Tom began with the *T*, for the Tabulating Machine Company, which produced a small minority of CTR's revenues. He favored this business over the Computing Scale Company. Tom's ambitions were too strong to dwell on coffee grinders and meat slicers, his early career as a butcher notwithstanding. The developer of the Census Bureau's tabulating machine, Herman Hollerith, discovered that clerks could work much more quickly by punching holes into cards, rather than writing down data into ledgers. Every hole punch represented a data point, and the cards could be sorted and tabulated by machine. Tom said, "You can punch a hole in the card . . . and you'll never have to write it down again. Machines can do the routine work. People shouldn't have to do that kind of work." [14] One of Tom's first stabs at synergy came when he realized that he could connect the punch card tabulators to printers. By marrying punch card machines to printers, he could make record keeping automatic for his customers. Who could resist? Few, it turned out. Over the next fifteen years, the profits of punch card tabulators grew from the lowest rung to the highest, delivering 85 percent of CTR's revenues. In 1935, the tabulators got their biggest push when President Franklin Roosevelt signed the Social Security Act. Suddenly, everyone needed a number, every company needed to keep track, and every government bureaucrat demanded access to the numbers. Tom literally and figuratively held the valuable cards. Whatever good Social Security did for old people, it did even more for Tom's company. Tom was a big fan of Franklin Roosevelt's before 1935, but his ardor intensified after that date.

In a near replay of events, thirty years later, a former IBM salesman with a Texas twang raked in billions of dollars when he helped the government computerize the new Medicare program. His name was Ross Perot.

In his day, Tom's punch card machines were sophisticated electric miracles. By betting on the punch cards, Tom left the meat grinders behind and seldom again thought about his early days in the butcher shop.

In 1924, Tom changed the name of CTR to International Business Machines. He liked the word "International," which connoted glamour and sophistication. And though he took his young family to Europe numerous times in the 1920s (he and Jeanette had two sons and two daughters), IBM was international in the same way as the World Series, that is, IBM had some sales in Canada. Tom had more places to take IBM and new ideas to promulgate.

TO INFINITY AND BEYOND

Here is how I picture Tom's business model. Imagine the two-looped symbol for infinity. On one loop ride the customers; on the other loop rides the sales force. The intersection is IBM. Tom sought to bind the customers to IBM, while also binding the sales force to IBM. He did this by inextricably, seamlessly, and smoothly tying the customers to the sales team.

Tying the Customers: Solutions, Not Slices

Tom realized that his customers needed solutions, not just hunks of metal equipment. Other manufacturers would send deliverymen to drop off equipment, collect the cash, and then drive off. Tom took a different approach. He trained IBMers to install and service the machines. More important, his sales force helped guide the customer to the right product in the first place. He turned the role of the salesman from con man to confidant.

Key to the IBM model was leasing. IBM would not simply dump the equipment on the front stoop of a customer because IBM actually owned the equipment. The customer made regular payments but was not locked into buying something that would become obsolete. Leasing created a reason for the salesman to check up regularly on the customer, binding them more closely together. Customers were reluctant to cancel leases because it would disrupt their operations and force them to spend time searching for alternatives. When a customer would ask why he should sign a lease, the salesman would assure him that "we'll send our customer service men around to inspect....We're selling service, not machines." [15] Tom pressed his sales force to provide feedback to the engineering team, creating a feedback mechanism to improve IBM's products. [16]

Leasing helped IBM's finances in several ways. First, lease payments created a steady stream of earnings, especially with IBM's strong renewals rates. If IBM had been outright selling machines for cash, it would naturally have experienced some strong months and some weak months. Under the leasing model, even if the sales force suffered a dry spell and could not win over any new customers, the company could still count on its monthly lease payments. Leasing helped insulate IBM against recessions. This same logic explains why cellular telephone companies are so desperate to get you hooked on a two-year service agreement. It also explains why Wall Street places such high value on "recurring revenue." A bird on the hook for twenty-four months is worth far more than a bird in the hand (even if it is for a blockbuster month). Some years ago I was the president and cofounder of a financial consulting firm that charged hundreds of thousands of dollars for advice, but one-tenth as much for a daily written report. Our investment bankers urged us to dump the consulting contracts, lucrative as they were, and focus solely on the daily letter. They calculated that a corporate acquirer would be far more interested in subscriptions with high renewal rates than with rich consulting arrangements.

Finally, leasing helped IBM scare off new competitors because those competitors generally required customers to pay cash up front. Few companies had enough capital to essentially lend the equipment to their customers. Tom's unmatchable leasing program became the "barrier to entry" that John Patterson had trouble erecting for cash registers.

In addition to the lease equipment, IBM earned handsome profits selling the punch cards themselves. Even if a customer did not want the IBM punch card machine, IBM dominated the market for the cards themselves. Most customers figured they might as well stick with IBM through the whole process. Think today about those amazingly cheap printers you can find at CompUSA and similar outlets or thrown in free with the purchase of a laptop. How, for example, can Hewlett-Packard pay its bills while selling a color copier for $75? It can't. But look at the ink! That's where the money is. Ever look at the confusing display of ink cartridges hanging in a computer supply store and wonder why Hewlett-Packard produces such a ridiculous variety? To foil the makers of cheaper knockoffs; imitators stumble trying to keep up with each new version that Hewlett-Packard unveils. It's like the old Soviet joke about a man who worked in a factory, and each day pushed a wheelbarrow past the guard post. Each day the same guard would lift up the canvas covering the wheelbarrow, suspicious that the worker was stealing something from the factory. Beneath the canvas were useless rocks. After twenty years the guard announced he was retiring and asked the worker to finally confess. "What have you been stealing?" "Wheelbarrows," answered the worker. Hewlett-Packard's ink is a Soviet wheelbarrow.

Tying the Sales Force

Tom Watson loved his sales team, and he especially loved to inspire them with songs, speeches, and money. He had started in the trenches, knew hunger, and knew how hard salesmen had to fight for their self-esteem. Remembering his lesson from Range at NCR, he insisted that managers accompany neophytes on sales calls. To his top executives, he repeated a mantra: "A manager is an *assistant* to his men." Despite his mighty ego, he even kept his door open, literally. He told his staff that any man who had a serious complaint could appeal directly to him. He figured that anyone willing to take him up on the offer must either be a fool or have a very serious issue to discuss. Tom instructed his managers to recruit salesmen on college campuses, looking especially for men with good looks and fine manners. Back in Tom's day, baseball scouts judged recruits not just by their quick feet or strong arms, but by their faces. The scouting reports would comment on whether the youngsters had "good faces," those sharp, alert features that signaled the heart of a winner (and looked good on a Wheaties box). I am not sure how Babe Ruth and Yogi Berra made it to the majors with faces that reminded fans not of a matinee idol, but of Magilla Gorilla.

Tom even hired men during the bleakest days of the Great Depression. In 1933, he joked with his biggest competitor, the chief of Remington Rand, who was startled that Tom was not firing men: "I'm getting along in years now. You know, I'm almost sixty now. A lot of things happen to men at that critical age. Some of them get to drinking too much. Some of them are interested in girls. But my weakness is hiring salesmen, and I'm just going to keep doing that." [17]

In IBM, Tom created a company and a corporate culture that he promised would go on forever. He assured his clean-cut team that he would hire their sons and grandsons. His ego apparently allowed him to contemplate that he would go on forever, too. He seemed immortal and paternalistic, before that latter word became pejorative. First of all, he paid good salesmen great sums of money. Second, he invested in his employees, building training schools and research facilities. By the 1930s, half of IBM's factory workers were taking at least one of the twenty-four courses offered in the Education Department, and thousands had graduated from the IBM "Schoolhouse." [18] Third, he provided health care for his employees and their families. Fourth, he encouraged healthy play, building a country club for IBM families. Like the Wizard of Oz, Tom began to address his entire staff by speaking into a microphone that rested on his desk. Following FDR, he also delivered fireside chats.

And then there were the songs. Tom created a religion around worshipping IBM, and in this religion, he was glorified like the Virgin Mary who had brought forth the Lord. Even the classrooms looked like altars. According to the rousing "Ever Onward," sung to the tune of "Stouthearted Men," Tom was more than just a man. He was a

> *man of men, our friend and guiding hand.*
> *The name of T. J. Watson means a courage none can stem:*
> *And we feel honored to be here to toast the IBM.*

In 1939, Tom pulled out all the stops and built a monument to IBM at the New York world's fair that outshone even the generals, namely, General Motors and General Electric. Never mind that IBM was like a gnat compared to these corporate behemoths. On "IBM Day" Tom delivered a speech and arranged for New York mayor Fiorello La Guardia to listen onstage. Not content to sing IBM's praises alone, he actually hired Metropolitan Opera superstars Lily Pons and Lawrence Tibbett to lead the musical revue.

Under Tom's guidance, IBMers sang their songs at meetings, as large portraits of Tom hung on the walls. They sang the songs at "Tent City" retreats, where thousands of IBM salesmen would gather in circus tents to award prizes and recharge their enthusiasm. If "Ever Onward" is not enough to make you squirm, consider the "IBM School Song":

> *With Mr. Watson leading*
> *To greater heights we'll rise*
> *And keep our IBM*
> *Respected in all eyes.*

Despite the hype, or maybe because of the esprit de corps, IBM profits rocketed from just half a million dollars when Tom joined in 1914 to $9.4 million in 1940. Revenues multiplied tenfold.[19]

During this glorious era, there was just one important man who hated the songs and blanched at the pomposity. The name of this mortified man was also Thomas J. Watson.

THOMAS J. WATSON JR.

Besides their name, about the only thing that the two Thomas J. Watsons shared in common was their height. They both stood about six feet two inches tall. But even this commonality served little good because it pressured Tommy Jr. to act more like an adult even when he was but a string bean teenager. Father dressed up his thirteen-year-old son like a mirror of himself, with a chesterfield coat, leather gloves, and a homburg hat. Father was a smart student; Junior got the grades of a dunce. Father shoved liquor off the table; Junior turned into a drunken practical joker. Father dreamed of owning his company; Junior dreamed of becoming a pilot for United Airlines and burst into tears when contemplating IBM.

I have had the opportunity to work for and advise the "Presidents Bush," and I am quite certain that powerful fathers and sons need not grind one another like lathes gone loony. In fact, when I asked George H.W. Bush whether his son calls home for advice, the elder president replied: "Of course. I answer the telephone, and George says, 'Hi, Dad. Is Mom home?' " No doubt, with all those posters of Thomas J. Watson Sr.'s face, and all the photographs of Father with FDR, Eisenhower, and King George, the force of Father's personality would have been inescapable, more akin to Kim Il Sung and his impact on the jumpsuit-wearing Kim Jong Il. When Junior entered school, he walked through hallways festooned with IBM clocks. He recalled that everything Father did made him feel "inconsequential." Perhaps Terrible Tommy, as he was called, suffered from an inferiority complex because he was, well, inferior. He was a lousy athlete who suffered from dyslexia, asthma, and depression. His depression was not just sadness, but a debilitating, suicide-inducing trauma. He confided in his younger brother, asking the nine-year-old boy to "help me, and if I die, be sure to tell Mother and Dad that it's not their fault."[20] With a stern, ambitious father, the Watson house was no funhouse.

In the beginning of this chapter, I discussed Tommy spiking his school's heating ducts with real skunk juice. Furious, Father chased him around the house roaring, "I don't need to discipline you! The world will discipline you, you little skunk!"[21]

Father was not all fire and brimstone; Tommy recalled his father occasionally horsing around and even dressing up as a woman. But for the most part, their matching chesterfield coats were buttoned awfully tight. When Tommy would spiral into his mood funks, Father would try to buck him up, assuring him that someday he would find the right path and become a great man.

It took a long time. Father used his connections to get Tommy into the best private schools. His marks at the Hun School in Princeton and on standardized tests were miserable, except for one ray of hope: a score on a standardized physics test that flew off the charts to beat all other students in New Jersey. Would Princeton University, the soon-to-be home of Albert Einstein, pounce on this physics prodigy? Father drove to the campus for a private meeting with the dean, flashed his own übercrendentials, and pleaded Tommy's case. The dean turned him down, calling the boy a "predetermined failure."

Brown University gave in to Father, with a resigned "He's not very good, but we'll take him." At Brown, Tommy excelled in carousing, clubbing, and shirking classes. Remember, this was during the Depression, and few families still had the resources to keep living like in the Roaring Twenties. Tommy noticed that many other students looked malnourished. But at this point, his diet was mainly the olives bouncing at the bottom of a martini glass. Around Rhode Island, laid-off workers stood in line for hot soup. But Tommy found a rich roommate (with a quadruple-barreled name) so flush with cash he bought a cafeteria meal ticket for his Great Dane. The dog would lumber down the block to the restaurant and tilt his massive head so that the waitress could punch the ticket.

Of course, Tommy got a job when he graduated (without much distinction) from Brown in 1937. Father arranged a worldwide trot as an assistant to a man helping to plan the 1939 world's fair. Tommy appeared not to know that his father had pulled the strings for this boondoggle to Moscow, Beijing, and Tokyo, but his ignorance just demonstrates how clueless he was at this point. "I love to buy things," Tommy said. He was so popular with merchants that when he left Beijing, local merchants sent their children with gifts to thank him for his patronage.[22]

Soon after the merry jaunt, his personal nightmare came true: Tommy showed up for work at IBM. He did not have to, of course, but like the powerful gravitational pull of Jupiter, IBM pulled him in. Like other budding IBM salesmen, Tommy attended classes at IBM's leading-edge training center in Endicott, New York. Like other newbies, Tommy began by learning the nuts and bolts of the punch-card machine, which was less nuts and bolts than wires and plugs, similar to an old-fashioned telephone operator's switchboard. He took a class in programming the machine, which could print paychecks, address labels, and make accounting calculations. Well, at least it could when someone else programmed the machine. Tommy's mind was tangled up in the wires and plugs. To avoid embarrassment, the school provided a personal tutor, which naturally embarrassed the young man. (Compare this experience to that of young David Sarnoff, who launched his career by proving his phenomenal hand-eye coordination and skill at handling the telegraph.)

After finally passing through Endicott, Tommy began his career in sales. He scored fantastic early successes, which was of course a disaster.

Why? It was a fix. His superiors assigned him the hottest territory, and within one day, he shot to the top of IBM's sales ranking when U.S. Steel filed a huge order. In that single day, he filled his quota for the entire year. Back in the 1970s, Yankee slugger Graig Nettles swung at a ball that cracked open his bat. Out popped little rubber balls. Like Nettles, Tommy felt humiliated by his success. But his situation was worse; Nettles chose to cheat; Tommy felt demeaned by other men trying to prop him up. This was, of course, before the day of steroids for athletes and of failed CEOs who would be paid tens of millions of dollars just to go away. Tommy began goofing off, missing sales meetings, and gallivanting around Manhattan nightclubs. It was like Brown all over again, but without the Great Dane and the meal ticket.

With all this fetid baggage and psychological trauma to haul around, how could Tommy ever mature into a great CEO? There was no way he could mature, or even survive, unless he figured out how to escape his father. He found the escape route in the one place that his father hated to go: the sky. Even as a young boy, Tommy was fascinated by flying. Growing up in Dayton, Ohio, home of the Wright brothers, had inspired Tommy to "fly" around the family kitchen on a broomstick, pretending to be airborne, while balancing a board under his feet as a rudder. When World War I pilots came back from Europe, they were heroes to Tommy. He begged just to sit in a cockpit. Here is the key point: Father hated flying. The larger-than-life CEO had met the Wright brothers and would later toast Lindbergh, but he was scared of leaving the ground. Father took the family across the Atlantic on luxury liners; airplanes were for daredevils. But Tommy, who fit in nowhere on the ground, found escape in the sky.

Now, Father was not a stupid man, and any sensible person would have been afraid of flying those early Jennys. In fact, in the early 1920s, Father took his children to a county fair at which a pilot offered rides. Tommy and his siblings waited in line, but then sneaked away for a few moments with Father to buy ice-cream cones. Before they could get back in line, they saw the plane hurtle down and crash in a field, killing the passengers.

Tommy was not deterred. As soon as he was old enough, he took flying lessons, and by the time of World War II, he was an experienced pilot. When he ditched IBM sales meetings in 1940, he headed either to the Stork Club or to the airfields to polish up his flying techniques. He longed to join the Army Air Corps, but he was worried that the Army's flight school might discover a little problem he had been hiding: he had no depth perception. An Air Corps doctor took him aside and warned him that he would crash an airplane. Determined to serve and to pursue his escape route, Tommy bought a copy of the Air Corps' eyesight-testing machine and practiced at home lining up the dots and lines. Instead of risking the Air Corps' testing, though, he joined the Air National Guard. He felt lucky when President Roosevelt called up the Guard in 1940 and quickly reported for overseas duty. Oddly, Tommy felt more free in the military than he did at IBM. Endicott was the toughest boot camp Tommy had ever faced. He was not angling for a desk job in the National Guard. He wanted to join a fighter squadron. This was not bravado or recklessness. The boy had finally developed a sense of duty. Sure, he had witnessed Germany's brutality toward Jews and Japan's rapacious militarism, but his real motivation came from a desire to serve his president and to prove himself. For the first time in his life, Tommy recalled, "I wasn't worried about being overshadowed by Dad."[23]

Father did not try to twist Tommy's arm or use his influence to have Tommy shunted to a desk job in a Biloxi bivouac. IBM was playing a role in the war. For every soldier, there was an IBM punch card. And the military employed IBM machines to tabulate casualties, bombing results, and payroll. IBM manufactured the Browning automatic rifle, and physicist Richard Feynman attested to the crucial role IBM calculators played in the Manhattan Project. Scientists deployed new IBM punch-card machines to simulate implosions. Feynman organized a race between them and a hand-computing group. "We set up a room with girls in it. Each one had a Marchant [desk calculator]. But one was the multiplier, and another was the adder, and this one cubed, and all she did was cube this number and send it to the next one," said Feynman. For one day, the hand computers kept up: "The only difference was that the IBM machines didn't get tired and could work three shifts. But the girls got tired after a while."[24]

When Tommy entered the service, Father commissioned a painting of his son. Tommy interpreted this as a sign that Father was preparing for Tommy to get killed.

Tommy's lucky break came when Major General Follett Bradley asked him to be his aide-de-camp. Bradley was the only man that Tommy had met who could command respect like his father. A bald man with deep-set eyes, Bradley looked like a silent movie version of a flier. Like FDR, he dangled a long cigarette holder from his lips and looked through pince-nez. He was an Air Corps pioneer and had been the first to test radio transmissions from the sky. Tommy wanted to impress Bradley and began writing detailed, incisive reports as Bradley inspected air stations around the world. Bradley praised the reports and ultimately rewarded Tommy with the rank of captain. The two men flew to dangerous locations in Russia, India, and China. While Tommy did not drop bombs on enemy targets, he demonstrated tungsten nerves, even under severe stress. Once while crossing the Caspian Sea, Tommy's leg got caught in a malfunctioning nosewheel apparatus. He was spread-eagled across the open hatch, a thousand feet above the oilfields. As the plane lurched toward a tragic landing, Bradley leaned down with a hacksaw. To cut off Tommy's leg and save the crew? No, Bradley sawed off the hinge of the landing-gear door, and Tommy was able to free his leg. On another occasion, they were crossing the South Atlantic from Brazil to Africa, ultimately en route to Moscow. With just enough fuel to make the distance, even experienced fliers like Tommy were anxious. Halfway across the ocean, Tommy checked on the navigator. He found a flummoxed man surrounded by crumpled balls of paper. The navigator was lost. He did not recognize the star formations of the Southern Hemisphere. At dawn, they peered out the windows, longing for land before the fuel gauges spun down to zero. Operating on those proverbial fumes, they found Africa just in time.

As the war was ending in 1945, Bradley asked Tommy what he would do next. Tommy replied that he would like to become a commercial airline pilot, perhaps for United Airlines. He expected Bradley, his wartime father figure, to bless the career plan. Instead, Bradley looked quizzical. Bradley said that he had always assumed Tommy would go back to run IBM. Thomas Watson Sr. was over seventy years old.

Tommy was stunned. That memory of sobbing on the curb returned to his mind. He gathered up the nerve to ask Bradley point-blank: Do you think I could run IBM? Of course, Bradley answered.

Tommy Watson came back from the war a changed man, not because he had seen destruction, torture, or liberation, but because he had seen a part of himself. And because a penetrating and powerful man like Major General Bradley had seen it, too. Tommy was finally ready.

After the War

Father was delighted both to hear that his son wanted to return to IBM and that his son had grown up. IBM would need the help. While Father had made sure that IBM had not profiteered from the war, two-thirds of its output was war related. IBM sales had sky rocketed, but its profit margins had been compressed. Where would the new business come from?

Junior looked for opportunities to help IBM and to prove himself to Father. He first found it in typewriters. Father liked electric typewriters because they saved time, and he thought they appealed to secretaries because they preserved their manicures. He had bought the ElectroMatic Typewriter Company in 1933, but the division bled money for fifteen years. Tommy looked at IBM's typewriter business and persuaded Father to fire the brand manager and replace him with a more innovative leader, "Wiz" Miller. Working with Wiz, Tommy invigorated the group and started paying attention to style, not just the *clickety-clack* of the keyboard. Instead of gunmetal gray, they produced colorful typewriters, including a white one that Father presented to the pope. Later Tommy drew inspiration from Olivetti's style, and the typewriter division began to grow at a 30 percent rate. By the 1970s, publisher Michael Korda was lauding IBM's Selectric as a critical symbol of office power, in his entertaining and ludicrous book, *Power! How to Get It, How to Use It.* If your secretary was not typing on a Selectric, you could be gobbled up and spat out in the Darwinian politics of the corporate office.[25]

In later years, Tommy launched a revamping of the entire IBM style palette. He hired the best industrial designers and commissioned Eero Saarinen, eminent architect of the St. Louis Arch and the space-age TWA terminal at JFK Airport, to create IBM's Rochester campus. In his memoirs, Tommy retells the story of building the San Jose, California, campus, which would be constructed on a walnut grove. The real estate manager told Tommy he had to wait eight months to break ground or else it would cost IBM an extra $800,000. Why? That was the value of the forthcoming walnut crop harvest.

Tommy's success with typewriters showed Father two aspects of Tommy's growth. First, he could choose managers well. Second, he could lead a product launch. Despite this quick postwar success, the two Tom Watsons could not stop bickering. Tommy felt that Father made him fight for every scrap of power within the firm, even setting Tommy up to duel with other executives. In IBM's offices on Madison Avenue in New York, Father commanded affairs from the seventeenth floor. He installed a button on his desk that sounded a buzzer in Tommy's office one floor below. At times it might as well have been a dog whistle. He summoned Tommy as an errand boy, a confidant, and an heir apparent. But until Tommy had climbed the flight of stairs, he had no idea how he would be treated. Like Churchill's speech rallying Britain to fight on the beach, on the landing grounds, etc., the two Thomases fought in the office, on the streets, and even in their homes. Tommy, who by 1950 was married and nearly middle-aged, would often collapse on a guest bed at his parents' Manhattan town house rather than commute home to his wife. This allowed the fighting to continue, for Father would rouse him to debate some sales deal gone awry. Why didn't Tommy just go home?

The Russian American painter Victor Nizovtsev has created a remarkable series juxtaposing an old king and a prince. The wizened king nervously cradles a timepiece, while his ambitious young heir wields a sword.[26] Nizovtsev could have used the Watsons as models for the tense relationship in his paintings. At one point Thomas Watson Sr. and family had an audience in Stockholm with the king of Sweden. Father turned to Tommy's wife, Nancy, telling her that her short dress was a "disgrace" to the Watson family. Tommy lit into him: "Look, old man. You can tell me anything you want. . . . But don't talk to Nancy that way. She is my wife and has nothing to do with you." Father reeled back and apologized.

In the 1950s, IBM began fighting and then negotiating with the Justice Department over antitrust infractions. Before Tommy left to attend a courthouse negotiation, his eighty-one-year-old father exploded, remembering his own conviction in 1913: "You're totally incompetent to do that! [D]on't you make any decisions!"[27] Tommy was still shaking with rage at Father's arrogant outburst as he sat in the courtroom. Then Father's personal secretary sneaked into the room and handed him a note. *Oh, God, Dad's had a stroke and died*, the son thought. But it was a little slip of paper torn out of Father's legendary notebook, with the header "THINK." Like a simple haiku, it read,

100%
Confidence
Appreciation
Admiration
Love
Dad

Slowly during the 1950s, the old man mellowed a bit. Hobbled by hernias, ulcers, and a conviction that surgeons would make him sicker, Father began to withdraw. Even when weakened, though, the old lion could surprise everyone and release a roar. Tommy remembered Father attending a sales meeting just before his death. The executive officiating did not expect him. Seeing the frail and stooped "man of men" loitering in the back of the room, he asked if the former CEO had a few words for the five hundred gathered salesmen. A wispy old man of eighty-two, Father began to shuffle down the aisle toward the stage. As Tommy tells it, "The men jumped to their feet and were clapping and shouting. The more they clapped and the farther he got down the aisle, the more erect he became. He stood up straighter and straighter and walked faster and faster until he finally got to the steps leading up to the stage. He went up them with such a surge of energy that he seemed to take them two at a time. . . . Dad shed about thirty years. . . . He grabbed the podium and made a very stirring speech, punching his fist into his hand . . . and telling the men how IBM was going on forever."[28]

When Thomas Sr. died in 1956, the *New York Times* called him the "World's Greatest Salesman," though the quotation marks suggested it was more an honorary title than an objective analysis. When he died, Tommy was, he said, the "most frightened man in America." Contemplating life without Father, Tommy's throat swelled up, his body erupted with rashes, and a doctor had to inject him with adrenaline to prevent him from choking to death. The future of IBM would not be easy.

LIFE WITHOUT FATHER

Despite Father's declining health in the 1950s, IBM's sales soared. Revenues jumped to $215 million in 1950 and then doubled by 1955. During this period, Tommy moved up from executive vice president to CEO. He also saved the company. In the late 1940s, IBM had no plans to introduce computers. To IBM, high technology was a calculator that performed arithmetic functions by mechanically sorting punch cards at about four calculations per second. Meanwhile, at the University of Pennsylvania a true computer called the Electronic Numerical Integrator and Computer (ENIAC) was flashing electrons around circuits and crunching five thousand numbers per second. Now, for all the magic of electronic computing, ENIAC had some drawbacks. It was too massive to fit in most offices, it contained thousands of vacuum tubes, it heated up the room like an old coal-burning locomotive, and it attracted moths and required debugging. Tommy visited ENIAC and was not impressed. Father was not interested either. Father loved punch cards almost as much as he loved his salesmen. Unlike magnetic tape or electronic memories, punch cards never forgot data and never got viruses. You could touch them, caress them, and count them by hand if you wanted to. They were as reliable as the Yankee dollar. Of course, this was before the inflationary 1970s and before the "dangling chads" of the 2000 presidential election in Florida. Electrons? They were flighty, unreliable, invisible, and, if you believed the quantum physicists, capable of devilishly irresponsible and unplanned behavior. The quantum theorists reported that electrons might act like Newtonian billiard balls at noon and then decide to act like wandering waves two minutes later.

In the battle between cardboard and electrons, IBM planted itself in cardboard's corner. In truth, IBM did not know much about electrons. IBM's engineers were, as Tommy called them, "monkey-wrench engineers," more comfortable with a screwdriver than a Zener diode. When Father had an idea for a new product, he would call in the monkey wrenchers, who would tinker in their garages and "put it in metal." After World War II, IBM was just pretending to be on the cutting age. But Tommy realized that the company could not be cutting-edge if it was merely cutting metal. IBM developed a massive, fancy punch-card calculator that was 120 feet long and displayed it behind the plate-glass window of its Madison Avenue showroom. It had all the blinking neon lights and spinning dials of a *Twilight Zone* episode. While it certainly looked like a futuristic computer, behind the glossy panels buzzed second-rate technologies. It would not do.

In the next few years, Tommy realized he had to take IBM forward and place his bet on the electron. He learned and taught some lasting lessons that apply today.

Listen to the Customer

What is the biggest resource a company has? Its customers. It began when Tommy learned that two of IBM's biggest clients, Prudential Insurance and the Census Bureau, were funding a successor to ENIAC called UNIVAC. Then the Metropolitan Life Company shot a warning. A vice president confided to Tommy that IBM would lose the company's business if it did not leap ahead. Met Life already had three floors of space filled with punch cards and punch-card machines. It needed magnetic tape, not cardboard. Then humiliation came. On the eve of the 1952 presidential election, on live television, Walter Cronkite, Edward R. Murrow, and Eric Sevareid consulted UNIVAC, which correctly forecast Dwight Eisenhower's trouncing of Adlai Stevenson. Cronkite even called the computer a "marvelous electronic brain."

Tommy realized that IBM should not be a company devoted to cardboard, but a company devoted to information and data processing. If the forces of technology were burying cardboard, so be it. He threw the throttle into overdrive and raced IBM to the front lines, hiring twenty thousand new employees and tripling the number of R&D employees to 9 percent of the workforce.[29] When Bell Labs brought forth a transistor to replace vacuum tubes and Texas Instruments began manufacturing them in 1956, Tommy forced his engineers to design transistor-based computers. Many engineers resisted. They had grown comfortable with tubes. Tommy issued a proclamation declaring that IBM would not design more vacuum tube computers. He helped negotiate volume discounts with Texas Instruments so that IBM could design new computers assuming that transistor prices would *fall*. This was prescient. Ten years before Gordon Moore of Intel suggested "Moore's Law," that computing capacity would double every eighteen months (and the dollar cost would decrease along the same curve), Tommy was taking advantage of the principle.

Tommy made sure IBM took advantage not just of new technology, but of its historically close ties between the sales force and the engineers. Even if UNIVAC was a more sophisticated piece of equipment than IBM's new 701 (also known as the Defense Calculator for its military uses), IBM's sales team knew how to show off the machine, hook customers, install the equipment, and hang on to the customers for years to come. IBM flew thousands of salesmen to Poughkeepsie, New York, for intensive seminars. They often invited customers, too. Remington Rand, which owned UNIVAC, did not bother to retrain its punch-card salesmen. Competing machines like UNIVAC would take a week to install. IBM's engineers designed their machines for easy shipping. They deployed modular technologies so that they could get a machine up and running within a few days. IBM also learned how to make money on the peripherals, such as printers and magnetic tape drives. IBM's "customer focus" was sharper than anyone else's. It paid off by the end of the 1950s, when IBM's revenues topped $1 billion, with two-thirds coming from real computers and peripherals. Tommy switched from cardboard to electrons and won.

Along the way, Tommy had learned from Father how to create a splashy unveiling for IBM's wares. For the Defense Calculator, William Shockley, David Sarnoff, John von Neumann, and even J. Robert Oppenheimer toasted IBM. Oppenheimer called IBM's work a "tribute to the human mind" that would "shatter the time barrier." One aside about the brilliant Oppenheimer, whose career became clouded by political machinations and accusations. He did have one youthful escapade in common with "Terrible Tommy" Watson. Remember young Tommy's being thrown out of school for his skunk juice prank? Malcolm Gladwell reports that as a student, Oppenheimer was kicked out of Cambridge for spiking his tutor's apple with poison![30]

Hook Them While They're Young

Since the 1980s, Apple Computer has done a wonderful job hooking young people, first with the Macintosh and more recently with the iPod. IBM has not. However, years before Apple's success, Tommy led IBM into classrooms. His motive was twofold. First, IBM needed to hire more computer scientists. If he could encourage the study of computers, IBM would have a bigger list of recruits. Second, IBM would always need more customers for its computers. Back in the 1950s, Tommy led an aggressive campaign to penetrate college campuses. He donated a large computer to MIT (at a time when computers were still rare and prized). Then he created a big discount program, giving colleges a 40 percent price break if they launched a course in data processing or scientific computing. For any college that launched both types of courses, Tommy slashed prices by 60 percent. Now, IBM was looking for institutional sales, not personal computer sales, as was Apple with its "Macs in the Classroom" program in the 1980s. Still, Tommy demonstrated a foresight that went missing at IBM in later years. Of course, as Tommy knew, IBM had some prior experience in the classroom. It had previously developed the scoring equipment for standardized tests. To this day, when you anxiously pick up a number 2 pencil, you can blame IBM for your jitters.

Make Yourself Obsolete

I believe that *it is better to make yourself obsolete than to wait for your competitors to do it for you.* Tommy Watson eclipsed his father and wrote his way into this book because he knew when to take a gamble. And, of course, he won. By the mid-1960s, IBM had grabbed an overwhelming market share for computers in the U.S. and even 75 percent in West Germany, Italy, and France.[31] U.S. competitors like Sperry Rand, Honeywell, NCR, and others were nicknamed the "Seven Dwarfs." Each year on the anniversary of his father's death, Tommy would follow a ritual. He would sit at home quietly, assess IBM's latest accomplishments, and say aloud, "That's another year I've made it alone."

Nonetheless, the Seven Dwarfs were always threatening to catch up. In 1961, Tommy took stock of IBM. His sales force and engineers were warning that Honeywell had a blockbuster new computer to unveil. Meanwhile, Tommy realized that IBM's dominant products had deep flaws. Computers designed for business were segregated from those designed for science. Most important, IBM's computers did not play well with others. The IBM catalog offered eight different computers, but the guts of each computer were totally different. Neither software, disk drives, nor even printers could be swapped. If a customer wanted to upgrade, he had to throw away everything he had invested in. This hurt the customer, and it required IBM to waste engineering resources. The Mazda Motor Company used to brag that it made something like one hundred different steering wheels, until some bright engineer asked, "Why are you bragging about creating so much extra work?" Was it possible to create a family of modular computers that could talk to one another, handle business and science, and allow customers to upgrade without first visiting a junk heap? Tommy thought the only possible answer was yes. And he bet $5 billion on that answer, far more money than IBM had. Heck, it was *thirty* times the size of its annual profit! *Fortune* magazine profiled the investment as the "$5,000,000,000 Gamble" and called it the most crucial and riskiest business judgment of recent times."[32] No other company could revolutionize computers as IBM would. Because it developed its own proprietary circuitry, it became the world's largest manufacturer of components and had tremendous incentive to stomp on the costs of memory. IBM would call the new computer System 360, for the 360 degrees in a circle.

The engineers liked the idea, but the salesmen nearly rioted. Salesmen did not want to give up their smorgasbord of choices. With a ridiculous variety of combinations, a salesman could always say, "We have the right machine for you."[33]

Tommy was determined to win the gamble. Like President Kennedy's announcement that the U.S. would put a man on the moon by the end of the 1960s, Tommy's audacious plan to unveil the System 360 in 1964 forced IBM to put a delivery date on a device that had not even been in-vented yet!

Like so much else in Tommy Watson's life, at times the System 360 looked like an absolute disaster. With all its resources leveraged to the 360, IBM could not afford to upgrade its existing line. Competitors started gobbling up market share, and IBM's sales force got panicky. In 1963, IBM sold just 7 percent more computers; competitors boosted their sales by more than twice that rate. Salesmen for Honeywell and the others scoffed and pulled customers aside, warning them that IBM's white ele-phant might never be born. Tommy saw his company "degrading" in the marketplace. Then IBM's financial records became a blur, and the company's frantic CFO could not even count the value of inventory. It lost its inventory? Wasn't this company supposed to be the premier data processor? IBM was forced to issue $370 million in stock, and vice presidents began to tell one another that IBM was becoming a "laugh-ingstock." Between 1961 and 1964, the rush to create System 360 de-stroyed nerves and destroyed Tommy's relationship with his younger brother Dick, whose engineers could not keep up with ever-changing specifications.

Everybody was scared and short of patience, Tommy reported. Tommy woke up an exhausted programmer who had ducked onto a cot to catch a little sleep and asked why the software was not coming along faster; the programmer snarled, "If you'd get the hell out of here and leave us alone, we would!" Tommy actually liked contention and often set his staff to debate one another. He liked scrappy fighters. But this was more tension than even he had bargained for.

Finally, bleeding in the balance sheet and reeling from lost sales, IBM unveiled the System 360. It was April 7, 1964, exactly fifty years to the day since Father had shown up for work at CTR. Tommy arranged nearly simultaneous press conferences in sixty-three cities, including fourteen foreign countries. He pulled the blanket back from six new computers and forty-four new peripherals. The oohs and ahhs came in the form of a flood of orders from NASA, Bank of America, and hundreds of others. It was the biggest blast since the Model T. Sales rocketed by a rate of 30 per-cent per year.[34] The System 360 inspired other companies to jump into software, leasing, and computer services, including the aforementioned

Ross Perot. By the 1970s, more than half the Fortune 500's chief information officers were proud alums of IBM.[35] Tommy had led IBM through enemy fire and into a golden era.

How Do We Solve a Problem Like Dell?

Tommy Watson was certainly not the first big CEO to make a big bet on a dangerous new direction. Consider Nokia. If you stop an old Finn on the streets (which may be tough in winter when he is ice-skating past you) and ask what Nokia is known for, he will answer "rubber boots." Before the 1980s, Nokia was best known by fishermen named Sven wading waist-high into rivers, looking for brown trout. Now Nokia means cellular phones to billions around the world.

Today, many companies could learn from the two Thomas Watsons. Consider Dell Computer. Dell's story is a marvel of entrepreneurship and audacity. Michael Dell started by selling computers from his dorm room at the University of Texas, Austin, in 1984 and quickly began stomping on Compaq, Hewlett-Packard, and Apple. His company custom-built computers, installing whatever capabilities the buyer needed. During the heyday of the 1990s, when Dell could do no wrong, when business magazines called him one of "America's Most Admired," and Wall Street awarded Dell a price earnings ratio twice that of his competitors, I visited his Austin factory to behold the wizardry of its efficiency. UPS trucks backed into cargo bays on one side of a very large room. There the components rolled onto the assembly line. Employees quickly screwed and riveted the pieces together. Before you knew it, the new computers were heading out the other end of the room. What was waiting for them at the other end? UPS trucks waiting to whisk them away. I realized that Michael Dell did not touch your computer; by the time the components were a fully integrated, completed item, your computer was out of his hands, and someone else was worrying about inventory costs. If possession was nine-tenths of the law, Michael Dell was the biggest crook in American economic history—because he never really had possession of your computer! It was a testament to his brilliant supply-chain management and engineering efficiency. I owned Dell laptops and lauded Dell in speeches around the world.

What happened? Why has Dell stumbled so badly in recent years? Did a brilliant person get stupid? Of course not. He is still terrific in supply-chain management, but the company lost the lessons of the two Tom Watsons. Remember Tom Sr.'s obsession to bind the customers and the sales force to the company, which I likened to the seamless infinity symbol? The seams have frayed at Dell. Tom Sr. figured out how to sell "solutions, not just slices." His salesmen could provide more than just the hunk of metal. His people could install, service, and hook the customer on new products and upgrades. Dell started as a customer-friendly outfit. Customization was rare among PCs when Dell launched his business. But now customers see a Dell computer as a hunk of plastic that shows up in the mail. They open up the computer and ask, "What do I do next?" Then they call a help line. In 2006 Dell admitted that 45 percent of those calls were transferred. Heavily accented helpers were no help. How could you follow Tom Jr.'s warning to "listen to the customer" if your employees could not even understand the customer? More intensive technical service from Dell requires paying large per-minute fees. As the comedian Lewis Black said, at "three dollars a minute, I'd just as soon have phone sex." Now, these complaints are not unique to Dell. Of course, they cannot provide free service or hold hands with dopey buyers who cannot find the on/off switch. But the point is that Dell was originally devised and billed as a more customer-friendly company. People expected more. Now, people feel more comfortable walking into a Circuit City and chatting with some smart kid named Josh or Justin who offers them some buying advice and a rebate check on a purchase. Dell is trying to correct its hands-off image, opening up more telephonic help centers in Canada, for example, as well as kiosks throughout shopping malls. Dell may not be able to hold hands with each customer, but for several years, the company actually appeared to be trying shake them loose.

Dell might also have to consider making itself obsolete. The laptop and PC look like low-priced commodities. How can Dell hold on and eke out a profit margin? It might have to break out of the commodity business and make a big bet. Instead of simply screwing together laptops and PCs that have largely the same specs as its competitors', Dell might have to dig deep into its pockets to develop something totally new, proprietary, and unmatchable by Josh or Justin at Circuit City. Is Dell an innovative, customer-friendly technology company—or just a workshop that puts things together?

LAST DAYS OF THOMAS J. WATSON JR.

After conquering the world of technology in the 1960s and the ghost of his father, Tommy got bored. In 1970, friends found him distracted; family found him irritable. While he moped in his executive suite, mobs of executives, lawyers, and bankers would stream in, seeking his signature. They would lay out for him folders containing billion-dollar expansion plans and notebooks bursting with antitrust documents. What he really wanted to look at was tucked into the top drawer of his desk. That's where he kept this intimate secret. When no one was around, he would furtively pull out the drawer and gaze at the secret. Was it a letter from Father? A devastating piece of evidence hidden from the Justice Department? A blackmailing letter from an illicit lover? For a man who had traveled as far financially and emotionally as Thomas Watson Jr., the possibilities were limitless. He disclosed the secret to no one until, at age fifty-six, he woke up in the middle of the night with a pain in his chest. Alone in the house, he rushed to the emergency room of the Greenwich, Connecticut, hospital, where he spent the rest of the night. By morning, the pain was gone, and he stood up to go home. The doctor looked at the monitors and said, "You're not going anywhere. You're having a heart attack." Father had lived to eighty-two and never had a heart problem. Incredulous and angry, Tommy was wheeled into an oxygen tent, where he lost consciousness.

Tommy survived this episode, though it took several weeks. He forged a close relationship with his internist, Dr. Newberg. When Tommy finally finished his recovery, Newberg asked what he would do next. Tommy had no choice. Go back to work. Maybe retire in a few years.

"Why don't you get out right now?"

Tommy was stunned. And relieved. He, who had fought Father for decades, who had followed in those frightening footsteps, had been wait-

ing for some authority figure to utter those words. Just as Major General
Bradley virtually gave him permission to lead IBM after the war, Dr. Newberg gave him permission to call it quits. From the hospital, he called the
office and ordered his assistant to open up the top drawer of his desk and
send him the secret paper. He tore open the envelope and peered at the
secret. It was a list of things he had hoped to do but never could before:
climb the Matterhorn, and sail to the Arctic, Greenland, and even Cape
Horn. In the next twenty years of his life, he at last found his escape.

2 ½

Mary Kay Ash and Estée Lauder:

The Most Beautiful Balance Sheets

A knock on the door. A brochure pinched under a windshield wiper. A Chinese menu slipped under an apartment door. A puff of perfume folded into a magazine advertisement. The marketing never stops. Who inspires these armies of marketing? Two of the most powerful and innovative generals were petite women who started all alone, Mary Kay Ash and Estée Lauder. The following chapters tell a tale of two women who came from different places, developed different sales techniques, and competed for different customers. One emerged from Texas, the daughter of a poor and luckless family. The other burst out of a humble apartment in Queens, New York, determined to regain the European grandeur that her forebears never really had. One sought customers amid coffee klatches and suburban homemakers in housedresses. The other knocked on the door of Saks until they let her in. One produced sales conferences modeled after evangelical revival meetings. The other steeped tea with Princess Grace. The more you learn about Mary Kay and Estée Lauder, the harder it is to get your brain to picture them in the same room. Imagine trying to seat Woody Guthrie next to Cole Porter at a dinner party. Guthrie would be looking for a toothpick while Porter would be looking for the oyster fork. And yet Mary Kay and Estée Lauder did share something essential: an unstoppable drive to knock over obstacles like bowling pins, whether those obstacles were sexist businessmen, niggardly financiers, or tiresome troops of neighbors who told women in the 1950s just to sit at home because Father knows best.

As we jump into the chapters on Mary Kay Ash and Estée Lauder, some readers might object that this book focuses on just two female CEOs. Moreover, both CEOs carved out their careers in cosmetics. Sounds awfully quaint and old-fashioned. But that is the point: for the overwhelming part of the twentieth century, women simply did not have the opportunity to rise to corporate CEO positions. Smart woman were shunted into education, which captured almost half of college-educated women in the 1930s. This was a huge boon for America's schools, an amazing hidden subsidy—smart women working at half price. But it was discriminatory. By the 1970s, only about 10 percent of college-educated women chose teaching.[1] As the father of three daughters, I am delighted that they have far more opportunities than their grandmothers. Today there are many successful woman CEOs such as Meg Whitman at eBay and Anne Mulcahy at Xerox. But today, happily, they are not dead and therefore not eligible for this book. I wish them long lives!

Okay, Todd, you did not have many women to choose from. But two cosmetics queens? Isn't that embarrassing? Not at all. First, I respect deeply anyone who can build a business from scratch. I see nothing intrinsically more noble and daring about selling spark plugs than selling eyeliner. Second, cosmetics provided one of the few open avenues for women. *Makeup is like professional boxing.* Not in its brutality (although those counters at Bloomingdale's are terribly competitive). Boxing has always attracted the poorest groups striving to make it big. In the early 1900s, Irishmen like John L. Sullivan dominated boxing. Later, Jews like Barney Ross, Italians like Rocky Marciano, and blacks like Joe Louis wore the championship belts. More recently, Hispanics like Oscar de la Hoya and Eastern Europeans like the Klitschko brothers have reigned. Cosmetics has played a similar role for women.

SARAH BREEDLOVE, AKA C. J. WALKER:
MADAM COURAGE

Consider the amazing Madam C. J. Walker. In 1867 a young girl named Sarah started life with virtually nothing, just the love of her ex-slave parents, Owen and Minerva Breedlove. They were sharecroppers living in a one-room cabin near Delta, Louisiana. Little Sarah tried to help her parents by spreading cotton seeds, carrying buckets of water, and even washing the clothing of white folks, using powerful lye soap. What little she had vanished at age six, when yellow fever swept across the fields, killing her parents. She moved in with an older sister, married at age fourteen, and spent the next twenty-five years washing other people's laundry, raising a daughter, and volunteering in her church, first in Mississippi, then in St. Louis. Lucky in neither work nor love, her first husband died, and she divorced a second.

In her thirties, Sarah realized that not only was her life falling apart, but also her hair was falling apart and falling out. She tried washing and rinsing with products on the market, but the breakage continued. Then, she claimed, she had a vision that would turn her into one of America's first female self-made millionaires: "One night I had a dream, and in that dream, a big black man appeared to me and told me what to mix up for my hair. Some of the remedy was grown in Africa, but I sent for it, mixed it, put it on my scalp, and in a few weeks, my hair was coming in faster than it had ever fallen out. I tried it on my friends; it helped them. I made up my mind I would begin to sell it." [2]

To pursue her entrepreneurial vision, she moved near her sister-in-law in Denver, rented an attic room, and prepared to launch a business while still taking in laundry and cooking to pay the rent. She had just $1.50 in savings, which even in today's dollars would not pay for much. She began walking door-to-door in African American neighborhoods, showing off her creations, which she colorfully named Wonderful Hair Grower, Glossine, and Vegetable Shampoo. Word began to spread, and soon she moved out of the attic. She married Joseph C. J. Walker and decided that "Madam C. J. Walker" provided the proper panache. *Her homemade remedies took off, not simply because they were better than store-bought, but also because stores simply did not cater to the hair of African American women.* In the next ten years, Madam Walker set up beauty salons, attracted a national sales force of five thousand, and launched a successful mail-order business.

Around 1916, Madam Walker turned business management over to others and bought a town house in Harlem and a villa on the toniest banks of the Hudson River, where her neighbors included John D. Rockefeller and Jay Gould. Until her death in 1919 at age fifty-one, Madam Walker spoke out for civil rights. She visited the White House to urge Woodrow Wilson to make lynching a federal crime. Her daughter A'Lelia became a key figure in the Harlem Renaissance in the 1920s, turning Walker's Harlem town house into a literary salon. Madam Walker not only understood that entrepreneurs need the help of others, but she also knew that no stranger and no friend could provide the ultimate spark: "I got myself a start by giving myself a start." [3]

Of course, Madam Walker's example inspired many others to go on their way, including Mary Kay Ash and Estée Lauder.

3

Mary Kay Ash:

The Billion Dollar Coffee Klatsch

Mary Kay Wagner was born in 1915 (or possibly earlier) in Hot Wells, Texas, a dying resort town served by the railroads. Apparently, those wells were not bubbly enough to keep even a handful of families living in the town, and the number of residents soon dwindled to zero. Mary Kay's family moved on to Houston, where her mother managed a restaurant. Her father could not work, for tuberculosis rendered him an invalid. As a young girl, Mary Kay witnessed her mother's rugged determination to be the breadwinner in the fragile family. With her father incapacitated and her mother constantly away at work, even at the age of seven, Mary Kay was hopping on streetcars by herself and trying to negotiate bargains in the department stores, reaching into her little purse to withdraw coins for a blouse or a sandwich. To a parent today, this seems terribly sad, but to Mary Kay, it instilled a boundless sense of confidence. Anybody who navigated the Wild West as a kid would have no doubts about taking on Avon ladies!

Mary Kay was not just street smart; she was book wise, too. She earned straight A's in school, and her competitive spirit drove her to win contests for typing and for extemporaneous speaking. She was inspired by a neighborhood rival who "had everything I wanted to have and did everything I wanted to do."[1] But like so many excellent high school students, Mary Kay could not afford college. While her friends packed their bags for nearby Rice Institute (later Rice University), Mary Kay started searching for a job and a husband.

In the 1930s, it was easier to find a spouse than a job, as the Great Depression ripped one-quarter of America's employees from their jobs, sending them scavenging for any work they could find. At a time when girls were encouraged to bring home "a good catch," Mary Kay reeled in Ben Rogers, a man who was known for two talents: playing guitar in a local band called the Hawaiian Strummers and filling gas tanks at a local service station. Ben was popular on the radio, and Mary later described him as a charismatic, provincial Elvis. Mary stayed home with their three children while Elvis entertained. Stuck at home in Houston, her future career in cosmetics seemed as far away as the Hawaiian Islands.

Before tracing Mary Kay's next steps, let's consider the state of the cosmetic industry during Mary Kay's youth. Prior to the Roaring Twenties, the average American spent only about $8 (in today's dollars) on cosmetics, toiletries, and dental goods—per year![2] For most Americans, the very idea of minty breath or fresh-scented underarms sounded like a page from Jules Verne. Now it is true that the upper classes had their own body-image priorities. First of all, they did not want to look skinny and hungry. A hundred years ago, those few Americans with spare time and spare change were more likely to sign up for a weight-*gaining* class than a weight-loss program.[3] Rich people stacked their vanity cabinets with fragrances and face whiteners. Dark skin suggested you labored in the hot sun. Apparently, in 1915 you could never be too fat or too white. Though companies like Colgate-Palmolive had marketed toiletries for decades, most Americans were suspicious of store-bought stuff, fearing lead or arsenic poisoning. Lola Montez, a popular Irish-born dancer who pretended to be Spanish, urged women in the 1850s to manufacture their own cosmetics or else risk ruining their complexions and nervous systems.[4] Most Americans simply did not have the disposable income to buy vanity products. In 1900, families spent over 40 percent of their incomes simply on food (compared to under 10 percent today).[5]

During the Depression, Mary Kay learned that professional musicians were a luxury, and her Elvis-like husband lost his radio show. Since everyone still needed to eat, Mary Kay and Ben found a job together selling pots and pans. They arranged marketing events that included dinners where Mary Kay would cook in some stranger's kitchen while her husband would charm the guest audience with the selling points of alloyed frying pans and pressure cookers. The menu was always the same, Mary Kay recalled: green beans, ham, sweet potatoes, and a cake. Since cooking was supposed to look like child's play, Mary Kay spent a lot of time preparing ingredients before she arrived at the house. "Each dinner was fabulous," she recalled, "but it was food we couldn't afford to buy for ourselves. If there was any food left over after the demonstration, it became our dinner. If our prospective customers ate it all, we just didn't eat that night."[6] A less honest person might have been tempted to bungle one dish each evening. But despite Mary Kay's fine cooking and scrupulous manner, the couple could not find enough people who could afford to spring for new cookware while the world economy was falling apart.

Mary Kay, who was religious all her life, prayed to God and soon found a job as the secretary of a Baptist church. It paid $125 per month— just enough to keep her out of somebody else's kitchen. Over the course of her life, incidentally, Mary Kay married a Catholic, a Protestant, and a Jew. World War II touched Mary Kay in a personal way: when her husband Ben came back from his service, he announced that he wanted a divorce. For someone so determined for personal and professional success, this was a devastating moment: "It was the lowest point of my life. . . . I felt a complete and total failure."[7] But with three children to support, she did not have the time to sit around and pity herself.

Mary Kay found an additional job, selling household cleaning products for a young Massachusetts-based company called Stanley Home Products. As in the cookware-selling business, Mary Kay once again found herself standing in other people's homes, this time demonstrating and hawking mops, brushes, and stain removers. It could not have been easy throwing dirt on some stranger's carpet. I recall a hilarious episode of the television show *Taxi,* in which Christopher Lloyd (portraying the burned-out Jim Ignatowski) grinds coffee, mud, and grit onto the rug of a protesting housewife. He then opens his box and, in shock, declares: "My God! I'm selling *encyclopedias!*"

Mary Kay was too organized to pack the wrong items. Still, she had trouble selling a lot of home cleaners. She liked the products, but suspected her sales methods needed fine-tuning. She started searching for any help she could find and traveled to Stanley's regional convention in Dallas. In Dallas she found not just hints, but also inspiration. After attending a series of meetings, she had written down twenty pages of notes. The ultimate meeting, though, was the "Crowning of the Sales Queen" to the heartfelt applause of the Stanley employees. Mary Kay got up the nerve to ask the queen to host a house party for her. Then she told the president and founder, Frank Stanley Beveridge, that she intended to earn the crown at the next convention. "He took my hand in both of his, looked me square in the eye, and after a moment said solemnly, 'Somehow I think you will!' Those five words changed my life."[8] Sure enough, a year later Mary Kay walked down the aisle wearing the crown.

Mary Kay's native enthusiasm made her money not just for selling cleaning supplies. At Stanley she also learned that she could earn money by recruiting other salespeople. Such recruiting later became a defining feature of Mary Kay Cosmetics. Over the next few years, Mary Kay attracted about 150 others to sell Stanley equipment, and thereby, reaped a small percentage from all of their sales efforts. Stanley asked her to beef up the firm's Dallas efforts, but when she moved from Houston, the company did not let her continue to benefit from the sales of her Houston recruits. Mary Kay pledged that she would fight to change this rule. After all, she had spent countless hours building up her Houston sales force. She could not change minds at Stanley headquarters, but years later when she started Mary Kay Cosmetics, she insisted that recruiting commissions be portable.

MOPS TO MASCARA

How did Mary Kay make the switch from mops to mascara? Once again the action took place in someone else's house. In the early 1950s, Mary Kay was showing off some mops and brooms for a group of twenty women when she noticed how youthful and smooth their faces looked, even the septuagenarians'. The ladies were users of special facial creams, offered by the hostess. The hostess stepped closer to examine Mary Kay's face and announced that she had whiteheads and aging skin. Mary Kay took home the special emollients—including a night cream, a cleaning cream, a masque, a skin freshener, and a foundation—and began applying them to her face. She and her new husband, Richard, immediately noticed her glowing face looking smoother and more youthful. Though Mary Kay stayed with Stanley a little longer before moving on to another direct sales firm called World Gift Company, she never forgot the extraordinary facial she received that day. She regularly returned to the lady's house to refill her bottles of magic. And so a decade later, in 1963, she bought the rights to the original formula used by that hostess.

Where did the hostess get the formula, this fountain of youth? Inventions are often spurred by accidental events rather than deductive laboratory research. In 1948 a Swiss hiker named George de Mestral found his trousers and his dog covered in burrs. With a microscope, he examined the tiny hooks that enabled the burr to cling so stubbornly. Velcro was born (named for "velour plus crochet").[9] As for the origins of Mary Kay's cosmetics, you need not look any farther than the buttocks of a cow or horse. Mary Kay learned that the father of the hostess was a tanner, who turned the speckled tough hides of livestock into beautiful soft gloves. As he applied the tanning fluids to the animal pelts, he realized that those fluids were restoring the suppleness of the skin on his own hands. Along with his daughter (the hostess), he began experimenting with the tanning ingredients, and ultimately, he got the courage to apply them to his face. Millions of satisfied Mary Kay users around the world today can thank some scarred horse's ass for their radiant complexions.

Mary Kay did not immediately jump on the idea of a cosmetics company. She spent the 1950s trying to raise her children while almost constantly traveling, building up a forty-three-state network of salespeople for World Gift. Mary Kay grew frustrated watching so many of her trainees far outearn her simply because they were men and, therefore, were deemed more deserving. The company explained, "They have families to support!" Of course, so did she, but that carried little weight. Mary Kay finally quit in a management dispute and decided to write a book about selling.

She sat in her living room, depressed and jobless after more than twenty-five years of toiling, wheeling, dealing, and sweet-talking: "I lived across the street from a mortuary, and I began to wonder if I should just call them up and tell them to 'come on over.'"[10] She began to write down her experiences in direct selling and her advice on how to improve the direct sales model. Perhaps she stroked her cheek or massaged her temples, and suddenly inspiration struck, and she realized she was still young enough to try again. This time, however, she would not answer to a long-distance, chauvinistic boss. She gathered Richard, who was good with finances, and her sons around the kitchen table and mapped out a strategy to buy the tanner's formulas. They had saved $5,000 (about $33,000 in today's dollars) and were willing to commit the entire bank account to secure a small office with two desks and to manufacture a small sample of supplies. Mary Kay quickly recruited ten saleswomen to work on commission.

The plan looked bold, and Mary Kay once again felt fearless. But suddenly the world spun against her. It was a month before the business was to open. Richard and Mary Kay were sitting at the breakfast table, assessing their chances, calculating the risks, and counting little sample jars labeled "Beauty by Mary Kay." Mary Kay might have thought Richard was grabbing for a bottle, but it was his chest he clutched. Richard's heart seized up, and he slumped in front of her. He was dead of a heart attack.

Their careful plan was shredded like black confetti. What could she do? What would she do? Most people, even most hardened entrepreneurs, would have called off the plan. After burying her husband, Mary Kay sat with her sons and pondered. Her attorney offered very prudent advice: liquidate immediately and recoup whatever cash you can. "If you don't, you'll end up penniless," he said.

As Mary Kay saw it, she faced a stark choice: she could salvage some cash and in four weeks time still be mourning Richard, or she could start a new morning for her life. Her son Ben, then twenty-seven, passed over to her his passbook savings account with $4,500. Her son Richard, just twenty and working for Prudential Life Insurance, offered to quit his job to help. How much could Mary Kay pay him? About $250 a month. That would be a 50 percent pay cut. He took the job with his mother: "I didn't view my offer as a sacrifice at all. Mary Kay had been a winner all her life, she understood direct selling as well as anyone in the world."[11]

Accountants and lawyers make very good accountants and lawyers.

They continued to pepper Mary Kay with missives and pamphlets explaining why her business model would fail. They were only trying to save her $5,000 life savings, along with her son's $4,500. They did not understand that she was building an empire. On September 13, 1963 (a Friday), Mary Kay opened up her five-hundred-square-foot store in Dallas. She stuffed her entire inventory on a single metal shelf she had bought at Sears. She wrote her goals in soap on her bathroom windows and stuck motivational note cards all over the inside of her car. She appointed her son Richard chief executive officer and sent him out to secure bank loans. Richard looked so youthful that he actually pasted a fake mustache on his face to appear older. As Mary Kay tried to make her customers look younger, her CEO had to go through an opposite charade!

The business was an immediate flop. Looking to create some customer traffic, Mary Kay even started selling wigs, a hot item in the early 1960s. But her floor space was so tight, she had to keep the inventory in a warehouse two blocks away. When she spotted a live customer for a wig, she would send her youthful CEO son running around the block to grab some samples. You could just imagine the kid with the fake mustache juggling hairpieces and bank loans as the creditors came calling.

Within months, however, Mary Kay began to compile a list of mistakes, and she began developing the model that would conquer Dallas and, later, the world. In 1966, she married Mel Ash, who would help guide her Dallas operations.

MARY KAY'S SECRET RECIPE

Mary Kay certainly did not invent the idea of cosmetics for women, and she was at the end of a very long line of women entrepreneurs who wanted to market to women. Helena Rubinstein, Elizabeth Arden, and Estée Lauder beat her to the punch. But while they chose to sell highbrow, hoity-toity Euro-luxurious creams that looked like they might have come right from the private collection of some czarina, Mary Kay chose to sell something simpler: soft skin. She did not hide with embarrassment the story of the tanner, nor did she consider for a moment inserting a "von" or "van" or "the III" into her name. She was a hard-driving, fearless Texan who could teach women to take better care of their faces. That was it.

Now, Mary Kay's folksy approach did not mean that she did not enjoy the riches she would later earn. In her heyday, she would welcome sales consultants to her palatial offices and have them photographed in a pink bathtub that would be wheeled in for such occasions. But she made it clear that she was not born to privilege, and that, by God, she had earned it. More important, she instilled in middle-class, and even lower-income, women the confidence that they, too, could smash obstacles and achieve great success. She liked to award people with diamond-studded bumblebees, a symbol of her unlikely success: "You see," she would explain, "a bee shouldn't be able to fly; its body is too heavy for its wings. But the bumblebee doesn't know this and it flies very well." She used this as a metaphor for the women who joined her company. "With help and encouragement, they find their wings—and then fly very well indeed." [12] Mary Kay proved to be the world's most successful female motivator since Queen Victoria. She was Oprah Winfrey with a map and a monthly sales target.

Thousands of women business leaders are good at making speeches and encouraging others. What made Mary Kay so noteworthy? She devised a clear business structure that exploited her talents and prodded others to follow. Her plan married monetary incentives and psychological inspiration.

First, she set up a far-flung sales organization that drove hundreds, and ultimately over a million, saleswomen to show off Mary Kay Cosmetics. Mary Kay had learned the strength of "network marketing" during her twenty-five years at Stanley and the World Gift Company. In network marketing, the distribution, sales force, and often the customers are the same people. Mary Kay inspired satisfied users of her cosmetics to become sellers. She called her sales force "beauty consultants." Then these women would encourage others to sell. Why would any Mary Kay salesperson want to encourage competition from other sellers? If beauty consultant Alexia recruited another representative, say, Katherine, Alexia would get a piece of the action, roughly 4 percent of Katherine's total sales. Most important, the 4 percent commission to Alexia would not get deducted from Katherine's compensation. This way, Alexia would seek out other recruits, and Katherine would not begrudge Alexia the commission. And if a beauty consultant recruited even more consultants, she would be eligible for even bigger commissions and fancier titles. For example, a salesperson who recruited eight active recruits would receive an 8 percent commission on their sales.

Critics often accused Mary Kay of setting up a pyramid scheme. But Mary Kay ingeniously avoided this trap. In a pyramid scheme, a recruit must bring in yet more recruits to stay afloat. The bottom layer of recruits sends its profits upstream and must recruit a new layer or else they go broke. Was Mary Kay building a pyramid scheme? Not at all. Mary Kay's bottom layer of recruits could earn fat profit margins—50 percent—even if they never bothered to find down-line recruits. Recruiting was a method to boost their profits, but they could still make a lot of money from their own direct selling. Mary Kay's 50 percent profit margin for beauty consultants was a significant leap from the typical 35 percent commission at the time.

During the bubble years of the 1990s, a former Xerox engineer named Bob Metcalfe, who helped develop the Ethernet, penned a formula for assessing the value of networks. Though he was discussing telecommunications networks, Metcalfe's insight would seem to support Mary Kay's approach. Metcalfe's Law states that the value of a network is proportional to the number of participants to the second power. In a simple example, the first facsimile machine was useless (whom could you fax to?), it grew more valuable as others rolled off the assembly line. If there were three facsimile machines, the economic value of the network would rise by a factor of nine (3^2). Long before the Internet, Mary Kay realized that with each additional sales recruit, she could multiply her outreach. There is an old sexist joke that asks what are the three fastest means of telecommunications: telephone, telegraph, and a telewoman (tell a woman). This was no joke to Mary Kay.

KNOW THY SALES FORCE

Mary Kay's system worked so well only because she knew the kind of people she was selling to and the kind of people who would be recruited.

In a "man's world" of sales, a salesman would fight like a badger to control his own territory, and he would chop off the legs of any interloper. In *The Music Man,* the opening number features traveling salesmen on a train chanting "You Gotta Know the Territory!" Yet Mary Kay insisted that her salespeople would not have defined sales territories. How could she get away with such a revolutionary concept that she claimed was "almost unexplainable to men"?[13] Mary Kay knew that her beauty consultants would not be full-time traveling salespeople armed with luggage filled with samples and a phone directory. They were mostly housewives looking to supplement the family income. Whom were they selling to? Their townsfolk. The butcher, baker, and dentist they passed in the streets each day. The beauty consultants were not opening up storefronts. Instead, Mary Kay showed them how to set up small house parties of six women, where they would teach the attendees how to apply the five basic skin care products aimed to (1) cleanse, (2) stimulate, (3) freshen, (4) moisturize, and (5) protect. Teaching was a key tenet of Mary Kay's system: "Instruct, don't sell" was the mantra. Mary Kay beauty consultants averaged a few thousand dollars in sales (in today's dollars). For most, it was not full-time work, though it was a satisfying sideline. They could still care for their children and help pay the family expenses.

DIMINISH DOWNSIDE RISK

As Mary Kay fostered a huge network of consultants, she needed to control her risk. After all, she did not start the business with a million-dollar endowment. So she introduced two key concepts. First, she paid virtually no salaries. Her sales force was composed of independent consultants. She launched thousands of micro-entrepreneurs and did not owe them weekly paychecks, health-care coverage, or paid vacation. They would derive their income from the generous 50 percent spread between the sales price and the wholesale price. Second, she insisted on "cash on the barrelhead," that is, a beauty consultant had to pay cash in advance for any cosmetics. That saved Mary Kay untold hours and expense in tracking down deadbeat salespeople. It also forced consultants to consider quite seriously the probability of actually making a sale. Now, Mary Kay may have been tough-minded, but she was not callous. The company would take back unsold inventory for credit if the consultant returned it within a year.

Third, Mary Kay insisted that the customer pay for her cosmetics on the spot (at the party) and that the consultant deliver the cosmetics simultaneously. That way the consultant would not be extending credit and creating awkward situations for her friends. This last requirement—a quick transaction—showed more than just a worry about credit. It revealed Mary Kay's insight into human psychology. Mary Kay knew that, unlike Stanley's mops and steelwool scrubbers, her pricey cosmetics relied on feelings and on impulses. Any delay in the ability to seal the deal would allow second thoughts, crying children, or even a nosy, niggardly husband to scupper the sale.

In her first year, Mary Kay and her team of three hundred consultants generated $198,514 in sales. Over the next decade, they averaged a nearly 30 percent annual growth rate. Her financial advisers suggested she offer local franchises, but she objected. It would ruin her commitment to "no territory." Furthermore, she worried that women entrepreneurs would require men to put up the capital and ultimately require a woman to work for a man. By the early 1980s, Mary Kay took great pride in reporting that her company had more women earning over $50,000 than any other company in the United States. During the early 1980s, her part-time beauty consultants earned about $4,000, while her four thousand sales directors averaged over $60,000 (both figures in 2006 dollars). From the late 1960s to the early 1980s, Mary Kay Cosmetics was publicly traded and enjoyed a 670 percent appreciation, until it participated in the leveraged-buyout wave.[14]

PINK CADILLACS

Like most men, I did not know a great deal about Mary Kay other than noticing an occasional pink Cadillac drive by. In 1969, Mary Kay introduced the Cadillac as a sales incentive in the color "Mountain Laurel," which matched lip and eye palettes in her cosmetics collection. But the Cadillac—now loaned to salespeople who generate $90,000 in sales over two consecutive quarters—is just one symbol of Mary Kay's charismatic motivational methods. The German sociologist Max Weber posited that charismatic leaders seem endowed with "exceptional powers or qualities" that are regarded as being of "divine origin or as exemplary, and on the basis of them the individual concerned is treated as a leader."[15] I do not believe that many of Mary Kay's followers thought that she had an exclusive route to God, but they did believe she had the inside track on earning profits while maintaining an upstanding life. She often spoke of applying the Golden Rule to business, and sure enough, when her sales consultants gave their best efforts, they received from Mary Kay Cosmetics some beautiful results, including gold bracelets, diamonds, and other gifts she called "Cinderella" rewards.

Mary Kay did not, of course, invent the idea of sales incentives, but she did hone the idea to perfectly fit and thereby maximize her constituents' output. She learned the hard way. As a young saleswoman, she won a sales contest and was confounded to discover her prize: a flounder light. A flounder light? A common tool for anyone enthusiastic about gigging a flatfish in the dark of night! Not a great gift for someone who would make her career in facial creams and lip liner. Mary Kay made sure that her gifts would bring tears of joy to her sales team, not tears of frustration. She called them "motivational compensation." When Mary Kay expanded internationally, she accommodated local tastes, so that top German sales consultants drove pink Mercedes-Benzes and Taiwanese women drove pink Toyotas. Incidentally, Mary Kay was not a huge fan of pink when she launched her company. She personally preferred wearing black, blues, and reds. Nonetheless, because pink prizes seemed to give her consultants a warm psychological glow of success, she accommodated them, too. Psychologists point out that pink has a calming effect, even on prisoners.[16] For this reason, the University of Iowa's football team paints its opponents' locker room pink. A calm opponent is a pushover. Former University of Michigan coach Bo Schembechler ordered his assistants to paper over the pink walls before the players entered.

Are pink Cadillacs tacky? When asked this question, Mary Kay would unleash a powerful riposte: "What color was the car *your* company gave *you*?" For many women, winning the pink Cadillac (there are about two thousand on the road) has been the highlight of their lives (outside of their children and husbands, of course). One Cadillac winner named Nancy zoomed straight to her local gas station—just to drive the attendants crazy by running back and forth over the hose that rang the bell inside. The attendants had sneered at her entrepreneurial dreams and her old jalopy when she joined Mary Kay. They knew her only as a low-wage laborer who had a dreary job loading shotgun shells during the graveyard shift.[17]

Mary Kay's "motivational compensation" went beyond jewelry and pink Cadillacs. Every summer the Dallas Convention Center bursts with nearly fifty thousand Mary Kay conventioneers attending the fabled "Seminar." They share success stories, crown sales princesses, award gleaming scepters, and share stories as they explain how to balance a family life with a desire for professional growth. It would be easy to make fun of the event, and Mary Kay herself would have a laugh as she entered in a hot air balloon or in a horse-drawn carriage. But Seminar is serious business for the women who would pay their own way for a brush with greatness and a few days of inspiration. Years before Jesse Jackson started leading poor kids in the chant "I am somebody," Mary Kay was doing the same for suburban (and ultimately urban and rural) women. "You are somebody. And after you've looked at yourself with new eyes, it's time for action: new clothes, new hairstyle, new friends. If you want to return to school, go. If you want to go to work, or change jobs, do it!"[18] Mary Kay had done it all, and she honestly believed that her audience could, too. She named her monthly magazine *Applause*.

ROUGH MOMENTS

The Mary Kay magic formula did start to look a little scratchy starting in the early 1980s. The share price of Mary Kay Cosmetics plummeted 65 percent during 1983. What happened? A demographic train collided into Mary Kay's roaring pink Cadillacs. Simply put, women left the house to go to work. When Mary Kay was selling Stanley products, only one-third of women worked outside the home. By 1980, two-thirds of adult women held jobs.[19] Women had many more opportunities to become lawyers, doctors, engineers, and accountants. At the same time, the pace of life in the U.S. quickened. Between car pools, children's clubs, and other commitments, fewer women had the time to attend leisurely makeup parties. When Avon rang the bell or Mary Kay's consultants called to set up parties, no one came to the door, and only an answering machine picked up the telephone. Stock investors got nervous when Mary Kay reported that the number of consultants had dropped from over two hundred thousand to one hundred thousand between 1983 and 1985.

Mary Kay, her family, and her top executives joined the leveraged-buyout wave in 1985. If public stock investors were not going to show confidence in their ability to turn things around, the Mary Kay team would do it themselves. They borrowed and paid $315 million to buy the company back.

Mary Kay's turnaround strategy involved three prongs: First, the company sweetened the commission to new consultants, something Wall Street would not have stomached. Second, Mary Kay set about attracting new consultants who already had full-time jobs, but wanted to supplement their income with an extra, say, $10,000. This was a key shift. Mary Kay's original model assumed that she could attract housewives who wanted extra "mad money." Now she accepted reality—women were working—but wanted to entice them to work a little more. Third, Mary Kay launched its "Direct Support" program, in which the company would create "personalized," professional mailings to customers on behalf of the sales consultants. The mailing would include a free gift with purchase that would be paid for by the parent company. These professional mailers appealed to customers and consultants who were pressed for time. The turnaround plan reinvigorated the business, and within a year of the buyout, sales revenue had rebounded to beyond the 1985 level.

RIDING DEMOGRAPHIC WAVES

Mary Kay's discovery that she could tap into housewives and other women who wanted a little extra cash still rings true today. An upscale firm called Arbonne has been penetrating hoity-toity country clubs, inspiring even women who already own Cadillacs to sell its moisturizers.

Arbonne's sales incentives feature a Mercedes (though it looks like a small one in the company's catalog).

Let's talk about some other demographic examples that are neither gender related nor cosmetic related. In the years ahead, senior citizens will be the untapped army that will be enticed into the workforce. As 76 million baby boomers rush toward senior citizenry and the ratio of workers to retirees narrows to just two to one, American companies will need to draw on seniors. Not everyone over sixty-five wants to play golf or can afford to go on cruises for thirty years. Some companies are already making their moves. Hoffmann–La Roche, Volkswagen of America, and the Principal Financial Group are enticing seniors by offering flextime, telecommuting, seasonal work, and job sharing.[20] Mary Kay did not think that idle hands were the "workshop of the devil." *To her, they were the workshop of her future.* The same may soon be true of the whole economy.

I also see another demographic wave for smart companies to ride. Toyota, perhaps the smartest manufacturer in the world, recently unveiled a spanking new truck plant in San Antonio, Texas. Toyota has hired thousands of Hispanic Americans for its billion-dollar plant. Hispanic Americans are, of course, the largest and fastest-growing minority group in the United States. The company chose San Antonio for a number of reasons. The cost of operating the plant, including prevailing wages, is comparatively low. Housing is not terribly expensive, either. Just as important, though, Toyota is tapping into the hearts and minds of Hispanic Americans, who will be crisscrossing Texas displaying huge signs on the back of their pickup trucks, advertising the Toyota name. Toyota is building a rabid and rapidly growing fan base. The people Toyota pay to build the trucks will themselves be the biggest promoters. Mary Kay would have approved.

FINAL BOW

Mary Kay was a dynamo, but a stroke slowed her in 1996. Her son Richard, formerly the twenty-year-old with the fake mustache, took over the company's day-to-day operations. She died in 2002, having built a company with 750,000 independent beauty consultants selling almost $1.5 billion worth of beauty supplies the world over. She was tough, ambitious, but, under all the makeup and froufrou, a genuine innovator. Recently I visited the Mary Kay headquarters outside Dallas, an imposing structure with a soaring lobby that also hosts the Mary Kay museum. While I looked at the displays—her first sales receipt, her famous gowns, her appearance on *Oprah*—I paid more attention to the other visitors. They were mostly women (the men's room is not conveniently located). Frequently the visitors were Mary Kay consultants, some of whom had large color photos of themselves framed on the wall. I noticed that the visitors all shared a look in their eyes. It was not blind worship or awe. It was the satisfied gleam that said, "You're damn right, Mary Kay. I could do it, too." In an era when other CEOs attained nicknames like "Chainsaw Al" or lauded books with titles like *Management Secrets of Attila the Hun,* a little pink pancake and mascara should have gotten more respect.

4

Estée Lauder:

Even the Rich Like Freebies

Estée Lauder would have wanted to touch your face. She would have opened her purse, squeezed a little cream onto her hand, and massaged it into your skin. Then she would have flashed a broad smile and proudly held a mirror to your face. She would not have asked permission. Here was a woman so determined and so confident that she would smear lotions on strangers, utterly convinced that they would fall in love with her products. She was usually right. If you walk into Bloomingdale's today and get sprayed, no, fumigated, by models wielding perfume, you can thank Estée Lauder, who virtually invented the idea of free samples. "I don't know her very well, but she keeps sending all these things," reported Princess Grace of Monaco, who later became a friend. Estée Lauder was a marketing genius, a quality-control freak, and a social climber who would ascend so high that the former king of England would send thank-you notes to *her*. As her many fallen competitors learned the hard way, it was better to let Estée Lauder touch your face than to say no. You were in good hands, two of the most capable hands ever to build a billion-dollar empire.

What kind of woman was Estée Lauder? She was tirelessly ambitious, determined, and elegant, and she could be exquisitely bitchy. She began her own autobiography by confessing to a fifty-year-old grudge that was still needling her: She was a young woman working in a fashionable New

York beauty salon when she complimented a wealthy customer on her blouse and asked politely where the patron had purchased it.

The woman smiled and looked straight into her eyes: "What difference could it possibly make? You could never afford it."

Estée walked away red-faced and burning inside. "Never, never . . . never will anyone say that to me again, I promised myself. Someday I will have whatever I want: jewels, exquisite art, gracious homes—everything." To top off the story, Estée assures us that "wherever she is, I'm sure her skin looks dreadful." [1]

With her perfectly coiffed blond hair and stylish clothes, Estée Lauder gave the impression that she rode in from a Hapsburg castle on a white horse. The truth was more humble. She was not royalty, though she was born in the New York City borough of Queens, the daughter of a Hungarian mother and a Czech father.

We do not know exactly what year Estée arrived. When she died in 2004, her company suggested she might have been ninety-seven. Or maybe ninety-five. Or perhaps a hundred. Once her extraordinarily talented son Leonard, who took over the CEO position, was asked how old he himself was. "My age? . . . I'll have to ask my mother. Every time she gives a different interview, I'm a different age. I'll check on what I am this week and let you know." [2] Estée's mother also shaded the truth about birth dates. She was embarrassed that she was much younger than Estée's father, so she added seven years to her husband's birth year.

I must confess that I know people like this. My maternal grandmother and her sisters were nicknamed the "Gabor Sisters" of Riverside Drive in New York. They did not have European accents, but like Eva, Zsa Zsa, and Magda, they always dressed fashionably and would never think of leaving the house without the right makeup and accessories. Also like the Gabors, no one ever knew their ages. My grandmother refused to celebrate her fiftieth wedding anniversary because it would make it difficult to keep up the ruse that she was not yet sixty-five. Her sister was even worse. My great-aunt lied on her husband's *tombstone* about his birthdate! If her husband had died at eighty-six, how could she possibly be in her fifties?

Estée Lauder entered the world with the name Josephine Esther Mentzer, though the family called her Esty. In the old country, her father liked to ride horses, but in America, he needed a job. With few practical skills, he finally managed to open a hardware store. The family lived above the store in working-class Corona, Queens. In this era in New York, it was not unusual for Jewish immigrants from Europe to keep a live carp in the bathtub before preparing it for dinner.[3] It is staggering to imagine that in a few decades little Esty Mentzer would go from a carp in the bathtub to caviar at Bergdorf. But Esty was not destined for fish-mongering. As a very young girl, she began playing with her mother's skin creams and toiletries and experimenting with all the faces around her. She gave "treatments" to her family members, even after her father, Max, warned her to "stop fiddling with other people's faces." Naturally, she said "Yes, Father" and then ignored him.

Estée was already showing sharper business acumen than her father, for the cosmetics industry was about to take off. Advertising spending for cosmetics was on its way to tripling between 1915 and 1925, and one-fifth of the female population was joining the workforce. The intrepid women who took jobs in offices and department stores wanted to display a pol-ished appearance.[4] Estée sensed that cosmetics would soon be considered not frivolities but necessities. While Estée seemed born with a desire to beautify, she learned hard-nosed business skills in her father's hardware store and in a small Corona department store called Pflaker & Rosenthal, which was owned by her half brother's sister. Though it was difficult to beautify a hardware store in the early 1900s, Estée worked on displays and helped her father keep tabs on inventory. She helped wrap holiday gifts of hammers and nails. Pflaker & Rosenthal, once known as the Macy's of Corona, was "dress-up land" for Estée. She learned an even more impor-tant skill than inventory watching: how to chitchat with customers and make them comfortable while they tried new products.[5] Corona was a melting pot, and Estée was happy to swim in the soup, as customers gos-siped in Yiddish, Italian, and Polish. "I whetted my appetite for the merry ring of the cash register. I learned early that being a perfectionist . . . was the only way to do business. The ladies in their furs came to buy, and smiled and bought more when I waited on them. I knew it. I felt it."[6]

The 1920s were beginning to roar, and flappers began creating new styles and testing new temptations. By 1929 in New York City alone, twelve thousand women worked as hairdressers, manicurists, and skin specialists.[7] Modern Millie said, "Painting lips and pencil-lining your brow now is quite respectable." But Estée Lauder would not simply follow the styling dictates of *Vanity Fair*. She would take her own entrepreneurial path. Who set her on this path? Oddly enough, it was a mysterious visitor from a far-off land who arrived on the Mentzers' doorstep.

John Schotz, the soft-spoken, bespectacled brother of Estée's mother, showed up from Hungary with a valise full of chemicals and the title "Doctor." It is not clear whether Schotz actually had a degree or was just a doctor in the way that Al Jolson called his musical conductor "professor." Regardless, Schotz seemed to know quite a lot about chemistry and skin care. In a tiny stable behind the hardware store, Schotz swirled together secret formulas of oils, creams, and enticing scents. Estée would dip her fingers in these magic potions and feel sweet-smelling, velvety mousses and frothy mixtures that she had to stroke across her cheek. In her middle-aged immigrant uncle, Estée found her teacher, mentor, and soul mate. Schotz taught her to avoid soap on her face and to rub oil-rich creams into her face immediately after washing with water. Before long Estée was sneaking the potions to Newtown High School and smearing them on her classmates. They made her very popular among pimply adolescents. Eager to expand her circle of makeover subjects, she even approached strangers and Salvation Army volunteers, her hands lathered in face creams.

John Schotz later opened his own little shop in Manhattan called New Way Laboratories. Apparently, his potions were almost as good as Estée imagined. Many years later a professional chemist from Revlon analyzed them and declared that they were "old-fashioned, but probably very efficacious."[8] One of his face creams even contained a sunscreen, though this may not have been a deliberate usage. Schotz was more down-to-earth than Estée, with her dreams of palaces, jewels, and social standing. She did not like to admit that in addition to magical skin-care potions, Schotz was also happy to sell his customers lice killers, embalming fluid, and cures for mangy dogs.

TRICKS OF THE TRADE

In 1930, Estée married Joseph Lauter, the son of a tailor. Lauter was a quick-witted young man, who lacked only the ferocious drive to rein-

vent everybody else's face. (A few years later, Estée and Joseph changed
their name to Lauder, which seemed to be the original Austrian spelling
before it was mangled by some U.S. immigration officer.) While Joseph
worked in the garment industry, Estée was what people call today a
"home-based mom." Their son Leonard was born in 1933, and Estée
cooked meals for him on the same grill on which she boiled facial creams
based on her uncle's old recipes. In 1933, she listed her own business in
the New York telephone directory as Lauter Chemists and shuttled to
beauty shops looking to sell her creations.

Though the Lauters were certainly not rolling in cash, Estée scrambled enough money each month to renew her blond hairdo at the House
of Ash Blondes on the Upper West Side. While the Great Depression
wiped out so many families and businesses, Estée discovered that Americans did keep spending on some services, even if they had to cut back
dramatically their overall spending. For example, more people went to
the movies during the Great Depression. Why? They had more time, and
it was about the only diversion they could afford. Florida vacations were
out of the question. Likewise, cosmetics spending rose. As Estée put it, a
woman in "hard times would first feed her children, then her husband,
but she would skip her own lunch to buy a fine face cream." [9] Economists call such goods "inferior" because they may attract more demand
in economic downturns, as when Hamburger Helper replaces a juicy
rib eye.

As a loyal customer at the House of Ash Blondes, Estée developed her
first clientele. She looked at the women under hair dryers and decided
they were a perfect captive audience. If she had the nerve to bombard
Salvation Army volunteers ringing bells, she had no qualms about approaching rich matrons. She would approach these immobilized women,
bored from the constant buzzing and humming, and ask whether they
would like to try a special cream—at no charge. They seldom refused;
where could they run with a gooey blue head of peroxide and Ivory soap
flakes? Soon the proprietor, a woman named Florence Morris, asked Estée if she would like a concession at the salon, where Estée would rent
space but keep any profits.

Here was Estée's big start. Quickly she began shuttling between her
space at the House of Ash Blondes and other highbrow salons. She began

to hone her sales techniques. She learned not to ask, "May I help you?" but instead to say, "I have something that would look perfect on you. May I show you how to apply it?" When her new clients asked for more products, Estée proved very resourceful. At this point, she had created only one lipstick color. She called it "Duchess Crimson." She did not know the Duchess of Windsor—yet; but her clients would feel as if they were buying from Wallis Simpson's own vanity.

Estée doted on her formulations as if they were children. Leonard Lauder later recalled that during his youth his mother spent more time in the lab and on the road than at home. She believed in her all-natural products as much as any mother believed in her children. Long before Whole Foods made billions of dollars on the word "organic," Estée boasted of her cosmetics' healthful, natural ingredients. One evening that boast was unexpectedly put to the test. A wealthy client asked Estée whether she could take jars of facial cream on a monthlong vacation. Would they stay fresh? Estée told the woman to store the creams in the refrigerator. Unfortunately, the labels on Estée's jars were defective and peeled off. Later that night at a formal dinner, the matron's maid served the facial cream as mayonnaise with the salad.

"Will my people die?" the dowager asked. Estée assured her that the cream would go down just fine, though apparently the client could never again eat a tuna salad sandwich.

LESSONS FROM ESTÉE

From the House of Ash Blondes, Estée Lauder began building a clientele of socialites. Later she moved into department stores. But what made Estée Lauder different from all the other entrepreneurs who tried to peddle their creations? Like Ray Kroc, who was about the last guy to throw a hamburger on the griddle, Estée Lauder was hardly the first woman who wanted to be paid for making other women beautiful. Helena Rubinstein and Madam C. J. Walker beat her to the punch by thirty years. Let's now take a look at the new and lasting ideas of Estée Lauder that businesses must still heed today.

Take Aim at Your Target Customer

Estée Lauder never dreamed of selling her creations at Woolworth or Walgreens or door-to-door like Avon. That would be a nightmare to her. Both Estée and Mary Kay would sell eyebrow mascara, but Estée was aiming for a much higher brow. She was aiming at the Palm Beach set and the would-be Gatsbys. Her autobiography features photographs of her with Prince Charles, Rose Kennedy, and a fabulously accessorized Terence Cardinal Cooke. I am sure her one regret is that she could not get Zelda Fitzgerald to pose. I do not cite these examples to make fun of her social climbing. Indeed, her socializing was a key business strategy for success. She recognized that by placing herself amid the "power elites," to borrow C. Wright Mills's phrase, she could more easily market her cosmetics to the strata just below them. And that is where the money was. By gaining the imprimatur of royalty, Estée Lauder would attract readers of *Vogue* and *Harper's Bazaar*.

Estée worked long hours and dreary days to make this happen. The merchants who supplied her with ingredients, jars, and even shipping boxes demanded not COD, cash on delivery, but CBD, cash *before* delivery. She reported that she cried more than she ate and that she routinely touched at least fifty faces a day. She would wear her most elegant dresses (which she could hardly afford in the 1930s and 1940s) and stroll into the snootiest hotels. The exclusive Lido Hotel in Long Beach, Long Island, was a Moorish-style hotel built in 1929 as a seaside country club, patterned after an Italian Riviera resort. I remember as a child visiting the Lido with my grandparents half a century later and marveling at the rococo columns and vaulted arches. In its days of glamour, Estée Lauder would spend weeks by the Lido's pool, showing the "beautiful people" how to appear even more beautiful. She realized that to be taken seriously by café society, she needed to look and act like them. How else to avoid hearing the dreaded acronym, NOKD, snob code for "not our kind, dear." From the pool at the Lido, Estée would be invited to the homes of the glitterati, where she would teach the dowagers and young jet-setters how to "bring out" their eyes with turquoise and to plump their lips.

All this pushing, prodding, and traveling took a toll on Estée's marriage to Joe. She could not turn down an invitation, and he could not bear to get dressed up every night to go trolling for business at a dinner party. During a trip to Miami in 1939, Estée filed for divorce. With both Estée and Joe looking after young Leonard, the parents never quite completed a full separation, and so in 1943, they remarried. A year later, son Ronald (future U.S. ambassador to Austria) came along. Estée and Joe decided that in order to keep their marriage partnership from fraying, they would become tight business partners as well. Together they opened the "world headquarters" of Estée Lauder Cosmetics in a former restaurant off of Central Park West, with money borrowed from Estée's father. A regular office would not have worked because Estée and Joe spent much of their time like novice cooks, brewing facial creams over the gas burners and pouring the emollients into bottles they sterilized themselves. With a newly secure marriage, Estée's business was ready to take a major turn.

Throughout the 1930s, Estée's career was really focused on picking off socialites just one or two at a time. It was hard for one woman to develop a consistent and growing clientele. While World War II, like the Great Depression, pinched the pocketbooks of many families, spending on cosmetics did not suffer—in fact, it rose by almost 25 percent during the war. In 1941, the U.S. government declared lipstick a wartime necessity.[10] The *New York Times* ran an article quoting efficiency experts stating that women factory workers worked more productively when they wore cosmetics.[11] Somehow Estée had to reach a wider range of clients, but without diluting her brand or scaring off her elite customers. During her first year working with Joe in the old restaurant with the discarded kitchen equipment, Estée grossed about $50,000. That was not enough to pay the bills.

Where could she go beyond the manses of Fifth Avenue and the spa at the Waldorf-Astoria? What were the alternatives? Helena Rubinstein and Elizabeth Arden had opened their own salons, which allowed them to push their products. But Estée knew that salons were very labor intensive and required a great deal of faith in hiring loyal, skillful haircutters. She was a two-person company and was not prepared to quickly hire many more. Besides, salon profit margins were quite low (even today they hover around 4 percent). Other routes existed, of course. Charles Revson of Revlon sold his wares at drugstore counters. How déclassé! And, of course, Avon ladies rang doorbells. Even worse! Estée sought a new path to her highbrow clientele.

She stood a few feet from St. Patrick's Cathedral on Fifth Avenue and began to knock on the doors. Not on the doors of the Catholic archdiocese, but of the cathedral of shopping next door: Saks. Estée had concluded that her best route to success would come from superhigh-premium department stores like Saks, Neiman Marcus, and Marshall Field's. Unfortunately, the managers of those swanky stores did not immediately agree. She would have had a much easier time with midlevel stores such as Macy's, but once again she was determined to hit her target audience. If she could just get some shelf space at Saks, the Saks name would deliver an automatic message to affluent buyers: Estée Lauder was high quality, highly reliable, effective, and, perhaps more important, "one of our kind, dear." Economists call this "signaling." [12]

To appreciate the rarefied air of such premium stores, we must step back to a snobbier, more elegant time in America's urban history, when men would not walk down Fifth Avenue without a sport jacket, when the back of every theater seat had a hook for a hat, and when women of means would spend the entire day in a single store, breaking only for lunch or tea in the in-store café. When I was a child, my mother took my siblings and me to a regal store called B. Altman on Fifth Avenue, where we would meet my grandmother. Of course, I hated clothes shopping, but I still loved to have lunch in the café called Charleston Gardens, which resembled a southern plantation. It was Tara meets the tomato-cucumber sandwich.

When Estée first knocked on the doors of Saks, she got little response. Nor did anyone answer the second or the fiftieth knock. Then good luck finally struck in the form of bad luck for others. First, an assistant buyer for Saks was scraped up in a car accident. Estée prescribed her Crème Pack treatment, which seemed to improve the woman's skin. Then, the daughter of a Saks executive showed up at Estée's kitchen/office wearing a veil. The veil was not an Islamic *niqab;* it was a shield to protect her from the embarrassment of pimpled skin. Sure enough, Estée's treatments cleared up the mess.

Having heard stories of scarred and pimply skin turned smooth, the cosmetics buyer at Saks acceded to, as Estée put it, her millionth request and ordered $800 worth of merchandise. Though the order was small, Estée figured out how to magnify it in the eyes of everybody else. She persuaded Saks to send out a little card to Estée's own customers and to those people who had charge accounts at Saks. The elegant gold-lettered card announced, "Saks Fifth Avenue is proud to present the Estée Lauder line of cosmetics: now available at our cosmetics department." Estée and Joe furiously got to work literally cooking up their Super-Rich All Purpose Crème, Cleansing Oil, Crème Pack, and Skin Lotion.

Take a moment to appreciate that Estée was sharp enough to realize the power of credit-card shoppers back in 1946. That was four years *before* the American Express card was issued to its first customers and before Diners Club sent cards to two hundred customers who could charge meals at a few dozen select New York restaurants. BankAmericard, the forerunner of Visa, did not show up until 1958. Estée had more than a hunch that Saks's charge-account customers had the money to buy on impulse. They could be entranced by a lipstick, a lotion, or an eyeliner and worry about the costs later in the month. Because Estée Lauder was selling to the most affluent stores and consumers, she was far more enthusiastic about riding the wave of America's credit expansion than Mary Kay Ash, who worried that credit expansion would leave her with a stack of IOUs.

Those little mailing cards apparently worked well. Saks was sold out in two days. Bathed in the glow of Saks, Estée hit the road, striking up deals with prestige cosmetic counters at I. Magnin in California, Himelhoch's in Detroit, and Frost Brothers in San Antonio. She was both tireless and tired as she hopped from train to bus, always looking her most elegant. She would visit every beauty editor at every local magazine and newspaper, hoping to gain a mention in the society column or the shopping circular.

Even the Rich Like Freebies

When Estée was pitching Saks in 1946, she unveiled an innovation that continues to remake retailing: the free gift. Today, any woman can walk into Nordstrom looking pale and plain, yet emerge with a makeover worthy of a *Vogue* photo shoot. Just as children attending birthday parties expect a "goody-bag" filled with candy or little toys, millionaires attending charity events expect a gift bag, with anything from cell phones to fine crystal. They call it "swag," meaning loot. Swag recipients today can thank Estée Lauder, who had launched her career by squeezing dollops of Uncle Joe's facial creams on wax paper and handing it to prospective customers.

In 1946, in front of a Saks's buyer, a man named Robert Fiske, Estée spoke at a charity luncheon at the Starlight Roof of the Waldorf-Astoria Hotel on Park Avenue. Not only did her words charm the audience, but also she had donated eighty-two Lauder lipsticks as table gifts. The lipstick came in a metal tube; metal was very scarce as a result of World War II. The reddish shade and texture were as striking as the metal, and word began to spread, since, as Estée surmised, every one of those eighty-two women belonged to approximately three other organizations. Fiske recounted that right after the event, the women walked right through the revolving doors of the Waldorf and straight across Fiftieth Street until they reached Saks, where they demanded to buy more.[13] Between the insistent socialites and the pockmarked Saks family members, Fiske had little choice but to stock up on Estée's products.

At Neiman Marcus she had to fight especially hard. The Dallas-based store was not terribly impressed that she had succeeded in New York. This was the Wild West, not Central Park West. She called, begged, and nagged the manager, Ben Eisner. He always had an excuse to say no. It was a bad time of day, a bad week, a bad season, and besides, the Korean War was about to start. Finally, he grudgingly allowed Estée a little piece of counter space the day after New Year's: "No one will come out," he said. "It's just too hot. Besides, every woman will have spent all her money on Christmas. Don't get your hopes up." Estée quickly developed a plan. She wheedled a local radio station to interview her for a local woman's program at 8:15 in the morning on New Year's Day. She introduced herself as "Estée Lauder, just in from Europe" with the newest ideas on beauty. Then she let it fly: there would be a gift for every woman who came in to see her. "Do let me personally show you how to accomplish the newest beauty tricks from Paris and London," she teased. And finally, she released a brilliant, timely slogan that she would deploy for years to come: *"Start the New Year with a new face."*[14]

Perhaps Estée had to give away free samples. It was the only kind of promotion her company could afford, considering its small revenue base. Madison Avenue advertising agencies turned down its business. In comparison, Charles Revson could spend tens of millions and later sponsored the hit game show *The $64,000 Question.* Instead of trying to meet with television executives in the RCA Building, Estée and Joe stuffed mailers with bits of rouge and eye shadow. Across the country women showed up at Estée Lauder counters looking for a makeover and a "gift with purchase." Unlike some of her imitators who reluctantly gave away inferior gifts and scuffed-up samples from last year's colors, Estée insisted that her customers receive only the best and the latest.

As long as Estée was telling women in Dallas that she had just arrived from Europe, she decided to expand her line to the finest stores in London and Paris. Once again, however, the head buyers thumbed their noses at her. And once again she pushed them over, partly with her charm, and mostly with her gall. While trying to squeeze by the gatekeepers at Harrods, she met with the hoity-toity editor of *Queen* magazine. "May I just put a bit of cream on your skin to show you how fresh and lovely it will make you feel?" she asked.[15]

"You certainly may not." Slam.

She flew to the heralded Galeries Lafayette store in Paris. The buyer repeatedly refused to see her despite Estée's numerous visits. After all, they had Chanel.

Estée showed her gall to the Gallic people. She did what any of us—no, what none of us—would ever have the nerve to do! She "accidentally" spilled her perfumed Youth Dew bath oil on the floor and watched as the sweet-smelling fragrance enshrouded the shoppers. They liked the scent. Soon French women could buy Youth Dew at the counter rather than sloshing their feet in it.

Today when you pass a Cinnabon bakery at a mall, you inhale the mouthwatering aroma that they pump into the air. Before there was Cinnabon, there was Estée Lauder getting even with recalcitrant buyers.

INNOVATION AND SOCIAL ECONOMICS

Estée's invention of the Youth Dew bath oil was a keen innovation, even more important than her idea of spilling fragrances on the floor. In the early 1950s, she realized that perfumes yielded a bigger profit margin (roughly 80 percent) than skin-care creams. But women did not buy nearly as much perfume and cologne as skin-care products. In fact, for most women, perfume was a gift to be used on special occasions. Most would not think of buying it themselves. That would be a narcissistic splurge. In their bathrooms, however, women proudly displayed shapely bottles of perfume that they did not buy and did not use. Nonetheless, they were delighted when a man or friend presented them with more. Estée wondered how she could enter the perfume market and actually "move product." The answer: change the name. Do not call it perfume. In 1953 Estée and her staff developed a perfumed bath oil called Youth Dew and invited women to buy it for themselves, without feeling guilty or waiting for their twenty-fifth wedding anniversary. Then she added an innovation in packaging: she did not tightly seal the bottles in impenetrable layers of metal wire and plastic. Instead, women in the store could quickly unscrew the cap and let the scent waft up. With Youth Dew Estée had found the secret to higher profit margins. Because customers poured several ounces of Youth Dew into a daily bath, rather than pumped a single spritz of perfume behind their ears, Estée also enjoyed higher gross sales revenue. Soon stores like Neiman Marcus saw their Estée Lauder sales multiply more than tenfold.

Estée's savvy and nervy insight that she could sell more perfume by avoiding the word "perfume" still inspires marketers today. Consider the prune. Americans under the age of sixty-five did not like to consider the lonely, wrinkled fruit. It conjured up church bingo night and Lawrence Welk television reruns. In the late 1990s, the California Prune Board petitioned the Food and Drug Administration to allow prune sellers to call their produce "dried plums." The FDA thought long and hard, commissioned expensive research, and then announced that, lo and behold, prunes are, indeed, dried plums. After this miraculous discovery, the Prune Board changed its name to the California Dried Plum Board. In 2001, prune/dried plum shipments jumped 14 percent, the first rise in six years.[16] Ever heard of a gooseberry? You probably know it as kiwi fruit, which sells much better than under its old name, the "Chinese gooseberry." Apparently during the cold war, the label "Chinese" hurt sales. Similarly, today, not many people would offer you an "Iranian pistachio."[17]

Restaurants frequently try new names to make old fish more appetizing. The wildly popular Chilean sea bass started as the Patagonian toothfish. The esteemed black cod, which sells for $25 a pound and graces the menus at Nobu and Ducasse, has been called the Cinderella fish because it started out as a throwaway fish on the Lower East Side under the name sablefish.[18] I recently ate a tender, delicious braised veal dish— delicious until the waiter explained it was veal cheeks. Suddenly, it felt mushy and seemed to be frowning in my mouth.

Estée's Youth Dew idea entailed more than changing names, though. By rejiggering the ingredients and the amount people used, she could boost profits. Heinz recently discovered that when children pour ketchup, they let loose an avalanche, whereas their parents pour a carefully controlled dollop. That's one reason squeezable bottles have come into fashion. Let the kids rule, and profits go up. When I was a kid, I remember a television ad for Harvey's Bristol Cream sherry. A stuffy British-accented actor paraded around a swimming pool, lamenting that Americans drank sherry in tiny little glasses, while Brits gulped the stuff in goblets. If only he could persuade the Yanks to pour more. Finally, take out a bottle of your shampoo and read the directions. "Shampoo. Rinse. Repeat." Whoever thought to add the word "Repeat" deserves a Nobel Prize for Marketing.

WHITE PEARLS, WHITE TAILS, AND HIP-HOP

Estée Lauder's battle to engage her target audience continues to teach us lessons. Cadillac and Chrysler have been aiming some of their most expensive vehicles at hip-hoppers. Cadillac traditionally enjoyed a following among African American households but not necessarily among the youngest and hippest. That has changed, as Caddy has played up the "bling" on the Escalade, even sponsoring a National Basketball Association contest called "King of the Bling." On the MTV show *Pimp My Ride,* the host, a rapper named Xzibit (I won't provide a pronunciation guide) called the Cadillac the "King of Cars." [19] Chrysler, too, has ridden along with tastemakers in the rap world. The rapper 50 Cent saw spy photos of the new, amped-up Chrysler 300C, with its tall, Bentley lines. Before long the car showed up in the rapper's music video, wearing shiny twenty-two-inch tire rims. In the video, the car rolls alongside 50 Cent's authentic $200,000 Bentley. The price on the Chrysler? About $33,000.

In Washington, D.C., the most formal social event of the year is the white-tie and tails National Symphony Ball. The dowagers come drooping out in their diamonds and pearls, and each year a foreign ambassador hosts the celebration. I have seen senators and celebrities jostle for the right table, alongside dignitaries whose chests puff out with decorations like the French Légion d'honneur or the Cross of the Order of the British Empire. What do these honored guests do on their way out, when the ball is over? They race to the side tables to grab their gift bags—the swag, which might contain fancy chocolates, perfume, or a cute electronic device. The symphony staffers watch them closely to make sure none of these ritzy people swipe an extra bag. Estée was right. Rich people love freebies.

A LOOK AND A LOCATION

In Terrence McNally's play *Master Class,* the Maria Callas character struts onto the stage and imperiously declares that you must "have a look." She picks out a patron in the first row, points down at him, and exclaims, "You don't have a look. Get one." Like the diva Callas, the diva Lauder knew that her company needed a look that would send a consistent message, whether on sale in San Antonio or in Tokyo. She started with the bottles and jars.

Estée spent a great deal of time snooping around other people's bathrooms. Mostly the beautifully furnished bathrooms of the beautifully appointed people. You could call her snooping "market research." She examined the decor of bathrooms to decide on the look of her jars and bottles. This research came to a conclusion: Estée's cosmetics packaging

would be a light turquoise, later known as "Estée Lauder blue." But unlike many of her competitors, Estée did not stop with the containers. She
required that all the Estée Lauder department store counters have the
same look, like a shining pale turquoise spa. A harried shopper could rush
off the street of Michigan Avenue into Marshall Field's, but when she
reached Estée Lauder, she had reached a soothing oasis. Whenever a new
counter opened up around the country, Estée would pack her bags and
stay a week to train the staff and ensure the Lauder look. She inspected
the new hires and made sure they were not "T and T girls," young women
more interested in the telephone and toilet breaks.

In spare moments at the store, she would network with people in
other departments. If she found a scarlet hat on display in the hat department, she would urge the saleswomen to send the customer to the Estée
Lauder counter for a smashing lipstick to match. Naturally, she would
give gifts and samples to those saleswomen. She figured out how to make
the whole store enthusiastic about her little spa on the first floor.

Estée studied location like a real estate developer. If Saks gave you a
counter, where would you want it? In the front? In the center? In the
back? Near the restroom? Estée wanted to know. She stood outside of
Saks for one whole week tracking women who entered the store. She
was already a bathroom snooper and a perfume spiller; why not add
stalker to the list? She discovered that 90 percent of women turned to the
right (probably related to handedness). From that moment on she bargained to get the Estée Lauder counter on the right side of the entrance
doors.

By the late 1950s, Estée Lauder was rolling into the big time with
sales over $1 million. Her predecessors in the industry, Helena Rubin-
stein and Elizabeth Arden, were about to fall into the hands of chemical
conglomerates. Estée was still small compared to the Revlon of Charles
Revson, who apparently tried to undermine her and copy her and even
ordered her counter removed from Bonwit Teller. She claimed that Revson had an "atomic absorption spectroscope" to break down and imitate
her creations. It did not matter. Even an atomic bomb would not have
stopped Estée from further developing her reputation for elegance and
shrewdness.

In the decades ahead came such innovations as Clinique, still a blockbuster line known for its hypoallergenic qualities. Here, too, Estée insisted on a "look." With its scientific patina, Clinique would have saleswomen wearing laboratory coats and wielding penlights to carefully examine the skin of customers. In 1964, Estée introduced one of the first skin product lines aimed at men and called it Aramis, after a Turkish aphrodisiac. At this time, the only skin-care tip a man knew about was to slap a sirloin steak on a black eye. Today, men's products are the fastest-growing cosmetics segment, and star quarterbacks are just as likely to be endorsing moisturizers as sports cars. Today racy "laddie" magazines like *Maxim* are filled with cologne and lotion advertisements; Estée Lauder and Aramis saw it coming forty years ago.

By the mid-1970s, Estée retreated from her dominant role in the company and allowed her son Leonard to lead the business into the billion-dollar powerhouse of today, with brands like Aveda, Bumble & Bumble, and even Sean John, after the rapper formerly known as Puff Daddy, P. Diddy, and just Diddy. Estée might have cringed for a moment, but Leonard Lauder knew that her brands needed to keep up with the times: "My mother always used to say when picking up a product, 'Would you give this to the Duchess of Windsor?' Well, that's lovely. But the Duchess of Windsor is dead." [20]

When Estée Lauder was a teen, she thought she knew what she wanted from life: her name in lights. She briefly tried acting. Instead she got her name on a bottle and on a thousand billboards in dozens of languages. There was not much that Estée Lauder did not achieve in her near century. She was awfully smart, staggeringly determined, but also willing to think quickly on her feet. Once, as an older woman, she looked in the mirror and realized that her ruby-and-diamond tiara clashed horribly with her turquoise dress. She immediately swapped the tiara for a more suitable gold-and-diamond crown. "You know how it is," she told a *New York Times* reporter. "You have to wear something." [21] And now millions wear Estée Lauder.

5

David Sarnoff: RCA

The Road to 30 Rock

David Sarnoff started life as a poor Jewish monk. At the age of five, his family sent the blue-eyed, precocious child to a Russian shtetl so remote and obscure that the Cossacks did not even bother to come by and burn the homes. For four years, the boy spent long days reading the Bible, studying the prophets, and tracing the arguments of the Talmud. He did not play games and had no friends. Each week his great uncle, a rabbi, tested him on thousands of Talmudic passages in Aramaic and Hebrew. It was 1896—Bell had strung telephone wires, Edison had generated electricity, and two bicycle makers named Wright were planning to fly. But for all that Davy Sarnoff knew, 1896 could have been the year 1096.

And yet this forced recluse, this ward of ancient texts and ramrod traditions, would do more than any man to pry open our houses to modern sight and sound. As a young boy, his eyes never saw more than a few hundred people. And yet he would teach us how to entertain the teeming masses. He would foretell and propel the spread of radio, of television, and of "living color" in our living rooms.

Pundits frequently condemn today's CEOs for looking ahead to quarterly reports and short-term gains. David Sarnoff teaches us to look years ahead and to work relentlessly. The CEO of RCA rolled up his sleeves, sweated with his intrepid scientists, and refused to leave their side until they could shout, "Eureka!" He learned how to navigate treacherous corporate competitors, antagonistic government lawyers, and skeptical consumers. Though he hurtled toward goals, he knew the value of sitting down, thinking, and writing a memo. How many CEOs today, shuttling from meeting to luncheon to fund-raiser to ribbon cutting, set aside time to sit in their offices and just think? Perhaps they fear their cerebral neurons would give off not a spark.

David Sarnoff had it all: all the virtues and all the vices of the great CEOs discussed in this book. He was blindingly bright, painfully pompous, an egotist, a patriot, a loyal friend, brutal in combat, and magnanimous in victory. George and Ira Gershwin wrote, "They all laughed at Rockefeller Center; now they're waiting to get in."[1] From his perch atop the RCA Building at 30 Rockefeller Center, David Sarnoff could peer out over the Atlantic Ocean toward the old country and then gaze downtown to the Statue of Liberty. He had climbed far more than seventy stories. He had climbed over staggering odds.

IN THE BEGINNING ...

Davy started with nothing. Estée Lauder could speak of long-lost family jewels, young A. P. Giannini could sell his father's fruit, and Akio Morita grew up a little prince. But Davy Sarnoff was born the son of a frail housepainter who could find no houses and no paint in a tiny town called Uzlian, a smudge on the map of Minsk Province (now in Belarus). Uzlian was poor, dull, and quiet. The trains did not bother to stop. The only sounds came from the harsh wind whistling through ramshackle wooden shacks. His mother, Leah, was sharper than her husband, Abraham, and she arranged for Davy's Talmudic boot camp after the skinny boy with the penetrating blue eyes demonstrated precocious reading and reasoning skills. For four years, Davy lived hundreds of miles from his parents and siblings, "hermetically sealed off from childhood," he recalled.[2] In today's world, a child psychologist would immediately call the Department of Social Welfare and warn that such a lonely, ascetic childhood would irreparably warp a young mind. Somehow, Davy Sarnoff overcame these years, explaining that those daily drills on religious texts instilled discipline, though he thought that "four years of prophets" was quite enough. He would have his own prophecies to share.

Around the time that Davy left Uzlian to live with his great-uncle, his father, Abraham, joined the tempest-tossed souls who fled Russia for New York. He was not abandoning the family, but hoping to earn enough money in America so that he could reach back and lift them all to safety in a land where streets were paved with gold. To the Sarnoff family, any pavement would be an improvement on dust. But Abraham's life in a humid, crammed Lower East Side tenement was rough and risky. Tuberculosis and pneumonia spread quickly through the dense and dirty neighborhood. Abraham scrambled to find work painting, hanging paper, and hauling boxes. After four years of sickness and physical labor that strained his malnourished body, Abraham finally had scraped together the $144 he would need to lift Leah, Davy, and his two younger brothers out of Russian poverty and into American poverty. But at least they would be free. Was the American dream just a fantasy? Sitting in his tenement, sore, exhausted, and ill, Abraham did not know. But he had slaved so that his children would have a chance to prove otherwise.

It was 1900. The rabbi woke up nine-year-old Davy, who would immediately have started to spout morning prayers, hoping not to trip over the intermingled passages in Yiddish, Aramaic, and Hebrew. But this morning was different from other mornings. The rabbi told Davy that he would, after four years, finally see his mother again. Four years! That was nearly half his life, and all Davy had was an old black-and-white photograph of the mother he hadn't seen since he was five—how reliable would his memories of her prove? When he reached Uzlian, he saw his mother, and they hugged each other tightly and joyfully. She was, as he remembered, brown haired with full lips and large round eyes spaced far apart. His memory had not failed. In later years colleagues would marvel at his recall of details. Leah then told Davy that they would leave Russia for America. The Sarnoff Library in Princeton has a photograph of the two taken just before leaving Russia.[3] Leah is sitting in a chair, Davy's little arm entwined in hers, his chin nestled on her broad shoulder. He would not leave her again.

Leah and her sons had little to pack and little to leave behind. First, they climbed aboard a horse-drawn wagon to ride to Minsk. Davy had never been to Minsk, never seen a building more than two stories tall. He looked in awe at the streetcars and the town squares. Maybe they should stay. Wasn't this civilization? Could America be more modern? Then Davy heard rumbling. The earth started to pound and dust started to fly. He and his brothers clutched Leah as strolling pedestrians suddenly huddled together, forming a large, frightening crowd. They heard screams. Leah and the boys backed up against a wall, looking for a safe nook, as the crowd trampled a few slow-moving peasants. The Cossacks, the czar's brutal cavalry, were here. Horseback-riding guards pulled out their whips and began lashing. Some of the peasants had taken part in a political demonstration. The horses reared up and stomped as sabers sliced through the air. Kandinsky would immortalize such brutal and fast-moving scenes by painting abstract red-hatted Cossacks wielding lances and knives, while carrion crows swoop above.[4]

Leah was able to shield her children, and they began a three-hundred-mile trek to the Baltic port of Libau, followed by passage through the North Sea and English Channel to Liverpool. Along the way, Leah realized that her oldest son had developed an indomitable spirit. After four years of study, he did not know how to play any children's games, but he did know how to battle, both verbally and physically. He often told a story about boarding the steamship in Liverpool. His mother had packed a box of kosher foods to sustain them during the rough transatlantic crossing. Davy was on the deck of the ship when he saw the package tossed together with other luggage and dropped into the ship's cargo hold. How would they ever retrieve it? Would they starve without it? He had no choice. As he watched the precious package tumble into the hatch, he pushed past the burly stevedores and dove in after it, falling many feet belowdecks. A seaman grabbed a rope and threw it down after the boy. Davy emerged, clutching his mother's package, as a sailor said, "Boy, you're going to do alright in America."[5]

The rescued box of food sustained them during the long and fetid crossing of the Atlantic to Montreal. They hopped a train to Albany and then a boat down the Hudson River to lower Manhattan. Davy did not look back to Russia. He had his mother, Leah, and never thought of the old country as "Mother Russia." He disliked Russia under the czars and later turned bitterly against it under the Communists. He would turn into a proud and vocal "cold warrior," bristling at biographers who called him "Russian American." A month after leaving Uzlian, Davy arrived in New York on July 2, 1900, but in his mind it was the Fourth of July. Over the course of his life, he would yield to no one in proclaiming his patriotism, not George M. Cohan, the Yankee Doodle Dandy, not even Bob Hope, who was also born abroad (in London). As an adult, he would wear the uniform of the U.S. Army and puff out his chest as if he had fought with George Washington himself.

When Leah and her boys stepped off the steamboat onto the dock in Manhattan, they looked for Abraham. He did not show up. They searched up and down the pier, panicked and lost in a city unimaginably large, raucous, and, in July, dripping with the sweat of nearly two million people, pushing, shoving, and clawing their way to prosperity, or maybe just their next meal. Mother and sons spent the day searching. As the sun set over this frightening and unforgiving city of skyscrapers, a steamship employee announced that he had found Abraham. He had been waiting at the wrong pier. When Leah saw her husband, he looked as if he had been waiting for decades. Old, hunched, and gaunt, Abraham had just enough energy to show them to their new American home, a fourth-floor flat in a brick tenement building. There was a single toilet down the hallway, shared by huddled masses yearning to breathe free in the foul summer heat.

To Davy it was a "slum whirlpool," a cacophony of Slavic, Irish, and Italian voices he could not understand. But it was also heaven. Boys played stickball in the streets and ran around with mischief on their minds. My grandfather, who grew up in Manhattan not too long after Sarnoff, told me that in the wintertime he and his boyhood friends would hop aboard carriages piled with coal and then paddle coal off the carriages into sacks, hoping the driver would not notice. They would bring home the coal, along with stories of being chased around Manhattan. The city that never sleeps finally awoke the child in David Sarnoff. But his family's poverty awoke the man in him, too. He looked at his father, who was getting too feeble for hard work, and his mother, who was busy caring for his younger brothers while trying to earn a few dollars sewing in the apartment.

It was time for Davy to work. But what could a nine-year-old offer?

What did he have besides a keen, focused mind and a capacity to work hard? The answer: fast feet and an even faster mouth. Also, a drive to beat out even the most vicious competitors: other nine-year-olds. Davy would race to the East Broadway railway station and grab a bundle of Yiddish newspapers hot off the press. He would race through his neighborhood hawking the papers before the other boys could catch up, earning a quarter for every fifty papers sold. Then he decided to "expand" his delivery franchise by training himself to wake up just as the 4:00 a.m. train dropped its bundle of morning papers. Again Davy would race to the station and tear through his neighborhood, even climbing across the narrowly spaced roofs to cover more ground. In *Annie Hall,* Woody Allen's character grows up in an apartment built under the Coney Island Cyclone roller coaster, which shakes the apartment like an earthquake each time the cars rumble by. Davy Sarnoff's home was slightly less comical but nearly as shaky. At the age of nine, though, he had learned to make the 4:00 a.m. shudder of the train an advantage, his own personal alarm clock.

When he was not delivering Yiddish papers, Davy was learning to speak English and expanding his vocabulary beyond schoolboy cursing. He attended night classes at the Educational Alliance, a settlement house that provided classes, clinics, camps, gyms, and job banks for new immigrants. The Educational Alliance was originally focused on Jews, but today provides social services for mostly non-Jews. In addition to Sarnoff, the Alliance helped launch the careers of Mark Rothko, Zero Mostel, and even Larry King. The Arthur Murray Correspondence School of Dancing began after Murray, the son of a downtown baker, took ballroom dance lessons at the Alliance. Davy had little interest in acting, art, or the rumba, but he was driven to speak English without an accent. He camped out in the library and read about Abraham Lincoln. He took part in formal debates and argued in favor of independence for the Philippines. By learning English, he would find his own independence.

He did not forget his Hebrew lessons, however; every weekend he sang in a synagogue choir and earned some more valuable change. When he reached the eight grade, his father's health worsened, and Davy realized he was now the family breadwinner. Racing to train stations and rushing up and down stairwells was not enough. He wanted his own newsstand. For this he would need $200, more than he had managed to save. As an adult, David Sarnoff never made clear where he got his start-up money, though a family tradition suggests an anonymous benefactor. Considering that the Educational Alliance was supported by many such contributors, it is not a far-fetched conjecture. In any event, like Pip from Dicken's *Great Expectations,* fourteen-year-old Davy began his climb out of the ghetto. First stop: a neighborhood in the West Thirties called Hell's Kitchen. It was light years from the Upper East Side. The nickname supposedly emerged in the late 1800s, when a rookie police-man stood off to the side, observing a riot, and said, "'The place is hell itself.' The retort, from 'Dutch Fred the Cop,' was 'Hell's a mild climate. This is hell's kitchen.'"[6]

Even his own newsstand could not bring in enough money to feed the family, though. Davy's English language skills were so commanding now that he decided to move out of mere sales and into the writing of the newspapers. He skipped over the Yiddish papers, dressed in his best and only suit, and marched right to the headquarters of the eminent *New York Herald*. Davy missed and knocked on the wrong door. And that sin-gle mistake proved to be the luckiest moment of Davy's life. Instead of knocking on the door of the *Herald,* he entered the office of the Com-mercial Cable Company, a firm that controlled transatlantic cable traffic. "I'd like a job with the *Herald,*" Davy announced. "You're in the wrong place," he was told. But the cable company hired him anyway as a mes-sage boy, offering $5 per week and 10¢ an hour overtime. Though he could not manage to find the right door in an office building, they trusted him to deliver confidential messages all over New York! He suited up and began bicycling across Manhattan, telegrams in hand. In between deliv-ery runs he watched and admired the telegraph operators, who could play the telegraph key with all the mastery of Rachmaninoff. The clickety-clack of the telegraph was music to Davy, even more entrancing than the click-clicking typewriters of the *Herald*. Davy would sit down at operator stations and teach himself this new language that allowed mes-sages to traverse the oceans. He was a quick learner and before long de-veloped a style or "swing" that receiving operators could identify. For the rest of his life—even in the age of spaceships and radar—Sarnoff would always have a telegraph key near his desk.

While Davy was working for Commercial Cable, he suffered another lucky unlucky break. The company fired him because he wanted to take three days off without pay for the Jewish High Holidays. He suspected anti-Semitism, but this was not the era of civil rights lawsuits. He got word of an opening at the Marconi Wireless Telegraph Company. Guglielmo Marconi! For a telegraph aficionado like Davy, this was like getting a job answering the telephone for Alexander Graham Bell or playing catch with Ty Cobb. In 1901 Marconi had transmitted a wireless message from England to Newfoundland deploying a four-hundred-foot-high antenna supported by a kite. Again, Davy put on his best suit, knocked on the door, and asked whether the Marconi firm could use "a man as a junior operator." The company offered him a job, not as a man, but as an office boy, sweeping and delivering. He took it, along with a 10 percent raise.

And then, in December 1906, when Davy was just fifteen, the Rachmaninoff, Bell, and Ty Cobb of wireless himself showed up in the Manhattan offices, caped and coiffed, from Italy. Who was the dandified stranger? Davy asked. "He's the man who makes lightning," replied a grizzled operator.[7] Marconi himself. Now, here was a test, not of Davy's brains, but of his backbone. How many fifteen-year-olds would have the self-confidence and chutzpah to introduce themselves to a god? What was at stake? The actor Kevin Spacey admitted that as a struggling young performer, he stole a party invitation from the pocket of a sleeping grande dame because he desperately needed to meet a famous director. But for the theft, the two-time Oscar winner might have returned to a dreary life in the San Fernando Valley. Young Bob Dylan, using the name Elston Gunn (three *n*s!), claimed to be Conway Twitty's pianist in order to get onstage, even though he could play only in the key of C. I have seen Washington, D.C., strivers step on their own children in order to shake hands with junior senators, much less presidents. In 1906, Davy Sarnoff did not have to resort to thievery or kid stomping. But as Marconi stepped outside the office into the street, Davy slipped out too and then thrust his hand into the inventor's face, introducing himself. Within moments, Marconi probably learned more than he needed to know about the road from Russia to Hell's Kitchen. But he also learned that this kid could not be stopped. He hired the kid as his personal messenger and aide. Davy would learn a great deal about running a technology business and even more about delivering flowers and running interference among Marconi's girl-friends scattered from the East Side to the West Side and from the East Coast to Western Europe. Marconi was the father Davy had longed for, albeit a father with a lot of extracurricular activities. His job came with a pay raise, the title "junior operator," and, most important, access to Marconi's technical files.

Davy dove into Marconi's science like a cryptographer trying to decode the Rosetta stone. This was key: *David Sarnoff conquered radio and television because he had the brainpower and the willpower to understand both the science and the business.* He was neither a genius inventor like Edison or Marconi himself, nor a flawless financial calculator like Rockefeller, but he devoted sleepless nights and every brain cell in his head to mastering all that had come before him. He would ride his bicycle while carrying books from night courses in electrical engineering, trigonometry, algebra, and geometry. Of fifty people who enrolled in the electrical engineering course at the Pratt Institute, only a dozen finished, and Davy was the only non-college graduate to do so.[8]

With his $7.50-a-week salary and proceeds from selling his Hell's Kitchen newsstand, Davy brought his family into the Brownsville section of Brooklyn. His father died soon after, but by then the family was more dependent on the son. The Sarnoff Library has a dandy photograph of Davy from 1907, as a junior operator. The skinny sixteen-year-old stares into the camera, chin thrust forward, eyebrows arched. With his bowtie and big handkerchief, he looks puckish, witty, and unflappable. The test would come soon.

TITANIC

Eighty-five years before Celine Dion started wailing about the *Titanic,* David Sarnoff was sitting in a chair at the Marconi station at the top of Wanamaker's department store on Broadway. He was manager of the local operation. In 1912, some vessels had Marconi wireless systems, the only lifeline for an injured ship. At 10:25 p.m. the world's most luxurious ship sent out a heartbreaking message relayed by its sister ship, the *Olympic,* which was five hundred miles from the frozen waters:

"*Titanic* ran into iceberg. Sinking fast." While the *Carpathia* heard the message and began steaming about sixty miles toward the listing disaster, closer ships, lacking the Marconi wireless, did not hear the SOS. David Sarnoff did. Along with two other men, Sarnoff began furiously reading the clickety-clack of the wireless through the static and storms of the North Atlantic. Before long, word spread that the boys wearing headphones at the top of Wanamaker's were receiving a list of survivors and casualties. Desperate families, even the Astors, the cream of New York society, descended on the Marconi station, begging for reports. Marconi, who was in New York, described to his wife harrowing scenes of frantic people. William Randolph Hearst's *American* newspaper described the breathless scenes and praised Sarnoff and his colleagues for their tireless efforts during the pandemonium, which lasted for days: "With every bit of energy at their command these men stood by their posts all night and fired scores of messages and captured scores concerning the wreck."[9]

The *Titanic* "made" wireless and, incidentally, helped make Sarnoff, too. He was no longer a boy, but had proven his stamina and his leadership. Critics point out that as years went by, David's heroism in the *Titanic* episode took on more grandeur, with some accounts even suggesting that he single-handedly received the messages, dispatched the *Carpathia,* and all but paddled the lifeboats to safety. He knew the value of publicity and did little to quell these exaggerations.

Marconi, who knew the facts, had little doubt in David, though. At age twenty-one, Marconi appointed him chief inspector of ships, an instructor at the Marconi Institute, and assistant chief engineer. David began to shop for good suits and good cigars and took on a striking resemblance to the elegant Marconi himself. He moved his family yet again, this time to a big apartment in a fashionable section of the Bronx. His mother had never lived with hot water, private toilets, electric lights, and modern kitchen appliances. When David turned the key to open that door for his mother, he was closing the door on immigrant poverty.

David had confidence in himself and Marconi Wireless. The *Titanic* disaster spurred Congress to require wireless devices on ships. After years of running close to its own financial iceberg, Marconi Wireless finally found itself with a surfeit of customers and a share price that doubled.

Eager to build up the Marconi brand, David put in nights walking the New York waterfront inspecting Marconi-equipped ships, but also visiting vessels with competitive devices. He soon carried the title "contract manager" and negotiated sales matters, linking his technological expertise and business acumen.

David Sarnoff had launched his career with a daring handshake and an unflappable command of the telegraph key. Now he would have a chance not just to operate someone else's equipment, but also to change the world.

PROPHETS AND PROFITS: THE MEMO

Throughout IBM offices hung portraits of Thomas Watson Sr. sitting below a sign that said "THINK." But of the CEOs profiled here, it was David Sarnoff who had the discipline actually to sit down at a desk, think for long periods of time, and bang out prophetic and powerful memoranda that would reshape American industry. The first was in 1916 (or possibly 1915). He was constantly twirling about in his head one dominant thought: how to deliver sound to *more* people. He was not content with a ship's telegraph room. That only delivered dots and dashes to other ships or the occasional Coast Guard station. Where else could sound go? A year after the *Titanic,* he had been featured in *Scientific American,* installing Marconi devices on railroad trains.[10] He made history deciphering messages that streamed from a speeding Erie Lackawanna express train, carrying five hundred members of the Society of Civil Engineers and a pack of press reporters. Even that was not enough. Why must wireless be relegated to slow ships and fast trains?

To press his thoughts further, in January 1913, David boarded a train down to the Jersey Shore to the beach at Belmar, accompanying an engineer named Edwin Howard Armstrong. They huddled in a rickety shack, trying to install Armstrong's new receiving technology, as bitter cold winds ripped through their coats. They began to hear hums and clicks and clacks. When they hooked up the speaker, the sounds became more clear and their sources more distant. A conversation between San Francisco and Portland. A weather report on a lightning storm about to hit Honolulu. David recalled that "whatever chills the air produced were more than extinguished by the warmth of the thrill which came to me at hearing for the first time signals from across the Atlantic and across the Pacific."[11]

Within a few months, David conducted another experiment. If wireless receivers could pick up clicks and clacks, why not the strums of a harp? Or the rat-tat-tat of a snare drum? Sitting at the top of the Wanamaker Building on Broadway, he gently laid a phonograph on a turntable and turned the knob to Play. At that moment he directed the Marconi operator at the Philadelphia Wanamaker's store to tune in. The Philadelphia man heard, not dashes and dots, but a swelling symphony of musical instruments. Twenty years later, David would lift up the quality of American entertainment by persuading the legendary Toscanini to conduct the newly formed NBC Orchestra.

What about that memorandum? Before 1916, almost every communications expert defined communications as one-to-one: J. P. Morgan orders his floor manager to buy one thousand shares of U.S. Steel. Andrew Carnegie orders five hundred tons of pig iron. President Taft orders a five-pound rump roast for dinner. Private, solitary transactions. If a message could be intercepted, that was a bad thing.

Most other executives would have spent the rest of their lives selling wireless tools to ships, trains, or stockbrokers. Not David Sarnoff. Today we too often hear clichés about CEOs wanting to "push the envelope." Frequently, it's the pay envelope they're pushing, directly into their own bank accounts. Or maybe they are pushing paper and little else. David was not focused on his paycheck or even on racking up the most sales possible. "THINK" was David's MO before it was Watson's motto. David's 1916 memorandum turned communications on its head. Interception was not a bad thing; *interception, that is, widespread reception, was a good thing.* To best appreciate this memorandum, I suggest you read it while cuddled up next to an old radio: "I have in mind a plan . . . to make radio a household utility . . . to bring music into the house by wireless. . . . The receiver can be designed in the form of a simple 'Radio Music Box' and arranged for several different wave lengths, which could be changeable with the throwing of a single switch or pressing of a single button."[12]

At this time, families entertained themselves by playing phonographs, by singing along while sisters plunked on the piano, or by attending live concerts, theater, and dances. The idea of enjoying Enrico Caruso in your house, *while others simultaneously did so,* sounded like something out of Jules Verne.

David's memorandum offered even more than music, though. He recognized that American culture was not confined to the highbrow: "Baseball scores can be transmitted in the air by the use of one set installed at the Polo Grounds.... Farmers and others living in outlying districts ... could enjoy concerts, lectures, music, recitals, etc."[13]

To foresee the value of sports broadcasting in 1916! Would Babe Ruth have earned more than Herbert Hoover without radio? Would Ronald Reagan have turned into the "Great Communicator" if he had not learned to enliven slowpokey baseball games for WHO in Iowa? Would professional football have thrived without the birth of the AFL on ABC and the Super Bowl? Take former ABC News president Roone Arledge. How did Arledge climb to the top of ABC News? By first turning ABC Sports into a global powerhouse. Sarnoff would not have been surprised to see sports drag the news business forward.

Why do sports make such an impression on radio and television networks today? Money, of course. Each year we marvel at the cost of a thirty-second advertising spot during the Super Bowl, most recently $2.5 million.[14] David's memo suggested "tremendous" advertising possibilities.

David went beyond content, though. He also sketched out the beginnings of network radio, with hundreds of thousands of families hearing broadcasts from stations located every twenty-five to fifty miles across the country. Nor did he ignore the simple economics of the "Radio Music Box." He posited that a radio would sell for $75. If only one million or 7 percent of the families bought a radio, the business could bring in $75 million, earning a hefty profit.

For its prescience and good sense, David's memorandum is almost without parallel in business. In the world of politics, you could cite George Kennan's 1946 "Long Telegram" on containing Soviet Communism and its fulfillment—Ronald Reagan's 1987 demand in Berlin that Gorbachev "tear down that wall."

Like Reagan's speech, which was at first shrugged off by the Kremlin, David Sarnoff's memorandum was thrown in the bottom drawer by the bosses at Marconi. It would not matter. Just as the infamous wall would fall down, the miraculous transmitter towers would go up.

BIRTH OF THE BLUES AND REDS

Throughout his life, David Sarnoff found bad luck and disasters, including sinking cruise ships, leaving him on higher ground. The mistaken door to Commercial Cable launched his career. His firing on the Jewish holidays pushed him to Marconi. The *Titanic* made him famous. World War I, of course, created a bloodbath in Europe. But it also showed that while German U-boats could slash the cables, they could not figure out how to slice wireless transmissions. Wireless became the only reliable link from Washington, D.C., to the boys fighting "over there."

In 1917, David's mother conspired at synagogue with a French immigrant woman who had a daughter just right for David. The two mothers set up their children for a date in the Bronx, and David was charmed by Lizzie Hermant's Paris-accented English.

Later that year, when the United States declared war on Germany, David, newly engaged to Lizzie, applied for a commission in the U.S. Navy communications office. He was turned down when the Navy's chief engineer claimed his civilian work was "absolutely" too important to interrupt. David spent the war installing Marconi devices for the Navy and commuting to Washington, D.C., for meetings with officials from the Department of War.

A few months after the Treaty of Versailles, President Woodrow Wilson marveled at how wireless had transformed the entire world, both for good and for evil:

> Do you not know that the world is all now one single whispering gallery? Those antennae on the wireless telegraph are the symbols of our age. All the impulses of mankind are thrown out upon the air and reach to the ends of the earth.... Quietly with the tongue of the wireless and the tongue of the telegraph, all the suggestions of disorder are spread throughout the world.[15]

There is always a risk when you see your government paying too much attention to you. Will Rogers likened it to watching a baby pick up a hammer. Wilson and the Department of War worried that foreigners could control U.S. telegraphs. As a result, they tried to force the Marconi company to surrender itself to the U.S. government, which would run wireless like a monopoly. After much shouting and protesting, a private-sector deal was reached, and Marconi shifted, not into the control of General Pershing, but into the arms of General Electric. They called the new firm Radio Corporation of America, or RCA. Twenty-eight-year-old David was the commercial manager but no longer under the protection of Marconi.

It could have been a disaster for David. But once again, he survived the turmoil and proved to GE executives that he best knew how to link technology and business. Here is a lesson for any employee in a takeover situation: Prove yourself indispensable. It is an obvious lesson, but David did not rely on tricks or becoming the prince of office gossip. Quite simply, he knew his stuff and could explain in both oral and written form what he knew and what he believed in.

In later years, pundits took potshots and accused David of puffery and taking credit for the work of others. The fact is, however, David Sarnoff's underlying competence and work ethic could not be challenged. Did Lance Armstrong sometimes receive credit for the superior cycling of his teammates? Perhaps. But no one ever doubted that the man could make a bike move like a Ferrari. Puffery from a genius does not grate as much as bragging by a malcontent. Carly Fiorina's recent screed on her debacle at Hewlett-Packard has been roundly denounced for fakery, egotism, and blindness to the facts. The company's fortunes have soared since she left, but she takes credit for everything, except of course her firing.[16] David Sarnoff did not invent radio, save passengers on the *Titanic*, or found RCA. But he did more than anyone else to draw families out of their kitchens, bedrooms, and backyards in order to gather around the radio and the television.

THE AUDIENCE IS LISTENING . . .

Who is the audience, anyhow? That is where David disagreed with other wireless pioneers. After World War I, everyone expected to go back to normalcy, as President Harding would put it. Messengers would ride bicycles delivering telegrams. But David would not let go of his "Radio Music

Box." What business are we in? David asked. Are we in the point-to-point messenger business? Or are we in communications by wireless? After World War I, he could hear the voice of the masses rumbling for radio. Telegraph operators who manned sets for the armed forces came home from Europe searching for civilian equipment so they could send messages from their homes, as ham operators. A man in Hollywood figured out how to play records for his neighbors using a five-watt transmitter in his bedroom. An engineer in Pittsburgh became the first disk jockey by introducing phonographs from a coatroom. The coats muffled the ambient noise, long before soundproof booths. These developments were akin to the birth of Internet blogs and Web sites; suddenly anyone could be a media star. Today, Matt Drudge in his fedora dresses like one of those 1920s pioneers.

The barriers to entry had collapsed. You did not have to be AT&T to send out messages. Radio started in the cellars, attics, and garages. David's 1916 memo may have been too early. But now the time was ripe; the audience was listening. And who was the potential audience? Everybody.

A CEO is truly tested just once or twice in his career, when he must decide whether to take advantage of a sweeping change or try to sweep it under the rug. Think about the CEOs of GM and Ford, who in the 1970s did not believe that Americans would ever care about the Japanese advantage in reliability and then spent ten years lobbying Congress to prevent Americans from buying Toyota's, Nissan's, and Honda's superior cars. David Sarnoff was not yet the CEO of RCA, but he was fighting for his ideas as forcefully as anyone could. How could he convince skeptical bosses at RCA that they should turn from singing telegrams to revolutionizing American life? How could he appeal to the bosses and the people? This was *broad*casting. Caruso and Heifetz would not do. He needed to throw raw meat to the hoi polloi. The raw meat was, of course, sports, and the rawest was boxing.

On a steamy July day in 1921, Jack Dempsey climbed through the ropes and scowled at the crowd of ninety thousand fans who had camped out in Jersey City, across the Hudson River, including H. L. Mencken, Al Jolson, and John D. Rockefeller. With a large, flat face and an unmistakable sneer, Dempsey looked the part of the villainous Manassa Mauler. To gain the heavyweight championship, Dempsey had ripped apart six-feet, six-and-a-half-inch Jess Willard, knocking the giant to the mat seven times in the first round. As ruthless as he was in the ring, many fans called him "chicken" for eluding World War I service. Tex Rickard, the master of sports hype, publicized the match as good versus evil, and a New York congressman tried to stop the fight because Dempsey was an alleged "draft dodger." [17] Clergymen protested that "the fight would serve to 'brutalize' the youth and foster juvenile delinquency; and the entire standards of Jersey City would be corrupted by allowing the match to be staged." [18]

Slowly, gracefully, like a predecessor to Fred Astaire, Dempsey's urbane opponent, Georges Carpentier, stepped into the ring. The French champion's robes rippled elegantly as the so-called "Orchid Man" bounced on his toes. He was fast, he was stylish, and he was a war hero in France, serving bravely as an aviator. He had the skills to keep Dempsey at bay and pick apart his flat face with lacerating jabs. He bowed to the crowd while a band played a rousing "La Marseillaise." The American crowd, many wearing summer straw hats, roared for the French war hero, angering Dempsey. Rickard had promoted the fight as a fund-raiser for the American Committee for Devastated France and the Navy Club of the United States. He promised Dempsey $300,000, Carpentier $200,000.

The bell struck for round one in the "Battle of the Century," and the men circled and pawed at each other like caged panthers. Who would land the first big punch and send blood streaming to the canvas?

David Sarnoff had some skin in the game. He was at ringside running a rogue operation, with virtually no support from RCA bosses. Sarnoff and a small team of engineers had jury-rigged a broadcast station with almost no budget. They knew of a huge transmitter that was on its way to the Navy in Washington. They diverted the delivery, and instead it showed up at a railroad shed outside the fight ring. They strung wires from the ring to the shed and created an antenna, as well as a telephone line to a ringside microphone. [19] Who could hear? An estimated three hundred thousand, including those who attended movie theaters, Elks Clubs, and school auditoriums where speakers were installed. The Dempsey-Carpentier fight was not just the first big broadcast; it also invented the closed-circuit broadcast to theaters. Over a thousand people jammed the Loew's New York Theater and Roof Garden. A clever entrepreneur on the boardwalk in Asbury Park, New Jersey, rigged a receiver to a golf cart and invited paying customers to listen to the fight on his "rolling chair." [20]

Who won, besides Sarnoff, who got a telegram from RCA's president announcing, "You have made history"?[21] You can watch the fight footage on YouTube, as I did.[22] Carpentier is cagey and much faster that Dempsey, who stalks Carpentier. Carpentier crouches and then flicks jabs. By round two, Dempsey draws blood from his opponent's nose. In response, Carpentier fires more jabs and seems unafraid of the larger man. He's got Dempsey against the ropes. Carpentier punches with his head down, giving Dempsey the chance to connect, adding bruises to the bloody nose. Round four opens. Dempsey launches a series of body blows as Carpentier suddenly looks more weary. Then a ripping right hand by Carpentier, but the punch does not stop Dempsey from marching forward. Carpentier's punches have lost their muscle. Carpentier jogs to the other side of the ring. Dempsey catches up. A quick left-right combination floors the Frenchman. He gets up on the count of eight, but Dempsey immediately rushes in to flatten him again. Carpentier is out for the count. At the sound of "ten," Dempsey rushes over to lift his foe to his corner. The mauler has a heart, after all.

Sarnoff would have been devastated had Carpentier gotten up for another round. It turned out that as Carpentier was crumpling to the mat, the transmitter shed was about to blow up. The heat of the Jersey July, combined with an electrical overload, was sizzling the equipment into a molten mess. Three hundred thousand boxing fans would have been left with a silent round five, and a bitter view of RCA's radio talents. Forty-seven years later, in 1968, RCA/NBC disgusted and amazed sports fans by cutting off the final minute of a football game between the Oakland Raiders and New York Jets in order to show the children's movie *Heidi*. The Raiders scored fourteen points in that last minute, rocketing to victory. Angry fans lodging protests blew the telephone switchboard at NBC and then called the police and the *New York Times*. The "Heidi Bowl" went down in the annals of sports infamy. Jets quarterback Joe Namath joked that while he didn't get to see *Heidi,* he heard the movie was great. Back in 1921, David Sarnoff had learned how powerful sports fans were and how important it was to keep them on your side.

FROM PROVIDENCE TO PATENTS

The Dempsey fight changed more than Georges Carpentier's bruised and misshapen nose. William Jennings Bryan's sonorous voice declared radio a "gift of Providence." Across the country, amateurs started building radio sets and nailing straw, burlap, and sponges to the walls in order to muffle interfering noises. Within a year of the fight, over six hundred entities applied for radio licenses. In 1922, President Wilson's former Navy secretary went overboard, giving a speech at North Carolina College claiming, "Nobody now fears that a Japanese fleet could deal an unexpected blow on our Pacific possessions. . . . Radio makes surprises impossible."

Remember David's 1916 estimate that Americans would buy $75 million of radio sets? In RCA's first year (1922), the number soared past $11 million. That sum was hefty, but RCA's competitors raked in nearly $50 million! Though RCA owned many of the founding patents for transmitters, receivers, and vacuum tubes, competitors ignored the patent filings. David realized that even the East Side of Manhattan was the Wild West. RCA could not manufacture every radio, yet RCA deserved compensation for its intellectual contributions. David needed to make it easy for competitors to comply with patent laws, so they could resist the urge simply to poach. He devised a royalty plan in which companies like Zenith and Philco would pay 7.5 percent to RCA; the plan soon covered about 90 percent of the radios in the United States.

Take a look at Qualcomm. In 1985, the company began in the cramped den of telecom visionary Irwin Jacobs, a former electrical engineering professor. Today Qualcomm holds 4,500 patents in cell phone chip technology, even though it no longer fabricates cell phones. A few years ago Qualcomm sold to Ericsson and Kyocera its base station and cellular-manufacturing arms. Instead it concentrates on developing and licensing wireless technologies and mobile chips. From India to China to Chicago, over 130 firms are sending checks to Qualcomm, even if the Qualcomm name does not appear prominently on their appliances. Qualcomm is following the example set by David Sarnoff in the 1920s.

Between the sound of Dempsey's punch and the crack of Babe Ruth's bat, sports made radio a household necessity. RCA broadcast the Rose

Bowl of 1927, the Jack Dempsey–Gene Tunney fight from Soldier Field in Chicago, and then the Kentucky Derby. Politics too was covered, as radio announcers tallied up votes in the 1924 and 1928 presidential elections. Al Smith, Herbert Hoover's opponent in the 1928 election, probably lost thousands of votes because his "Noo Yawk" voice grated on midwestern ears.

In the mid-twenties, David persuaded RCA to create two separate networks, the Red and the Blue, Red for comedy and Blue for music and drama (later the Blue became ABC, and Red remained NBC's flagship). The Roaring Twenties roared as loudly at RCA as at any place in America, as radio sales skyrocketed to $400 million in 1929. F. Scott Fitzgerald created Jay Gatsby in the early 1920s, but Fitzgerald starting living like Gatsby after he invested in RCA shares, whose price rose nearly twentyfold between 1923 and 1929. David, who was not yet CEO, said, "I may not be a millionaire yet, but I'm beginning to live like one."[23]

EXPAND THE BRAND:
SURROUND THEM WITH SOUND

David consistently scooped his competitors by asking, "What business am I in?" Companies that forget to ask this question show up in corporate obituaries. They stick with producing carbon paper instead of photocopiers. Or fax machines instead of laptops. David decided he was in the business of beaming sound waves to any place where a human ear would listen. He was no longer in the business of sending bilateral messages; let Western Union handle that. *Where can I find more ears?* David wondered. He started, of course, in American homes and proposed to the Victor Talking Machine Company a deal in which Victor would place an RCA radio receiver in its record players. Victor, home of Nipper, the terrier who hears "His Master's Voice," said no. Too confusing for the public, they replied. David made a beeline to Victor's competitor, Brunswick, which agreed to a $1.5 million contract. Soon after, Nipper and Victor executives showed up with their tails between their legs and asked David to reconsider. He did, and combination radio–record players showed up everywhere.

David was not content with just homes. Where else could he find those ears? Radios should be portable, he argued in a 1922 memorandum to his GE bosses. He suggested that someday automobiles would provide music. But in 1922 automobiles were lucky to provide a door. By 1929, GM figured out how to put a radio in a dashboard, and David hopped a train to Detroit to negotiate a joint venture. GM embraced the idea. In those days, having GM on your side lifted the prestige of any endeavor.

To appreciate David's revolutionary goal of spreading sound in the 1920s, think about the radical shift from landline telephones to cell phones that took place in the 1990s. In the 1970s and 1980s, mobile phones still seemed like a fantasy from *Star Trek* (the Motorola flip phone looked just like William Shatner's prop). In the 1970s, people thought that a telephone number identified a specific house, not a specific person. A telephone number could not move any more than a street address could. It was a law of nature, as if declared by Isaac Newton. If you traveled, you would need a new number. Today our telephone numbers and e-mail addresses are like tattoos on a body; wherever your buttocks travel, so does your telephone number. Cingular's (now AT&T) ad campaign declares that it is "raising the bar" on reception and service. AT&T, Verizon, et al. spend billions of dollars advertising that you can hear your calls no matter how far you go. True enough, my AT&T cell phone worked flawlessly off the coast of Zihuatanejo, Mexico. Of course, I can't hear callers when I'm in my own driveway in California.

After the GM deal, David had put RCA on ships and trains, in homes and automobiles. Where next? Among the ringside celebrities at the Dempsey-Carpentier fight was Al Jolson, the self-proclaimed "World's Greatest Entertainer." In 1927 Jolson made waves by starring in the world's first feature-length talkie, *The Jazz Singer.* Hollywood could never be the same. Suddenly silent movies were like yesterday's sushi, and ticket sales exploded. I watched the Jolson movie recently and found Jolson's hamminess rather touching, especially for a man playing a lapsed synagogue cantor. You could also watch *Singing in the Rain* to see the hilarious sequences when the leading lady of silent movies reveals she has a speaking voice like the screech of a rusty caboose. David Sarnoff knew that RCA had to be in talkies. While in Boston, he met a young son of immigrants who was just as much a striver as he. This man on the move was also on the make and had little guilt about cutting corners or rum-running under the name Dewar's. Joseph P. Kennedy owned part of a flimsy network of theaters around the country that vaudevillians called the Orpheum Circuit. Kennedy also had a hand in movie production through a small firm called Film Box Office (FBO). After preliminary discussions, David and Kennedy met at the Oyster Bar in Grand Central Station in New York and hammered out a deal for RCA to buy into a merged firm called RKO Pictures. Kennedy got $150,000 in cash and stock that he soon sold for $20 million. David, who was now RCA's executive vice president, was not after the money. He got RCA sound systems installed throughout the country and achieved RCA's entrée into Hollywood filmmaking, which led to such stars as King Kong and Fay Wray. David's domain now encompassed ships, planes, automobiles, homes, and crowded theaters. He and Kennedy got what they wanted, including the opportunity to launch the duet of Fred Astaire and Ginger Rogers in ten RKO musicals. Like Sarnoff and Kennedy, the pairing of the two dancers created extraordinary synergy. They say Fred gave Ginger class; and Ginger gave Fred sex.

FIGHTING A DEPRESSION

What do you do when the music stops and the screams begin? The twenties ended disastrously, with RCA shares plunging off a cliff alongside those of GE, GM, and the others.

Like the *Titanic,* the terrible stock market crash of October 1929 pushed David's career upward, not down under water. In contrast, RCA's president, Owen Young, lost his $3 million fortune and resigned while battling to avoid personal bankruptcy. The board appointed thirty-nine-year-old David as president. David had sold his RCA shares in June 1929. He'd had no idea the crash was coming, but unlike many others, he was not greedy or determined to become the richest man on the block. Make no mistake: David wanted power and fame, but money came in a distant third. In his forty-year career leading RCA, he never owned more than

0.5 percent of RCA, nor did he negotiate for himself the stunning profit-sharing percentage that Thomas Watson Sr. had at IBM.

With RCA's presidency in hand, David Sarnoff, an immigrant who had shown up on the wrong pier without money, without food, and without knowing English, now commanded America's radio networks, the most powerful instruments in the world. But his adopted country was reeling, soup kitchens were spreading, and RCA's profits were collapsing by two-thirds. What could David do?

What better way to test a leader than to throw him into the control room just as the machinery is exploding? In 1932 radio sales tumbled by one-third and RCA racked up a $1 million loss. Great CEOs keep their cool and learn to manage. Watson Sr. kept hiring salesmen, figuring they would pay for themselves by drumming up much-needed revenues. Watson cherished the salesman; David exalted the scientist. David slashed salaries, including his own, but kept his scientists at work exploring a new frontier: it was called television.

David felt confident that radio would survive the Depression. Many of his colleagues thought he was deluded. But David argued that for a guy out of work, radio was the cheapest source of entertainment. Even a poor country needed comic relief. RCA introduced portable radios that allowed people to leave their homes and listen as Bob Hope or Will Rogers cheered them up. Radios had become such necessities that people would sooner give up their refrigerators or telephones than their radios. Following the 1932 election, Americans listened to radio's best salesman, Franklin Roosevelt. His fireside radio chats gathered families around the radio to watch. Take a look at photographs of the era; Americans are watching the radio, as if FDR would somehow appear in the mesh speakers, like an unworldly saint.[24] FDR became the very symbol of radio, almost replacing Nipper, the RCA dog with the tilted head. In 1940, at FDR's request, David outfitted the White House with a tape recorder. The tape caught FDR discussing whether to start a rumor about Wendell Willkie having a girlfriend. FDR then unplugged the microphone, proving he was more media savvy than Richard Nixon.

In 1933, David moved RCA's headquarters into a brand-new project called Rockefeller Center, which was desperately hungry for tenants. The Rockefellers had been counting on the Metropolitan Opera, but nonprofit groups do not have much money when their for-profit donors are jumping out of windows. David took a corner suite in the Art Deco masterpiece, lined it with white oak, and awarded himself with a private bathroom and a barber's chair, so his thinning hair could look as good as possible. Perhaps you would be self-conscious, too, if you were constantly photographed with the likes of Clark Gable and John Barrymore. He also had installed an old telegraph key, allowing him to tap messages through the telegraph system, in a quaint old style. In bright red lights, seventy stories above Manhattan and defying America's falling fortunes, the sign "RCA" glowed.[25] In 1934, when the country suffered with a 22 percent jobless rate, RCA clawed back into profitability and paid back virtually all its debt.

SEEING THE BATTLEFIELD: TELEVISION

No cliché is more common to business school students than the "first-mover advantage." To which you should reply, "Oh yeah? Was Google the first search engine? The iPod the first music downloader? Was eBay the first auction site?" No, no, no. Have you ever bought a Chux disposable diaper? Or Reychler laundry detergent? They beat Pampers and Tide by years. And as we discuss in our chapter on Ray Kroc, McDonald's was hardly the first food stand to quickly fry up a burger and shoestring potatoes.[26] It's better to bet on the "best" advantage than the "first" advantage.

Who invented television? You cannot ask that question without facing an army of bruised egos, men who feel they should have gotten Nobel Prizes and billions of dollars. After Marconi proved he could send dots and dashes across the air, many people imagined sending black-and-white dots, which could form a picture. At the turn of the twentieth century, the patent office started receiving various applications, none of which really did the trick. One was filed by Alexander Graham Bell, another by a man with the curious surname Frankenstein. A few years later, a team of Russians named Boris Rosing and Vladimir Zworykin experimented with a cathode-ray tube.

While all these professional scientists toiled in their laboratories, a fourteen-year-old kid in Idaho began peppering his science teacher with his own promising ideas. The kid, named Philo Farnsworth, began to tinker and ultimately revealed some critical concepts behind the science of television. Aaron Sorkin's masterful new play, *The Farnsworth Invention,* dramatizes the long-distance and sometimes tense relationship between this wunderkind of television *science* and David Sarnoff, the wunderkind of television *business.*[27]

David Sarnoff did not invent television. But Sarnoff had the unique ability to "see the battlefield," command the right forces, and inspire the troops more effectively than anyone else. Imagine the battlefield and all the forces pulsing before him: the regulators in Washington, the War Department, the scientists, the competitors, the shareholders, the financiers, the advertisers, etc. When developing a society-changing technology, a CEO must figure out how to navigate the treacherous path to success. Perhaps this is the most important lesson that Sarnoff teaches: See the battlefield clearly; do not be blindsided.

When David was an office boy at Marconi, he had delved into the emerging science, absorbing technical manuals and patent applications. In 1923, as a young executive at RCA, he once again sat down at the table, collected his thoughts, and produced another prescient memorandum. Instead of the "Music Radio Box," he forecast a television "for home use," allowing people to "see as well as hear what is going on." It would be the "ultimate and greatest step in mass communications."[28] In 1923, RCA's best scientists were still seven years away from passing the crudest test: transmitting across a room the fuzzy, grainy image of a Felix the Cat doll. Most communications businessmen were not too impressed even in 1930. After all, passing the Felix test involved an immobile doll and required unbearable heat and light. Television would have to send images of moving people who would faint under intense heat and light.

Still, David was not discouraged. He asked Vladimir Zworykin, his chief scientist, how much money it would take to achieve moving images that looked somewhat sharper than a Monet waterlily. Zworykin replied $100,000. Years later David declared Vladimir Zworykin not only a great inventor, but history's greatest salesman. Zworykin put a price tag of $100,000 on television, David said, and "I bought it" for millions more. David never regretted the investment. He was a missionary for the electron; television was the next altar after radio. During the 1930s, he defended

RCA's research patents against others, fended off government regulators, and eventually paid to license young Philo Farnsworth's patents, too. He showed both zeal and patience, unwilling to unveil the television before it was ready for public viewing. From 1931 to 1937, he encouraged researchers to sharpen the image, leading the "line count" on screen to grow from 48 to 441. (Today HDTV can produce 1,080 progressively scanned lines.) He also pushed to create the right palette of blacks, whites, and grays. Early television performers painted their lips black and their faces blue in order to look normal on monitors. In 1938 David declared to the Radio Manufacturers Association that television was ready for the home, ready for prime time. But it was not yet perfect. RCA needed practical trial-and-error experience in people's living rooms.

David was finally ready for his moment and television's moment. He needed a big splash for the revolutionary device. RCA/NBC would turn on its first programming. But where could he achieve the most publicity? He studied history and read about the frenzy that erupted when Bell showed off the telephone at the 1876 world's fair. Could lightning strike twice at a world's fair? David thought so and chose the 1939 New York world's fair (where Thomas Watson Sr. hoped for his own publicity coup). Television had progressed far beyond a grainy Felix the Cat doll, but the cameras still required a great deal of light. What if the world's fair opening was rainy or the sky was filled with dark clouds? How foolish David and RCA would look, transmitting black and gray splotches instead of people.

On opening day, David drove to the fair, leading an RCA/NBC bus that would serve as a mobile broadcasting unit, very similar to the buses that today pull up to stadiums to broadcast *Monday Night Football*. They parked the bus fifty feet from the speaker's stand. It was a cool April day, and men showed up in overcoats and their customary hats as David helped set up the apparatus in front of the RCA Exhibition Hall. Photos show a man in a sweater, hugging himself to stay warm. Who would stand on the speakers' platform? None other than radio's best salesman, President Franklin Roosevelt. But would television viewers be able to see him? RCA had set up about a hundred television sets in area homes, along with monitors on the fairgrounds and in the RCA Building.[29]

The cameraman aimed his instrument down the road in front of the hall and turned it on. The immigrant from Uzlian looked at the camera and then up at the sky. The sun broke through clouds and shone down on the camera, which desperately needed light waves in order to shoot electron beams and transmit a clear moving image. Then FDR's motorcade roared into view, the images and the sounds captured by the camera and microphones. Mayor La Guardia, the charismatic and plucky "Little Flower," darted straight at the camera to peer into it, creating the world's first close-up. A bugler played as the viewers saw the American flag climb a tall pole, the stripes waving clearly in the breeze. After FDR toasted world peace, David stepped forward. If luck had taken a different turn, he might still have been a poor peasant in Russia, sheltered from technological progress and from freedom. Instead he proclaimed a new era: "We now add radio to sight and sound . . . a new art . . . that is bound to affect all society. It is an art which shines like a torch of hope in a troubled world. It is a creative force which we must learn to utilize for the benefit of all mankind." Thrilling, prophetic. What would he have said if he had known that television would bring the haunting images of Nazi concentration camps, the Vietnam War, and even *Baywatch* into the viewers' living rooms?

Eager men, women, and children crowded into RCA's Exhibition Hall to stare at RCA's seven-by-ten-inch black-and-white sets. They were astonished. But none of them placed an order for the sets (which were priced between $400 and $700). NBC quickly began broadcasting about ten hours each day, including the Brooklyn Dodgers, *Truth or Consequences,* and dramas. Too often, though, the screen would show only a test pattern as NBC tried to invent more programming. If radio took off like a prairie fire, television flickered like a flimsy match torn from a damp matchbook. By midsummer 1939, fewer than a thousand sets had sold, and the wags at *Radio Daily* called the phenomenon "Sarnoff's Folly."

David slashed prices, promised regular programming with big stars, and began to attract the medium's first advertiser: the ticking clock of Bulova (the company that Sony would later snub). It cost Bulova $4 to tick off a minute. In time, those prices would rise. David would not give up or give in.

THE REAL BATTLEFIELD

David Sarnoff had the talent to see business battlefields with more clarity than his competitors. In World War II, he had the chance to see real battlefields, too. During the 1920s and 1930s, he had served as a faithful reservist in the Signal Corps, earning the rank of colonel. He also began to hone his ideas on how future wars would be fought. Ten years before World War II began, he told an Army War College audience that someday radio transmitters and television cameras would enable reconnaissance planes to fire artillery with pinpoint accuracy. A few months before Pearl Harbor, David assured FDR that RCA's communications channels could provide vital services to the military. When the Japanese attacked, he fired off a message to the Oval Office offering up "all our facilities . . . at your instant service. We await your commands." This was not a formality. David was willing to devote his company to saving the West from Hitler and Hirohito. His childhood memory of the vicious Cossacks in Minsk trampling innocent people helped inspire his patriotism. He was also willing to devote his own life and his three sons, who served in uniform. During World War II, he directed his factories for wartime use, and RCA delivered over four thousand television cameras to guide pilotless planes, missiles, and Navy artillery, along with millions of electronic tubes used for sonar, navigation, and walkie-talkies.

Then David's role became more personal than that of an efficient and patriotic CEO. He was fifty years old and in no shape to lead a parachute troop or a beach landing. Yet his telephone rang on a spring day in 1944. It was Eisenhower's office. The general ordered David to hop on the first military transport plane available from New York to London. David did not know his assignment, but he did know that Nazi bombs had been blasting through London. After the long flight, he reported to Eisenhower. Eisenhower had asked his generals in Washington to send him the best man in the country to organize critical communications links for the D-Day invasion. They told him that David Sarnoff was the man. Eisenhower did not reveal to David the precise date of D-Day, nor the precise landing targets in Normandy. He simply gave David his marching orders: create a whole new radio network and broadcasting station to link American, Canadian, and British forces in time for the treacherous launch into

Normandy. How much time did David have? A matter of months, maybe weeks, depending on weather, Nazi advances, Churchill's spirits, etc. Weeks? Hadn't it taken years to develop NBC in peacetime, where the only threats were Bob Hope's gibes and his crippling salary?

Eisenhower's assignment called on all of David's energies and all of his experience in politics, technology, and business. It was the role of a lifetime. Working around the clock, he requisitioned transmitters and negotiated with American officers, as well as British officers and BBC officials, in order to create a new network. Without a reliable system, Eisenhower would not be able to direct the perilous invasion. He also wanted to establish a media "pool" so that reporters could share their coverage of the war. Watching Churchill's masterful command of British radio, Eisenhower realized that propaganda was a powerful tool to bolster morale. Today such media pools are routine. But the BBC rejected his request for help. Under pressure from Eisenhower, David appealed to the British minister of information. The minister turned him down flat, worried that Americans would be calling all of the shots in the communications network. Time was running short; David needed the network up and running. He still did not know when Eisenhower would pull the trigger for D-Day. There was only one man who could overrule the British minister of information. David got in a car and rode to 10 Downing Street. He would not be able to face Eisenhower if he failed in this diplomatic mission. In the private chambers, he unveiled his communications plans, argued for a unified Allied front, and pleaded with Churchill to overrule his own minister. Churchill listened and shook his head. He disagreed with David. But, Churchill continued, with all the agony that lay ahead and all the pressures building to splinter the Allied forces, he would not stand in the way of the American communications plan. Churchill reversed his own minister's decision.[30]

David completed his mission well before D-Day. Eisenhower had the communications tools he needed to organize and perform the most daring and deadly invasion in history. The general had indeed chosen the right man. And when you next see photos and video footage of the Normandy invasion, remember that meeting at 10 Downing Street.

David was not an infantryman, but he did see some action. Before leaving London, he huddled with Londoners in a bomb shelter as the

Luftwaffe fired the screeching V-1 "doodlebug" bombs, forerunners of today's cruise missiles. After D-Day Eisenhower posted him in Normandy, where he got caught up in a firefight with German troops. And when the Germans fled Paris, he commandeered a jeep and sped into Paris, where he quickly turned Radio France, a tool of Goebbels and Nazi collaborators, into the public voice of liberation. He proudly told friends that he beat de Gaulle to Paris by one day. The French Republic awarded him the medal of Commander in the Legion of Honor. In David's proudest moment, the U.S. Army pinned on his uniform the silver star of a brigadier general.

This is a book about CEOs, not generals. You might ask why I have bothered to describe David Sarnoff's war service. After all, he was not an Army Ranger who bravely scaled Pointe du Hoc and repelled the Nazis firing down. After World War II, David became known as General Sarnoff, and, of course, he was delighted with that appellation. Perhaps he was too proud of the title, which reinforced his pomposity. But his war service proved that he indeed had the goods. In 1944, under the wrenching pressure of time and against the bitter resistance of bureaucrats, he built and delivered a vital network to the supreme Allied commander. He did it on time and with superior performance. When, in the most daring moments of twentieth-century history, General Eisenhower needed competence, diligence, and audacity, he was lucky that David Sarnoff eagerly answered the call.

COLOR WARS

After World War II, Americans had more money in their pockets and less worry about being sent into battle. NBC had more programming, and by 1948, RCA was selling two hundred thousand sets, with an 80 percent market share. RCA was also making money on cameras, programming, advertising, and the vacuum tubes that went into the sets of competitors. In those days, televisions were rather temperamental. Vacuum tubes blew, and owners felt an overpowering urge to kick the sets right in the face. David realized that RCA needed to stand out for its service, too, or else owners would blame RCA for any mishaps. He created the RCA Service

Company, which trained thousands of repairmen and sold service contracts. This was in an era when doctors made house calls, and television viewers were delighted to see the RCA man trot up to their front porch with his box of tools. (As I write this, my Internet access has failed, and I long in vain to see a Time Warner repairman at my door.)

By the late 1940s, "Sarnoff's Folly" had turned the corner with great speed, and the Radio and Television Manufacturers' Association anointed him the "Father of American Television." But the Father would soon be on the defensive again. William Paley, the wily CEO of CBS, announced that CBS had perfected color television. David was aghast at being beaten to the punch. He liked Paley, a fellow son of Russian Jews, but he knew that the man had no brains for technology. Paley could not understand a toaster, much less color television. From 1940 to 1953, CBS and NBC battled each other at the Federal Communications Commission, in the laboratory, and in the marketplace. The CBS version came first, years before NBC's, but CBS's technology suffered from a fatal flaw: its color broadcasts were invisible to owners of black-and-white sets. They would see a blank screen. David insisted that RCA/NBC create color broadcasts that owners of black-and-white sets could watch, too, even if the images appeared only in black and white. He insisted that the first mover was not the best mover. David spent sixteen-hour days at the laboratories in Princeton, encouraging his researchers, helping with experiments, and providing whatever support they needed. The man with the sweeping corner office overlooking Manhattan would have been happy holding a beaker and test tube if it would have helped his scientists. If during World War II, he could string together a brand-new network to help Eisenhower beat the Nazis, then he could surely figure out how to beat CBS!

The FCC would not wait for David, though. In 1951, it declared CBS the winner and officially adopted CBS's technical standard. Paley rejoiced, and the RCA scientists were devastated. Then, a break for RCA. The Pentagon declares color phosphors to be a critical war material. The CBS assembly lines screech to a halt. CBS had spent $60 million. For David Sarnoff, this was like a boxer saved by the bell. He sped back down to Princeton and virtually camped out in the labs, not wanting to miss a moment of the reprieve. Given more time, the RCA scientists achieved a breakthrough: vivid broadcasts that even owners of black-and-white sets can watch. Paley ordered his staff to set up for him a side-by-side competition between CBS's and NBC's color. His staffers brought two televisions onto a stage. Imagine the nervousness of the CBS executives as their dominant chairman sat back in his chair and turned on the competing sets. He was testing a lifetime of their work. They had persuaded him to spend CBS nearly to bankruptcy on their technology. Paley later wrote, "We watched in tense silence for fifteen minutes.... There was a deadly pause before anyone would venture an opinion. I knew exactly what I thought. I stood up and said, 'Gentlemen, I'll be glad to speak first. I think the RCA camera has us beat.' ... No one spoke. So I walked out and that was the end." [31] The FCC ensured the end when it reversed its decision and declared RCA the final winner of the color wars.

Congratulations came pouring into RCA's mailroom, but not into the sales desk. Color was a flop, and the term "Sarnoff's Folly" came back once again. I recently discovered a horrendously downbeat article that appeared in *Time* on October 22, 1956, entitled "Faded Rainbow." [32] The writer describes Sarnoff's optimism as "rusty" and quotes a naysayer: "I know the grass is green at Ebbets Field," he said. "It isn't worth $400 more to find out how green." The president of archrival Zenith complained that Sarnoff was "tub-thumping," overhyping the promise of color. The president of rival GE announced, "If you have a color set, you've almost got to have an engineer living in the house." Zenith, Westinghouse, and GE had actually closed down their color assembly lines, while color sets collected dust in retail stores.

Had David lost his edge? Or his mind? He was sixty-five years old. The RCA Building murmured with rumors that the old man was through. But David did not feel old. He would not go out to pasture peacefully. At least not until he had won again. But how could David turn around this color disaster? Looking down at Rockefeller Center, he literally saw more color in the streets: brighter ties, suits, lipstick, and cars. *The Man in the Gray Flannel Suit* appeared in 1956 and must have meant the peaking of gray flannel. Rent the 1998 movie *Pleasantville,* and you will get a sense for how the shift from black and white to color accompanied changing mores and flashier times. Surely the raging rock 'n' roll music did not make sense in black, white, and gray. David was hardly a rocker or a partier, and he hated the chitchat circuit of Manhattan that CBS's Paley cherished. But he did pay attention to social trends. He figured that if Cadillac could sell over 150,000 luxury cars in 1956, he could sell as many color televisions. In 1956 Elvis Presley bought his mother a pink Cadillac. David had an idea. He began a series of steps to mobilize demand for his televisions. He began with celebrities and politicians. Gift-wrapped televisions began to arrive for congressmen, editors, financiers, and performers. He persuaded President Eisenhower to accept color at Blair House, the home for visiting dignitaries. Then he opened up his factories to his competitors, offering blueprints and cost details. Today some computer makers and software writers offer "open architecture" in order to spread their influence and draw more people into their network. David foreshadowed this kind of maneuver by trying to build up a wider constituency for color—even among competitors. He also cut retail prices and, as we discuss in the chapter of Walt Disney, persuaded the myth-maker to switch from ABC to NBC in order to create Sunday night's startling show, The *Walt Disney's Wonderful World of Color.* In the first episode, Donald Duck's bumbling Uncle Ludwig von Drake explained how color imagery worked. CBS and ABC resisted, since color shows cost about one-quarter more to produce than black and white. But then studies began to trickle into David's office showing that owners of color sets watched one-quarter more television! In 1960, David announced that color television was, for the first time, earning profits for RCA—though the word "profit" may have meant about 99¢. In response, Admiral and Packard Bell placed some orders for RCA picture tubes. Sheepishly, in February 1961, Zenith's president phoned RCA and asked for fifty thousand picture tubes, swallowing a heap of crow along the way. Within a few years, twenty companies jumped into the billion-dollar market to satisfy the rabid demand. No longer did David look like a rusty tub-thumper.

Thirty years later Paley paid tribute to his rival in the color wars: "The way he refused to accept defeat . . . the way he kept coming back to Washington and rallying his people . . . the way he drove those scientists to perfect his system. No doubt about it, he was magnificent in color." [33] Bob Hope had a different answer when asked how NBC won the color wars: David Sarnoff stood behind the sets with color crayons.

. . .

Corporate battles today can inspire just as much drama, and the battle-field can look just as treacherous. Boeing and Airbus have been jousting for years. Their sales forces must worry about government regulators, enormous R&D costs, and even foreign policy, as national airlines decide whether to buy a symbol of U.S. or European might. Of course, when we look at the components of a Boeing or Airbus jet, we see the contributions of dozens of countries. Airbuses could not be built without Americans or Boeings without Europeans. The forthcoming Boeing 787 will feature fuselage parts from Italy, along with wings from Japan's Mitsubishi, Kawasaki, and Fuji. And both Boeing and Airbus are offering to send some work to China, since China will spend about $280 billion on aircraft in the next twenty years, making it the second-largest buyer, after the United States.[34]

While Airbus nudged aside Boeing for the title of top airplane builder at the beginning of the twenty-first century, in 2006, Airbus skidded off the track, ignoring some of the lessons of David Sarnoff. David urged his scientists onward, but resisted selling color televisions until they had figured it out. In contrast, Airbus gathered orders for the behemoth A380 jet before the company knew how to build it. The airplane has been delayed for several years because Airbus cannot figure out how to string together the hundred thousand wires that weave for hundreds of miles throughout the aircraft's belly. Moreover, divergent software systems don't seem to like to talk to one another. Delays to date have cost the firm about $6 billion, as airlines have canceled orders, and Airbus has been forced to pay out hundreds of millions of dollars for breaching delivery schedules. Three chief executives have been axed in a year, and Airbus's chief salesman, John Leahy, has publicly called the company an "absolute mess."[35] *He's* kept *his* job. At the A380's original rollout in Toulouse, French president Jacques Chirac had said, "This veritable ocean liner of the sky will go down in history like the Concorde."[36] Perhaps the irony did not translate well.

Unlike CBS, David Sarnoff refused to sell color televisions that made it impossible to watch black and white. He tried to change the world of technology without tossing everyone's life into a Waring blender. In contrast, Airbus is selling a jet that makes airports obsolete, requiring airport authorities to invest many millions of dollars so that gates and runways can handle the superjumbo jet. Further, aviation scientists are now warning that the wake of an A380 could endanger planes that follow it. Big planes produce little tornados spiraling behind their wingtips. The International Civil Aviation Organization issued a surprising recommendation that planes maintain three times as much distance behind an A380 as behind a Boeing 747 jumbo. That means planes would wait longer on the runway before taking off, possibly clogging up airports, even though the A380 is supposed to reduce traffic by piling more people into one fat metal tube.[37]

At the moment, Airbus's technological leap is annoying rather than enriching people. In the future, the Airbus A380 might prove to be a wonderful plane. But the path to its flight has ruined the careers of Airbus chiefs in the executive dining room while threatening the jobs of working stiffs who carry lunch pails.

FINAL DAYS

When the color wars ended in the 1960s, David Sarnoff was headed toward retirement, turning over the reins to his son Robert. It would be nice to write that he lived out his years watching NBC on an RCA television and planning for new ideas like the Internet. Unfortunately, in 1968, at the age of seventy-seven, his body began to fail in terrible ways, leading to three years of operations on his mastoids and intensive care for infections that followed. Robbed of certain motor skills, he could still exhibit extraordinary lucidity and insisted that his aides read him the newspapers and keep him updated on the latest in technology.

David Sarnoff died on December 12, 1971. New York governor Nelson Rockefeller eulogized his "life of greatness" while standing next to the flag-draped coffin: "His genius lay in his capacity to look at the same thing as others were looking at—but to see far more." Others thought radio and television were mere gadgets; he saw precious instruments that would enrich lives. The front door of the Sarnoff mausoleum in New York shows the path of an electron orbiting its atomic nucleus.

He had often joked that he and the electron were twins, born in the same year.

In David's final year, Lizzie Sarnoff, his wife of fifty-four years, placed his old telegraph key next to his bed. As a boy the clickety-clack had entranced him. Now in his final moments, he could be close to the faint memories of his extraordinary life—those urgent, tragic, and uplifting sounds that pierced through lightning and static from the *Titanic,* from the legend of Marconi, and from the beaches at Normandy. In those crackling signals, which confused most everyone else, he could hear and make the future.

6

Ray Kroc: McDonald's

King of the Road

It is 1954. You are trying to pick out from a crowd the man who will revolutionize the food business and inspire millions of little children throughout the world to tug on their parents' shirttails and beg for a Happy Meal. You will not choose Ray Kroc. He was neither a sharp young hipster nor the classic 1950s corporate Man in the Gray Flannel Suit, as played by Gregory Peck. When Ray Kroc drove his rental car across the barren California desert to an oddly shaped octagonal hamburger stand in San Bernardino, he was fifty-two years old with a lot of miles on him. He was suffering from diabetes and a thyroid condition and had already lost his gallbladder. He looked more like Gregory Peck's weatherbeaten gardener than like the leading man. Yet, when Ray Kroc pulled into the parking lot of that hamburger stand, he knew that the best years of his life were in front of him, not in the rearview mirror. What Kroc saw through his front windshield would reinvigorate his tired body. But more important, the word *lunch*, translated into the languages of 120 countries, would never be the same again.

Ray Kroc's life teaches us lessons, not just about perseverance, but about how companies should treat their partners, their suppliers, and the public. These lessons show up every day when you wait in line for a cup of coffee, curse the post office, or wonder whether to dump that stock that cannot seem to go up.

THE EARLY YEARS

"I am an American, Chicago born—Chicago, that somber city—and go at things as I have taught myself, free style, and will make the record in my own way: first to knock, first admitted; sometimes an innocent knock, sometimes a not so innocent." [1]

That was Saul Bellow's Augie March speaking. That was fiction. Ray Kroc was the real deal, born in 1902. Kroc's father, Luis, had started running Western Union messages when Ray was just twelve. Though Luis urged Ray to graduate from high school, Ray could not sit still long enough. He did not apply himself as the teachers demanded. His parents called him Danny Dreamer. In today's world, he would have been diagnosed with ADD and forced to take medication. Instead, he yearned to hit the road. His mother, Rose, a piano teacher, had taught him to play, and Ray had quite a knack. He played organ at a local church, but even there he had trouble following all the rules. This was the age of ragtime, and Ray found both the choirmaster and the somber chords oppressive. He could not stop himself from ending stately hymns with the vaudeville riff, "Shave and a haircut: two bits!" Since this was not quite the standard ending to "Nearer My God to Thee," Ray got booted from the church choir. He also played the bugle in Boy Scouts, but he felt trapped in the narrow repertoire. They insisted on "Taps." He would have been happier tooting the emerging Chicago jazz.

Though often frustrated, Kroc's musical talent encouraged him to open his first business, a sheet music store. This was, of course, before radio and iPods. The money was in selling sheet music to middle-class folks with pianos in their living rooms. Stores like Woolworth and Marshall Field's hired piano players to bang out popular songs and encourage shoppers to buy the music. That is how Irving Berlin and George Gershwin got their start. Today, Nordstrom hires pianists, but the motivation is very different. Rather than hawking sheet music, their job is to inspire shoppers into feeling relaxed, giddy, and irresponsibly affluent. Kroc and two of his friends rented a hole-in-the-wall joint and sold ukuleles, harmonicas, and the hottest new songs. You might have noted that there is not a McMusic store near you. Kroc did not sell enough to meet the $25 monthly rent. The boys closed down, and Kroc went back to fidgeting in school.

He did not last long in high school. He and algebra had a disagreement that could not be solved even with imaginary numbers. Once again music called the teenager, but instead of the church choirmaster or the Boy Scouts, it was the enticing rhythms of a suburban Chicago cabaret. Or so Kroc thought as he hopped buses and trains to get to the gig. When he walked into the garish Gay Nineties–style cabaret, he smelled cheap perfume. A two-hundred-pound woman rolled up to him. He was no sophisticate, but Ray could tell this was no ordinary cabaret. The woman leaning over him was the madam of the bordello. Ray dutifully played his sets, even indulging the madam's wish to sing along in her gravelly voice. Then he grabbed his pay, stuffed it in a sock, and ran out the door, hoping that the linebacker-sized madam could not catch up.[2]

KING OF THE ROAD

Not many people could keep up with young Ray Kroc. He heard George M. Cohan's World War I anthem, "Over There," and decided to go. He lied about his age, quit school, and signed up for the Army. That is when he joined forces with Walt Disney. What? You had not heard that Kroc and Disney were partners forty years before Disneyland and McDonald's? Almost. Both Kroc and Disney signed up to be ambulance drivers in the Army. In fact, they served together in the same company, which trained in Sound Beach, Connecticut. Someone should write a book about World War I ambulance drivers, for they included not just Disney and Kroc, but also Ernest Hemingway, John Dos Passos, Somerset Maugham, and e. e. cummings. (Perhaps it was a German bomb that knocked out of cummings's head the ability to capitalize.) Kroc recalled that Disney "was always drawing pictures while the rest of us were chasing girls. . . . Therein lies a lesson, because his drawings have gone on forever—and most of the girls are dead now."[3] Kroc never got far from Connecticut, for the Great War ended before he could get shipped to Europe. Still, many years later, as Disney was constructing his first theme park in Anaheim and Kroc was desperate to land an account, Kroc wrote to him, seeking the opportunity to link their businesses:

> Dear Walt,
> I feel somewhat presumptuous addressing you in this way. Yet I am sure you would not want me to address you any other way.... My name is Ray A. Kroc.... I look over the Company A picture we had taken in Sound Beach, Conn. many times and recall a lot of pleasant memories.
>   I have very recently taken over the national franchise of the McDonald's system. I would like to inquiry if there may be an opportunity for a McDonald's in your Disneyland Development.[4]

Disney did not respond in 1954. He was not interested in sharing his brand success with an upstart. Even today, though you can buy McDonald's french fries in Disneyland, the McDonald's brand name is blocked from full view. The fries are sold at a counter called Conestoga Fries. Today, the market capitalization of Disney is $72 billion, compared to $55 billion for McDonald's.

After the war, this ambitious, worldly young man turned to the sexy business of ... paper cups. Good thing they were lightweight because young Kroc would hit the streets early in the morning and spend ten hours a day knocking on the doors of restaurants, cajoling managers and soda jerks to buy cups made by the Lily company. He was twenty years old, trying to pitch a newfangled product to a crusty old crowd. Immigrant owners would shake their heads and turn down his sales pitch in broken English: "Naw, I hev glasses, dey costs my chipper." They could reuse glass; this foolish kid was trying to hook them on a continuous monthly fee. Many of those stores were still using glassware from the last century! He might as well have been hawking encyclopedias to the illiterate. He looked like a feckless failure. Yet, toting those samples and pounding those hot streets taught Kroc more about America's future than anything he could have learned in school.

What did he learn? Most important, he learned to shut up. While salesmen had an obvious reputation for being motormouths, Kroc figured out how to keep his sales pitch concise. Whenever he would notice his prospect fidgeting or "shuffling papers on his desk, [he'd] stop talking right then and ask for the order."

Selling door to door does not work so well during Chicago winters, so one season Kroc took a leave of absence and, with his young bride, Ethel, drove a Model T to Miami, where he learned another valuable lesson that would pay dividends thirty years later. They stayed at a flophouse, and Kroc made some money selling swampland and playing the piano at a plush nightclub on Palm Island called the Silent Night. Palm Island was a place where Al Capone made a home and where Barbara Walters's father, Lou, opened the famous Latin Quarter club. Kroc described the Silent Night's ballroom as "fabulous—gorgeous, glamorous and illegal." [5] The owner was a rumrunner who bootlegged booze from the Bahamas. The place was hidden by high hedges, and the doorman would announce the entry of clients by pushing one of two buzzers. Buzzer number one would send the maître d' hurrying out to bow. Buzzer number two meant revenue agents—it was an alarm signaling the staff to scatter and stash the goods. One night the g-men successfully broke the code and invaded the Silent Night. Ray spent three hours in the pokey. Still, it seemed a big step up from the linebacker madam at the edge of town.

What could he learn from this illicit club, besides the need to run fast? Kroc noticed the quick service of the waiters who seemed so eager to please. He also noticed the simplicity of the menu. The Silent Night was lavish, with a marble dance floor and its own yacht. If the owners could supply rum, brandy, and bourbon, they could have served any food available on earth. Yet, they chose to limit the menu to just three items: Maine lobster, steak, and roast duckling. These were highbrow dishes served by elegant Swiss waiters. Nonetheless, Kroc understood that by limiting the menu, the place could be run more efficiently, and the clients would feel comfortable relying on the chefs. When Kroc took over McDonald's, he was competing against roadside diners with foldout menus that unraveled like medieval scrolls. Because of his experience with the shady but sumptuous Silent Night, he chose simplicity and efficiency over excess and developed his first McDonald's motto, the now clichéd KISS: Keep it simple stupid.

Even today, when I enter a new restaurant, I am not impressed if I see two dozen entrée choices. How fresh can the food be if a restaurant that seats fifty is offering me fifteen kinds of fish, eight soups, and a chef's special called "Seafood Surprise"? I like my surprises wrapped in a Tiffany box, not on a dinner plate. I recently ate at a Cheesecake Factory restaurant. The spiral-bound menu was so large, my friend could not find the page that listed the salads, and the waitress showed us her "trick" to fold the menu back into proper order. It is tough enough folding a road map, which is probably why automobile navigation systems sell so well.

THINK LIKE A CUSTOMER

After the ordeal in jail, Kroc returned to Chicago and to the Lily Cup Company. Kroc turned into a wonderful salesman because he could get excited over seemingly mundane matters. Ask a very old person today about the late 1920s and 1930s, and you will hear stories about Babe Ruth "calling" his home run, Lindbergh battling the Atlantic winds, and Roosevelt warning of a "rendezvous with destiny." They will recall the excitement of Jack Dempsey and the terror of the 1929 stock market crash. Here is how Ray Kroc begins a chapter of his autobiography: "The ten years between 1927 and 1937 were a decade of destiny for the paper cup industry."[6] Destiny? Cups? Kroc wrote that without sarcasm, but with a sincere belief that you must focus on details.

Back in Chicago, Kroc began to think like a customer, not like a salesman. He would spend hours at Wrigley Field watching ball games but also watching fans. What did they drink? How did they drink? What did they do with the cups when they were done? He realized that the future of his career was linked to a new phenomenon: carryout foods. We take it for granted today that Chinese restaurants deliver chow mein, that coffee comes in a cardboard cup, and that station wagons stacked with pizza boxes whiz through our neighborhoods, stopping at the corner to wave at FedEx truck drivers. But in 1930 you could stand on a street corner for a long time before seeing anything like that. Kroc's success started by sidling up, not to the owners of sit-down restaurants, but to the itinerant summertime vendors of Italian ices. They preferred paper cups because they had no room to lug heavy glassware on their carts. Nor did they have a convenient place to wash them. That was a pretty easy sell.

Kroc's big opening came with more resistance. He had already achieved a modest account at the Walgreens Drug Company, which had soda counters in its stores. Walgreens bought little pleated cups from Kroc and used them for serving small portions of ketchup and other sauces. You see similar cups today next to the ketchup and mustard pumps at fast-food restaurants. But that was not good enough for Kroc. He noticed that at lunchtime a line of Walgreens customers snaked around the counter waiting for their malt shakes and ice-cream sodas. How could he solve this for Walgreens? Of course, the company could just hire more countermen. But that would drive up labor costs. And besides, Kroc correctly perceived that the real problem was not slow service. The problem was lack of stools. If a few customers lingered and slurped too slowly, it created a line. Kroc's answer seems obvious today, but back then the food-service manager, named McNamara, said: "You're crazy, or else you think I am!"[7]

What was the groundbreaking solution? A carryout counter, of course. But Walgreens was not equipped for carryout—because it used only glassware! You could not have Walgreens customers sucking on straws in the streets and carrying stemware. Kroc's answer served Walgreens's purposes and, of course, his own: use paper cups.

How could the Walgreens manager deem this idea crazy? All McNamara saw was the cost: "I get the same fifteen cents for a malted if it's drunk at the counter, so why the hell should I pay a cent and a half for your cup and earn less?" Kroc argued that Walgreens's volume would go up because he had seen customers give up after waiting in the lunch line. He proposed—and financed—a test. He gave Walgreens free cups and set up a takeout counter. Sure enough, the Chicago street teemed with happy customers carrying paper cups, many of whom were Walgreens employees who worked at the nearby headquarters.

Kroc's Walgreens experiment proved a few things worth remembering. First, look for ways to make your client more efficient. Kroc hung out at Walgreens to figure this out. As Yogi Berra said, sometimes you can see a lot just by looking. Second, be willing to pay for your client's research. Kroc gladly gave away the paper cups until he could prove his case.

Third, try to build your client's profits, not just by pleasing his existing customers, but by attracting new customers who have never bothered to shop there before. Fourth, hang around growing businesses. Walgreens was a quickly expanding client, and each time a new Walgreens store went up, there was Ray Kroc setting up the lunch counter. Kroc did not stop with Walgreens, of course. When he saw all those Walgreens employees on the street during their lunch break, he decided to get into the "employee lunch break" business and grabbed accounts at factories including Swift, Armour, and U.S. Steel. For Kroc, selling paper cups did seem like his destiny.

Kroc achieved his success by putting himself in the shoes of his customers. He asked himself, *How can I help build* their *businesses?* This approach gained their trust. Pretty soon, he had fifteen men working for him, and he was not just dropping off new cups from a truck; he was actually checking their inventories, roaming around their stockrooms, and placing orders on their behalf. He would even tip them off to imminent price increases, and make sure he overordered so that they could beat the price hike.

I do not know whether anyone at Lily ever asked Kroc, "Just whose side are you on?" But by protecting and exalting his paper cup clients, he developed the key discipline that eventually allowed McDonald's to trample over its competitors: McDonald's was virtually the only fast-food company that protected and exalted its franchisees. In contrast, competing burger joints almost always exploited their own franchisees. Ray Kroc would never have become the hamburger king had he not first learned how to hawk little paper cups.

FROM CUPS TO SHAKES

How do you make a milk shake? That seems like a pretty low-tech question. Personally, I grab my Waring blender, pour in some milk, add a couple scoops of ice cream and some chocolate sauce, and then push the Frappe button. When I cannot stand the screeching whir any longer, I turn it off.

Though Kroc could become passionate about almost anything, including the tiny creases of a paper cup, technology especially fascinated him. He was not a scientist and paid little attention in school, but he admired the gee-whiz devices quickly coming on line in the 1930s and 1940s. One day he was in Chicago when his friend Earl Prince, who owned a chain of dairy bars, unveiled a newfangled mixing machine. Instead of a single spindle that blended one milk shake at time, Prince had figured out how to use one large motor to drive five spindles at once. The whirring sound would produce five drinks simultanously. Kroc, then thirty-seven years old, was hooked on the magical machine that Prince called the "Multimixer." This was even more exciting than paper cups! Kroc negotiated for the exclusive marketing rights and began traveling from dairy bar to soda fountain touting this miracle of engineering. The Multimixer saved on labor, space, and time. Many businessmen already knew that "time is money." But Kroc recognized that "time is money" both for the businessman *and* for the customer. Quicker service could bring bigger profits for the operator, but it would also make the customer happier. Kroc remembered the long lines snaking out of the Walgreens. If a soda fountain had a Multimixer, it could make drinks faster, and if it used paper cups, it could make more money in less time because no one would have to wait for a stool at the counter.

Do you ever get the feeling that some businesses do not think your time is worth very much? A few years ago, I flew to Los Angeles to take my kids to Disneyland. We arranged to rent a car from Alamo and rode the little shuttle bus to its off-site location. When I got off the bus, I immediately had the urge to climb back on and head back to LAX. Why? Alamo had set up a zigzagging rope line with several dozen stanchions. In other words, Alamo was telling us right from the start that we would be standing in line; that our time was not worth very much to the company. I do not like doing business with firms that scoff at my time, especially my vacation time with my kids. Schoolkids get only a few weeks off during the year; we should not waste it waiting to attack the Alamo agent. Perhaps Alamo learned this behavior from Disneyland, where families will spend hours of their spring break weaving in and out of lines for the Indiana Jones ride. The ride takes three minutes. The entire movie lasted two hours! Would they make Harrison Ford wait? Now, I must admit that after nearly a half century, Disney finally introduced an effective "Fast Pass" system, which basically allows savvy visitors to make a reservation for a popular ride. So today, only dim-witted people wait for hours. Too bad it took so many years to come up with this solution. Ray Kroc would never have let things get out of hand: he had spent too many years of his life as a frustrated salesman forced to loiter in reception areas, waiting to meet with prospective customers.

Kroc turned the Multimixer into a roaring, whirring success. He went beyond soda fountains and tried to penetrate cocktail lounges by inventing new drinks with Kahlúa, curaçao, and other exotic mixers. He thought he had finally hit the jackpot, selling eight thousand mixers a year at about $300 apiece. He joined a country club, played golf, and hobnobbed with other successful entrepreneurs in the Chicago suburbs. He even sold a Multimixer to a fellow who had just opened a drive-in stand in Washington, D.C., called A&W Root Beer. At the time, he was just another customer to Kroc. Later Kroc would look at the name on the contract and recognize J. Willard Marriott.[8]

TESTING HIS METTLE AND HIS MULTIMIXER

Just when Kroc seemed content to glide into a happy state of affluence, three obstacles popped up to twist his business and test his mettle. First, World War II shook up the U.S. economy, shipping young men to Europe and Asia, but also sparking embargoes on key wartime products. For example, copper. Who cares about copper? It turned out the little motor inside the Multimixer was laced with copper wires to conduct electricity. The Roosevelt administration even closed down nonessential gold mines and directed gold miners to extract critical minerals like copper instead. The Multimixer business got another slap in May 1943 when the government began rationing sugar by issuing "Sugar Buying Coupon Books." Even if you could build a Multimixer with alternative wiring, how could the dairy bars and soda fountains make a decent milk shake without sugar? Kroc's business started faltering. By the mid-1940s, he had a sizable payroll to meet. "A salesman without a product is like a violinist without a bow," Kroc said. While others might have whined and retreated to selling used cars or insurance, Kroc searched for a way to salvage the business: "I just had to finagle around for something else."[9]

To figure out Kroc's solution to the sugar embargo, I suggest you simply walk to your freezer. Take out a half gallon of ice cream and read the ingredients. My freezer is stocked with Dreyer's (marketed as Edy's east of the Rocky Mountains). Here are the first ingredients: "milk, cream, sugar, corn syrup. . . ." There is the answer. Corn syrup is a decent substitute for sugar. Today it is everywhere, replacing sugar in jams, jellies, and apple sauce. Even "maple syrup" is corn syrup these days. Recently, I held in my hand a bottle of Log Cabin pancake syrup, which declares itself "A Family Tradition Since 1887." Some tradition. You cannot find maple syrup anywhere on the list of ingredients, though corn syrup ranks very high. Not even the label's homey illustration of the log cabin shows a maple tree. They must have chopped down the last maple because the tiny cabin is surrounded by pine trees!

We overuse corn syrup today because the U.S. government restricts imports of sugar, thereby giving incentives to agriculture companies to overproduce corn syrup.[10] Nonetheless, during World War II, the discovery of corn syrup for ice cream and milk shakes was an innovative idea. While Kroc did not actually discover the usage, he networked aggressively enough to meet Harry Burke, the son of the founder of the Good Humor ice-cream vending company. Burke cleverly mixed corn syrup into ice milk. Kroc slurped a shake and realized that Burke's recipe could fool enough palates to survive the World War II embargoes. Kroc struck up a marketing deal with Burke so he could sell Burke's recipe to soda fountain owners, who would then have the confidence to buy Kroc's Multimixers.

World War II embargoes stressed Americans everywhere. On a more mundane level, they provided a "stress test" for Kroc's business model. They forced him to demonstrate his flexibility and resourcefulness. He lost money during that period, but gained confidence in himself. Still, the obstacles kept coming on.

The second obstacle was obviously not as dire as a world war. Nor was it a surprise. It was called competition. When Ray Kroc was just a child, a few guys named Frederick Osius, Chester Beach, and Louis Hamilton started a motor-making company in Racine, Wisconsin. You will not find the name Osius on your kitchen counter because Frederick did not like his surname. However, Hamilton and Beach were quite pleased to screw their nameplates on all sorts of appliances. They got a nearly thirty-year head start on Kroc by patenting a drink-mixing machine in 1911. By the 1930s, Hamilton Beach was selling mixers, juice extractors, fans, floor polishers, meat grinders, and jewelers' motors to businesses and homemakers across the country.[11] They should have beaten Kroc and Prince to the Multimixer, but it sometimes takes big companies a long time to sniff out squirrelly competitors. By the late 1940s, Hamilton Beach finally realized that the five-spindle Multimixer was stealing sales from its single-spindle brand. Of course, it could have beaten Kroc by inventing a six-spindle job (which reminds me of the guy in *There's Something About Mary* who hawks a *Seven Minute Abs* video to trump the best-selling *Eight Minute Abs* tape). Instead, Hamilton Beach unveiled a cheaper, more efficient three-spindle competitor. Very few soda fountains needed more than three spindles.

Kroc was in trouble again, as Multimixer sales plunged. He could not meet his payroll and had to fire his salesmen. Then a third obstacle hit. It hit not just Kroc but all of American society: the explosion of the automobile and suburban life. Car sales rocketed from about three million cars in 1947 to five million in 1954. Instead of soda fountains at the urban Woolworth, families zoomed up to carhop and drive-in joints with names like Dairy Queen, Tastee-Freez, and Howard Johnson. These suburban locales made much bigger profits selling fancy sundaes than simple milk shakes. To them a five-spindle drink mixer might be a good way to lose money on a family that would otherwise buy an expensive "Satellite Sparkler"—a sundae topped with a lighted sparkler spraying magical pixie dust all over the table.

At first Kroc could not figure out how to win on this new turf. He tried some dreadful ideas, including the Fold-A-Nook. It was a kitchen table connected to a bench, which folded out of a cabinet. Remember, this was still the era of Murphy beds tucked into the wall. In the early 1940s, a Sicilian immigrant named Bernard Castro patented a "Feather-lift" mechanism so that even a child could unfold a convertible sofa. Now Kroc was yelling, "Look, Mom, no hands—instant nook!" It is a good thing the Fold-A-Nook never took off because today's tort lawyers would probably stuff children in the darn thing just to concoct lawsuits. At the time, though, Kroc had high hopes and actually pitched the idea at the

Beverly Hills Hotel in California. Kroc adorned the elegant hotel room with fresh flowers, hors d'oeuvres, and a sample Fold-A-Nook. The hors d'oeuvres were a big hit. No one dared to sit in the nook.

Imagine a depressed Kroc sitting alone in his nook, nearly bankrupt. The telephone rang. Some drive-in out west had ordered eight Multi-mixers. Eight? That was forty shakes at a time! Must be an ordering mistake. Only the U.S. Army could use that many, but the war had ended almost nine years before. Kroc double-checked the order, looked for a town called San Bernardino on the map, and bought a ticket on the red-eye to Los Angeles.

MEET THE MCDONALD'S

Kroc took a morning drive fifty miles east of Los Angeles and was not impressed. The landscape was brown and so was the air. He pulled his car up to a modest, octagonally shaped drive-in tucked onto a two-hundred-square-foot lot. No other cars were parked there. There was little hint that this hovel could change the world. Then around eleven o'clock, a few employees dressed in spiffy white shirts and paper hats rolled in. Kroc liked that. Though he was once known as Danny Dreamer, even as a child Ray Kroc took neatness and cleanliness very seriously. He bragged that he could make a bed with crisper sheets than any other kid in Chicago. Kroc still did not see how this place could use all those Multimixers. Then two parades began. The first parade consisted of busy employees darting back and forth from a back shed carting sacks of potatoes, boxes of meat, and crates of milk. The second parade was even more impressive. Like true believers congregating for a Billy Graham rally, cars started arriving, and people jumped out to get in line in front of the octagonal building. After they reached the front of the line, they turned around, and Kroc watched them grabbing hamburgers and french fries from the paper bags. He saw construction workers and would-be Hollywood starlets devouring the food. He asked a man with a carpenter's apron how often he came for lunch.

"Every damned day," he said without a pause in his chewing. "It sure beats the old lady's cold meat loaf sandwiches." [12]

Even if the "old lady" made great meat loaf, Kroc realized she could not compete with the taste, addictiveness, and efficiency of this small operation. Kroc's pulse began to hammer with excitement, and he knew he must introduce himself to the owners, Dick and Mac McDonald. The McDonald brothers were not native Californians. They were Yankees from New Hampshire who had moved to Hollywood after high school to try their hands working for the studios. Then they opened a movie theater, which lasted just a few years. In 1937 they opened their first drive-in, located in Pasadena, followed by the San Bernardino branch in 1940. The McDonald's originally employed twenty carhops, serving barbecued beef and pork ribs. Teenagers loved it, and the brothers got rich.

A few years later, new competitors showed up, though, and the McDonalds realized that the carhop business had several drawbacks. First, young families shunned the teenager and carhop phenomenon. Carhop joints had a reputation for loose morals. Those of us who grew up with innocent nostalgic television shows like *Happy Days* might not have known that those girls on skates sometimes sneaked into the backseats of the cars to deliver more than soda pop. Second, and more important from a business perspective, carhop joints were very labor and land intensive. As more drive-ins sprouted up, they drove up the cost of hiring carhop talent. Carhop joints also required bigger parking lots because the customers ate in their vehicles. Third, carhop joints generally used real dinner plates and utensils, which required McDonald's to hire vast numbers of dishwashers.

In 1948, Dick and Mac decided to shut the store and revamp. They reopened and offered a cheaper menu, plasticware instead of china, and a walk-up counter instead of carhops. At first it was a flop. Yet, within a year, a new kind of customer started to belly up to the counter: children. Children and working-class families began to enjoy the pleasures and cost savings of the new system. By 1954, the brothers were generating about $275,000 in annual sales. That was 40 percent more than their old drive-in, while they spent only one-third as much on labor and capital.[13] No wonder that when Ray Kroc drove up in 1954, he wanted a piece of the action.

If the McDonald brothers had this secret recipe for making money, why in the world did they get involved with the fifty-two-year-old salesman from Chicago? And why does this chapter focus on Ray Kroc, who stumbled upon McDonald's many years after the brothers flipped their first burger? This is a controversial subject. In fact, McDonald's.com, the official Web site of the company, begins its corporate history with Kroc in 1954. Moreover, Dick and Mac often complained that corporate officials at the headquarters in Illinois sometimes denied that the McDonald brothers ever existed. They were fictitious stooges, no more real than the Hamburglar or Ronald. Of course, the McDonald brothers were real, and they were innovative. So what did Kroc bring to the table, or should we say, to the self-serve counter?

- First of all, Kroc brought ambition. The McDonald brothers were easily contented. They had big bank accounts, fancy Cadillacs, and the most prestigious home addresses in town. (Of course, the town was San Bernardino.) Kroc had spent his career crisscrossing the country by plane, train, automobile, and sometimes horse in order to make a sale. Only he was inspired to turn McDonald's into a national name.

- Second, Kroc had even more confidence in the McDonald *system* than the brothers themselves. Before Kroc showed up, the brothers did allow a few entrepreneurs to license the name and copy the business model. But, unlike Kroc, they did not insist that their franchisees follow their rules. Kroc knew that a national brand required uniformity. Dick McDonald did not even recognize that his name had brand value. When a man named Neil Fox from Phoenix proposed a franchise, McDonald assumed he would call it "Fox's." When Fox surprised Dick by announcing his plans to call it McDonald's, Dick replied, "What the hell for? McDonald's means nothing in Phoenix." The brothers watched blithely as a local telephone repairman named Glenn Bell "borrowed" their quick-service concepts and opened up his own drive-in, which he named after himself, calling it Taco Bell.

- Third, Kroc's experience taught him that he must continually cut costs and raise efficiency. That meant hard bargaining with suppliers. The McDonald brothers were not fat and happy, but they seemed too happy to wield a whip with their suppliers.

THE DEAL

For a sharp businessman, Ray Kroc struck a pretty lousy deal with the McDonald brothers. He made the same mistake a novice car buyer makes when he struts into a showroom and drools over his favorite model. Better to play it cool. Not Kroc. He was tired of hawking Multimixers amid the fierce competition from Hamilton Beach. He couldn't bear to think about the abandoned Fold-A-Nook. He was desperate. Watching the little San Bernardino hamburger stand reinvigorated his exhausted body. He dreaded getting onto the flight back to Chicago without an agreement to market the McDonald's company. The McDonald brothers quickly agreed to a bare-bones deal. He could launch franchises around the country, as long as he limited his fees to a $950 payment plus 1.9 percent of sales revenue. However, the agreement also required him to kick back 0.5 percent of the 1.9 percent, more than one-fourth of his commission, back to Dick and Mac.[14] In other words, even if Kroc could find a franchisee, teach him the McDonald's system, and spark sales of $100,000, he would keep only about $1,400 of the take. And of course, Kroc would have to pay for hiring trainers, real estate professionals, and others in order to grow new franchises. Under these terms, Kroc would starve unless he could dot the country with McDonald's drive-ins. He nearly did. In fact, the McDonald's company turned many franchisees and suppliers into millionaires long before Kroc himself could cash in.

Kroc's experience with McDonald's got off to a rough start. Shortly after inking the deal and returning to Illinois, he discovered that the brothers had not disclosed all of their prior dealings. For example, they forgot to tell Kroc that though he was based outside Chicago, they had already franchised a McDonald's in his neighborhood! While he purportedly had national rights to the business, he could exert absolutely no control over the local McDonald's branch. When Kroc found out, he asked how much the franchisee, a company named Frejlack, had paid. The answer: $5,000. Now Kroc was faced with a choice. Either buy out Frejlack or try to build up the McDonald's brand while competing against another McDonald's. He chose the former, and it cost him $25,000.[15] A nice profit for Frejlack and a lousy launch for the McDonald's dynasty. A furious Kroc never quite got over the loose and lackadaisical ways of

Dick and Mac. By 1961, he grew so frustrated with the brothers that he dove deep into debt to buy them out for their asking price, $2.7 million. Kroc still had not made any money on the business.

NEW IDEAS FROM RAY KROC

First, Make Your Partners Rich

In an era of outlandish CEO pay where compensation calculations require scientific notation, Ray Kroc is a refreshing story. While he turned humble, middle-class mom-and-pop franchisees into millionaires, Kroc did not withdraw his first dollar from McDonald's until 1961, six years after meeting Dick and Mac McDonald. Compare that to today's golden parachutes that flutter open after just one day on the job. Kroc did not invent the idea of franchising restaurants. As we will see, everyone from Howard Johnson to Dairy Queen to Bob's Big Boy beat him to the punch. By the late 1950s, he was competing against all those plus Taco Bell, Burger Chef, Burger King, Kentucky Fried Chicken, Chicken Delight, and dozens of other places that were eager to give children free hats, aprons, and buttons. And decades before restaurant franchises cropped up, Singer sewing machines, auto parts stores, and drugstores struck up franchising deals.

So why did Kroc and McDonald's survive and thrive while others struggled? The secret was not under the sesame bun. Though Kroc focused more closely on the burger than others, his real innovation was to turn the business of franchising on its head. Typically, franchising deals were struck by firms that wanted to get rich quick by being paid up front for licensing their brand name and menu and supplying products. They were not confident in their long-term survival, so they wanted to pocket money now. Kroc burst with confidence in McDonald's future, and that's why he was willing to get rich at a slower pace, if it meant that his franchisees would prosper. Think of President Kennedy's inaugural command: "Ask not what your country can do for you—ask what you can do for your country." Kroc believed his Illinois headquarters had an obligation to help its franchisees. Others saw their franchisees as an oilman looks at a depleting well: "Pump till it's dry and then move on." How so? Tastee-Freez forced its franchisees to buy their expensive freezers. Burger Chef was owned by General Equipment. General Equipment's biggest concern was to sell as many shake machines and fryers to Burger Chef stores as possible. Three-quarters of the equipment on the premises was slapped with a General Equipment insignia. Likewise, Burger King's parent company wanted to sell as many broilers as possible. Dairy Queen headquarters tacked a 32 percent profit margin onto the ice-cream mix it forced franchisees to buy.

When I was a kid, I loved Carvel's soft serve ice cream and the tacky television advertisements narrated by founder Tom Carvel. During December, Carvel would advertise a Santa Claus cake. Then in March, a leprechaun. Then in the off-season, "Fudgy the Whale." Tom Carvel never disclosed that they were all made with the same mold. Fudgy tilted sideways looked like he was wearing a hat. This did not get Carvel into trouble. But "tying" arrangements did. Carvel broke antitrust laws by forcing its own partners to buy not just ice cream, but even trivial items like paper napkins, from the parent. Now what happens when a company tries to squeeze its franchisees by driving up costs? Well, they can quit, go broke, or try to escape the regulations by buying on the black market. Kroc claimed that many Howard Johnson locations were buying bootlegged food.

Kroc felt that his competitors cared only about jamming profitable stuff down the throats of their partners, rather than long-term growth. This was not just a hunch. He noticed how casually and negligently the companies supervised their stores. Big Boy employed only five men to supervise in the field. Tastee-Freez had just five who were supposed to oversee quality control at 1,500 branches! They must have been very tired, or more likely, they did not manage to see much at all. Charles Bresler, coowner of Bresler's ice cream and the Henry's hamburger chain, tells the story of his Phoenix franchisee. Henry's home office signed up a new franchisee, apparently sight unseen. When Bresler visited the store, he was shocked to find that the man had just one arm. Bresler asked whether the man had any employees or even relatives to help him. "No, I'm all by myself." Bresler later stated, "You can't blame a guy for having one arm, but how the hell can you sell a franchise to a guy who couldn't even wrap hamburgers?"[16]

Reacting to these fiascoes, Kroc felt passionately that his job was to make his franchisees rich by cutting their costs and improving their products. He refused kickbacks from his suppliers. When a big supplier of cooking oil offered him a Christmas gift, Kroc turned it down: he just wanted better oil at a better price that he could pass on to his franchisees. Kroc did not want to get paid on the basis of each store's capital expenditure, but on each store's profits. Nor did Kroc want to make money on extraneous profit centers. He banned jukeboxes, pay telephones, and vending machines. Why? Hasn't Starbucks made a bundle on music CDs and shiny Italian cappuccino machines? Yes, but those offerings reinforce the "Starbucks experience." Kroc argued that jukeboxes and vending machines created unproductive traffic and loitering. Furthermore, "vending machines were controlled by the crime syndicate, and I wanted no part of that," he explained.

Kroc's business model required an extra helping of patience. Many of his former business colleagues must have thought him foolish. Why would he trust his life to a bunch of novice franchisees, most of whom did not yet know the difference between a pickle and profit? Kroc may have been confident, but he was not completely naive. No lifelong salesman could be. Kroc was not simply giving away franchises to any stumblebum who showed up with a spatula. He slowly distributed the stores, testing and training the franchisees and requiring them to meet his excruciating standards for quality, cleanliness, and service. Because other companies were eager to collect big bucks fast, they sold off vast statewide territories to rich speculators. Kroc sold just one at a time and refused to sell a second franchise to an operator unless his performance was stellar. This meant that McDonald's operators tended to be more middle-class than others. They had stronger incentives to succeed. And they had a shorter leash to run with because Kroc did not want to relinquish a great deal of control. That was the deal. You sign with Kroc, you get a leader devoted to your success. In return, however, you get a leader who will be watching you closely.

Ray Kroc pursued uniformity because he wanted a McDonald's

hamburger and a bag of fries to be dependable. He did not want to hear that the burgers in Memphis were even better than those in Nashville. He told the McDonald brothers that "we are not going to stand for any monkey business. . . . Once they sign [the franchise agreement], they are going to conform." In one heralded story, Kroc confronted a quirky California operator who decided to serve freshly carved roast beef. And if that was not a big enough breach of the standardized menu, the man actually dressed like a chef and carved the roast in the front window of the store. He was becoming his own mascot. "Take down your arches," Kroc demanded. The man acknowledged that Kroc had to take a tough approach with outlaws: "McDonald's can thank God that I was such a scalawag, because it made them more careful in selecting franchisees." [17]

Kroc liked franchise uniformity. On a personal level, he had many pet peeves. He hated beards, gum chewing, white socks, and comic books. He also had a temper and was constantly "firing" people. I place the verb in quotation marks because he usually backed down after an hour. Ray Kroc's explosive behavior reminds me of the Billy Crystal movie *Mr. Saturday Night,* in which a television variety show host starts firing his staff after a poor performance. "You're fired! You're fired! You're fired!" he screams while pointing his finger to the huddle around him. Then a small voice pipes up. "But I don't even work here, sir." The Crystal character smiles. "All right, you are hired." Beat. "Now you're fired!"

Yet, despite these foibles and peeves, Ray Kroc did not demand that his partners look like they came from a cookie-cutter mold. McDonald's is a Scottish name, but the names of the key players sounded like a roll call at the United Nations. Kroc's family came from Bohemia (now a region in the Czech Republic). His assistant, who became a huge equity holder, was of Italian descent. His key CEO during the explosive years was a Jewish man named Harry Sonneborn. Kroc was slow to bring women into the business but reached out to black proprietors quite early compared to other corporate moguls.

Growing up in Chicago made Kroc keenly aware of the American melting pot. When he sold paper cups, he noticed that he was selling many in old Polish neighborhoods. What did they use them for? *Povidla,* a prune butter. "Those folks ate an awful lot of prune butter," he remembered. As chairman of McDonald's in the early 1960s, he fielded a call from a franchisee whose store was in the middle of a Roman Catholic neighborhood in Cincinnati. The operator had a problem. His customers would not eat hamburgers on Friday. "I had to have a damn fish sandwich," the man demanded. Quite a religious statement! Under Kroc's leadership, McDonald's performed the world's most thorough and expensive research on haddock and cod and developed the Filet-O-Fish. The Filet-O-Fish now satisfies customers throughout the world, but it all started with a religious request to feed Catholics a damn sandwich on Fridays.

Raising the Steaks

Back in the early 1980s, Wendy's had a huge advertising hit with a little old lady sneering at a puny burger and shouting at a fast-food server, "Where's the beef?" That tagline helped derail Gary Hart's attempt to win the Democratic presidential nomination. Ray Kroc's question was even more penetrating: He asked, "*What* is in the beef?"

Nowadays, it is easy to scoff at a lowly McDonald's hamburger. As a kid, I remember McDonald's wrapping its burgers in a paper sleeve that said "100% beef." That did not seem like a big deal to me, but my father was impressed. You have no idea what was stuffed into a hamburger back in the 1950s. Nobody does because the options were so great and scary. If you were lucky, most of the burger at least came from a cow. Nonetheless, it typically had the same kind of ambiguous ingredients you would find on a can of Alpo, that is, "meat and meat by-products." By-products? What's that? A lot of things come from and come out of a cow, pig, or a horse. Upton Sinclair's *The Jungle* disclosed the horrors of the meatpacking industry in 1906. But when Ray Kroc took over McDonald's, hamburgers were still generally made from scraps and frequently pumped up with fillers like blood and soy. White Castle tried to shave beef costs by cutting five holes in the center of their tiny patties. Today the U.S. government merely requires that the fat content be limited to 30 percent. Kroc demanded a uniform and fairly healthful hamburger. Under his watch, McDonald's required hamburgers to be 83 percent lean chuck from grass-fed cattle and 17 percent choice from grain-fed cattle.

Kroc did not immediately trust his suppliers and franchisees. A team of inspectors traveled the country administering a comprehensive "meat test." Burgers that looked too red were likely juiced with nitrates. Burgers that felt gummy were probably derived from bull meat. Burgers that sparkled with mist when grilled were laced with soy. Kroc's team brought science to the griddle. Literally. They distributed to their franchisees small vials of hydrochloric acid so that they could gauge the fat content. Sometimes Kroc's team would burst into the warehouse of a suspect supplier after midnight, searching for telltale signs of filler and other shenanigans. The economics of fast-food franchising depends on strong supervision so that consumers can rely on the menu. Because of Ray Kroc, consumers can answer the question, *What* is in that meat?

Americans eat about 140 pounds of potatoes each year.[18] That's roughly equal to their weight. And, of course, if they are larding them up with sour cream or butter, their weight becomes a moving target. The first day Kroc parked his car in the San Bernardino lot, he realized he would be selling more than hamburgers. Dick and Mac served up intoxicating french fries. Burger King spent almost half a century trying to concoct better fries, and only in the past few years has it had the nerve to even *claim* that it can compete on taste and texture. Have you ever tried to make your own french fry? I have, and I would not invite guests over to try them. Even doused with ketchup, something is not quite right. Ray Kroc asked a simple question: Why are the San Bernardino fries so good? He received a quick answer. We dunno. In fact, in the 1950s, no one really knew how to make a consistently good fry.

Kroc wondered about the science of french frying. "Are you kidding?" potato sellers replied. Potato growers were a motley group of farmers who looked like they had just stumbled off the set of *Green Acres.* The search for the perfect fry began. Kroc and two of his employees, Fred Turner, a fresh-faced former Army clerk, and Nick Karos, the son of a sandwich shop owner, turned to the usual suspects. Was it the temperature of the fryer machines? They dipped thermometers into oil vats and tested. Was it the type of potatoes? Most agreed that No. 1 Idaho russets worked best, but within that category, you could get inconsistent fries. They examined potato after potato, batch after batch of french fries. They made two discoveries that revolutionized agriculture. First, some russet potatoes contained more water than others. They learned that the best french fries came from potatoes with less water and more solids. A more solid potato absorbed less oil, creating a crisper fry. More solid potatoes also shrank less, so a franchisee would get more fries per pound of spuds. Once again, Kroc's team did not just perform laboratory research—they demanded that their suppliers comply with their findings. McDonald's field managers swooped down on potato fields wielding hydrometers, a floating instrument to measure the water-to-solids ratio, or more precisely, the "specific gravity," of spuds dunked in buckets of water. Imagine the rustic-looking potato farmer in his overalls watching his crop turned into a science fair experiment. But the promise of McDonald's gleamed so brightly, he went along with the plan.

The second french fry discovery involved storage. Where do you keep your potatoes? The pantry? The garage? The refrigerator? You are miles ahead of potato farmers in the 1950s and 1960s. The best potato processors in Idaho did not even use silos or temperature-controlled barns. Instead, they just tossed the russets into caves dug into the ground and covered with sod. Tasty, no? What did they do if the caves felt a little too steamy on a humid summer day? They flung open the door to the cave and let in some "fresh" farm air. Life on the farm had not made much progress since van Gogh painted *The Potato Eaters* in 1885. Kroc was not content to be frozen in time. Once again he clamped down on the growers, urging them to develop more reliable storage systems. At first they balked, but those who complied soon saw their orders pouring in.

When other fast-food firms like Burger Chef were working with virtually no supervisors, Kroc devoted scarce dollars to a research laboratory outside Chicago. That concept ultimately turned into the highly regarded Hamburger University, but at the outset, his competitors must have doubled over in laughter as Kroc struggled to pay his bills. Their recipe: Just dunk the old potatoes in the oil. Just pound the meat and flip. Just grab as much cash as you can and damn the future, they thought. But as Ira Gershwin wrote, "Who's Got the Last Laugh Now?"

Taming Suppliers by Making Them Rich

From the point of view of a potato grower or a meat packer, Ray Kroc must have been a pain. He wanted better prices *and* better quality. In the 1950s and early 1960s, who had ever heard of Ray Kroc or McDonald's? Why would any big organization kowtow to those names? It turns out that the big players did not kowtow. In almost every case, Kroc negotiated better deals with small suppliers who were hungry for his emerging business. Kraft had the McDonald's cheese account early on, but when Kroc requested a sharper-tasting cheddar for the burgers, Kraft was too busy or too comfortable to develop a new recipe. When Kroc went looking for good-quality beef, major players like Armour and Swift refused to extend credit. A too-proud baking company called Bays refused Kroc's request for a uniform English muffin. That would flout its proud tradition of jagged muffins. Even Hires root beer lost McDonald's business in the early years.

So what happened instead? Ray Kroc made multimillionaires of the quick and hungry suppliers. When Kraft failed him, Kroc turned to a cheesehead in Green Bay, Wisconsin, named L. D. Schreiber. Today the Schreiber Company is a multibillion-dollar firm. Kroc could not negotiate great deals with Wesson Oil and Procter & Gamble. Instead he turned an upstart named Harry Smargon into a very rich man. At the time Kroc met Smargon, though, the oil purveyor was far from the major leagues. Smargon's oil contained some beef fat (along with vegetable shortening) because he could not afford the equipment to make all-vegetable oil! Yet, Kroc placed his faith in Smargon. In return Smargon placed his faith in Ray Kroc.

Why did Smargon and the others trust that Kroc was worth doing business with? Two reasons. First, Kroc was a hell of a salesman. When he launched into his vision of a nation border-to-border with McDonald's franchises, he entranced the suppliers. "You could see the bun!" one supplier commented as Kroc described the menu by waving his arms in the air. His enthusiasm allowed him to negotiate volume discounts even before there was any volume. When the Wessons and Swifts said no, Kroc sought those with a lean and hungry look. A seasoned salesman, Kroc always looked for clues. When he sent out his real estate team to scout out new locations, he urged them, "Look for schools, churches, and new houses." That's where the money was.

Second, despite this awesome salesmanship, Kroc reeked of integrity. He turned down bribes, gifts, and even a legitimate salary. He refused the easy tricks to puff up the food and the profits. More important, while he negotiated hard for good pricing deals, once he agreed to a price, he did not try to beat down the supplier for even more concessions. Nor did he expect the suppliers to cut their prices every time the commodity markets hit a soft patch. He was a loyal customer. Was there a risk here? Wouldn't sharper buyers diversify their business among numerous suppliers and insist that they slash prices every time commodity prices slipped by one-tenth of a penny? Many would. But stingier buyers would endure more pain when commodity prices spiked or when shortages forced suppliers to choose which customers to send deliveries to. Kroc was reliable and tough. And his suppliers realized that with every penny of savings Kroc negotiated, McDonald's franchisees would profit, and more orders would come rushing in.

Finally, as McDonald's growth exploded, many of the suppliers became almost dependent on the Golden Arches. Economists call this a monopsony; that is, a situation when a single buyer dominates the market. Ray Kroc, who started off begging for cooking oil and buns, ultimately achieved enormous market leverage. Thankfully, it did not occur to him to use that leverage to smash the little people who trusted him in the early years.

RONALD AND RAY

Ray Kroc had a touch of showbiz in him. The very idea that he would rent the Beverly Hills Hotel to show off the Fold-A-Nook tells us that. But Kroc also knew that he had to make McDonald's a kind of entertainment destination. Though he had banned jukeboxes and other diversions, he did recognize the appeal of McDonald's to children. As a child, I collected rectangular paper hats that McDonald's gave away, long before Happy Meals and collectible toys with movie tie-ins. Even in the late 1950s, Kroc insisted that franchisees spend 2.5 percent of their sales revenue on advertising. The very idea of a glass-enclosed kitchen, a "fishbowl," added entertainment value. Kroc hired a public relations firm in Chicago to feed witticisms to local newspaper columnists. "If you've got time to lean, you've got time to clean," he offered. In the 1960s, McDonald's drummed up the mayor of Hamburg, Germany, in a publicity stunt to "return" the burger to its birthplace. And then there was Ronald. The joyful clown began as Bozo on a local Washington, D.C., television station. Who played Bozo, and then Ronald? Willard Scott, later the jovial and plump weatherman on NBC's *Today* show. According to John Mariani in his book *America Eats Out,* "Within six years of airing his first national TV ad in 1965, the Ronald McDonald clown character was familiar to 96% of American children, far more than knew the name of the President of the United States."[19] In Japan, McDonald's changed the clown's first name to Donald to avoid challenging the Japanese tongue. When the company sent Ronald McDonald around the world riding bicycles and roller-skating and developed catchy television jingles, franchisees could easily see that they were getting their money's worth. That was very different from other fast-food companies, which spent decades trying to develop a theme or a look. Further, franchisees from other companies often suspected that their advertising contributions were just kickbacks to management, to go along with the unnecessarily expensive broilers, fryers, and napkins.

Ray Kroc's devotion to cleanliness was legendary. When he would visit a franchise, he would have a car drop him off several blocks away. He would show up at the manager's door juggling the trash that he had picked up in the nearby neighborhood. No wonder that McDonald's commissioned a successful television advertising campaign showing a bunch of workers grabbing buckets and mops. During the booming 1960s and 1970s, McDonald's jingles might have been Top 40 hits: "You Deserve a Break Today" and "Two All-Beef Patties, Special Sauce...." A few years ago, I was in my kitchen, too lazy to get in the car. So I thought about making my own Egg McMuffin. What's in it? Suddenly, the old theme song chimed in, giving me the receipe, to the old tune "Carolina in the Morning": "Nothing, I mean nothing beats McDonald's Egg McMuffin in the morning. Eggs, Canadian bacon, cheese, and muffin are the making of your morning...." Before McDonald's launched that tune and that sandwich, most of America did not even know what an English muffin was. Back in the 1970s, before McDonald's unveiled the "Ham & Egg Cheese Bagel," even bagels seemed exotic, mentioned in rural areas only to hurl an anti-Semitic epithet. Today, if Norman Rockwell were painting an American breakfast scene, he'd depict the old Yankee grandmother chewing on a poppy seed bagel with a schmear of cream cheese and some McDonald's hash browns.

GLAZED AND CONFUSED: KRISPY KREME'S SLIDE

Ray Kroc's mantra, QSC&V—quality, service, cleanliness, and value—was easily memorized by competitors. It sounds like a cliché from an old Cub Scout handbook. The very idea of franchising, which Kroc did not invent, has spread beyond fast food into tax preparation, travel agencies, dry cleaning, kitchen-cabinet refinishing, and even tennis lessons. The basic concept—local owners handle daily operations, while the franchisor markets and builds the brand—has not changed very much. Franchises now span nearly one hundred different industries and contribute more than $1 trillion annually to the U.S. economy. Almost half of that comes from the food-service sector.

Yet, despite the surge in franchising, almost all fail to perform as well as Ray Kroc and his disciples. In this chapter, we have explored some key principles that worked for Kroc. If he carved the path in the wilderness fifty years ago, how can anyone get lost or cut up in the stinging nettles? Have a doughnut. In particular a Krispy Kreme. Like the original McDonald's stand in San Bernardino, Krispy Kreme started with a cultlike appeal. Customers in the South would line up salivating when a new store opened up in the neighborhood. Rosie O'Donnell complained on television that she could not buy Krispy Kremes in New York. It reminded me of my junior high school teacher who lauded Coors beer, which could not be bought east of the Rockies. I don't know why he was talking to fourteen-year-olds about beer, but I know we could not wait to have a taste. We want what we cannot touch. When Krispy Kreme finally started cutting ribbons nationwide, Wall Street investment bankers started salivating. In 2000, the share price soared from an initial offering at $21 a share to $105. Then a two-for-one stock split created even more furor. Krispy Kreme opened 435 stores across the U.S. and as far away as England and Australia. What a hit! Krispy Kreme was on easy street. But it was not Kroc's path they followed. By 2004, shares in Krispy Kreme had plummeted by 90 percent, and the company shuttered almost 100 stores, as average store sales collapsed by 20 percent.

What went wrong? What would Ray Kroc say? First of all, Krispy Kreme's management was too greedy toward franchisees, requiring them to "overpay" for the privilege of selling jelly doughnuts. Management got rich immediately, while franchisees were struggling. Management admitted this in 2004, when it offered to buy out failing franchisees for $32 million. It might have avoided a free fall in its share price if it had made those franchising deals $32 million cheaper at the outset.[20] Instead, it expanded too fast. Remember, Ray Kroc allocated just one restaurant at a time, after carefully inspecting the applicants.

Second, Krispy Kreme did a miserable job of watching its own books and was forced to restate earnings, inviting a federal investigation. Kroc was always boasting about the *future* of McDonald's, but he did not lie to investors about current cash flow.

Third, Krispy Kreme diluted its brand. Kroc insisted that franchises follow the McDonald's architecture and the precise layout of the kitchen. In contrast, you could pick up a Krispy Kreme doughnut at a Krispy Kreme counter or in a box at Safeway or at the Piggly Wiggly. Sometimes they were stale because Krispy Kreme was not as punctilious about supply-chain kinks. How could Krispy Kreme control the Krispy Kreme "experience" if you could bite into a jelly doughnut while pumping gas at an Exxon station? Krispy Kreme defenders lament that the rise of the doughnut business had the bad luck to coincide with the Atkins low-carb craze. This sounds more like an excuse, since Dunkin' Donuts and Panera Bread did much better during this period. Can Krispy Kreme be saved? Sure, but it will require a huge dose of honesty and modesty to defang those angry franchisees who got snookered. Nor would it hurt to sell some fancy, high-margin coffee with those doughnuts. After all, caffeine is even more addicting than a cruller.

THE KROC LEGACY

Ray Kroc died in San Diego in 1984, a very rich man. His buyout of the McDonald brothers, which strained him in 1961, paid dividends with every sign that reported how many million—or billion—burgers sold. Despite fame and money, he never forgot his frugal and efficient ways. His driver would deliver Kroc in his Rolls-Royce to the Price Club (the forerunner of Costco) so that Kroc could check out the bargains. Witnesses reported that Kroc once scolded his wife, Joan, for wasting a napkin, in which she had wrapped a slice of orange for her husband. At the time, they were flying on his $8 million Gulfstream jet.

Kroc was not perfect, and he committed enough blunders just to prove it. He tried to introduce the HulaBurger, a pineapple-and-cheese sandwich. It led people to ask, literally, "Where's the beef?" At one point he was convinced that America needed fast-food pound cake. He also bought the San Diego Padres and contributed $250,000 to Richard Nixon after Watergate. After a particularly miserable performance by the Padres, Kroc grabbed the public address microphone and bellowed: "This is Ray Kroc speaking. . . . I apologize. . . . I'm disgusted. . . . This is the most stupid baseball playing I've ever seen." A player protested, "Who the hell does he think he's talking to, a bunch of short-order cooks?"[21] Kroc told the press that the player had insulted short-order cooks. He offered free tickets to anyone who showed up at the stadium wearing a chef's hat. At the next game thousands of fans lined up waving their hats. They knew that Ray Kroc would live up to his promise.

7

Akio Morita: Sony

The Sound of the People

As the sun rose, the young lieutenant nervously reached for his sword. His forefathers were samurai, but he hadn't slept well the previous night. Maybe one did not inherit bravery. He methodically buttoned up his navy uniform, straightened his tie, and brushed the gold anchor on his collar. He stood at attention and awaited the message from the emperor. Already thousands of Japanese had been killed fleeing Tokyo as swarms of American B-29s bombarded the old town, scorching the wooden buildings and whipping up winds that turned into firestorms. As city residents ran for cover, their coats and hats ignited.

Akio Morita had been spared, so far. He was shielded in a navy laboratory working with other physicists to design heat-seeking weapons to repel the American onslaught. But now his turn might come, and the emperor might ask—no, command—that he step from behind his desk and march into the fiery battle. He could not refuse. In 1945 almost four thousand of his countrymen had flown kamikaze missions, diving their airplanes into Allied navy ships. The kamikaze manual ordered pilots to "transcend life and death . . . totally disregard your earthly life . . . concentrate your attention on eradicating the enemy with unwavering determination."[1] Countless soldiers committed seppuku (ritual suicide or hara-kiri) rather than surrender to the Americans.

Life was not cheap, but it could be spent quickly in the name of the godlike emperor. Akio, the firstborn son of a prominent family that traced its roots back fifteen generations, could not think of disobeying. What would Emperor Hirohito demand of him? Akio had been taught never even to glance at the supreme leader, for fear of going blind. Train conductors instructed passengers to bow when the railroad car passed the imperial palace. They were subjects of the crown. No one but the emperor's closest family members and advisers had ever heard his voice. He was like the burning bush of the Old Testament, too awesome for mere mortals to view and too wise and powerful to ignore.

Akio clutched his sword, turned on the radio, and listened for the emperor's voice over the state-run radio station. He was surprised. It was not the thundering tone of an angry god. The timbre was thin and high and made even tinnier as it passed through the crackling static of the electrical circuits. The words were not imperious or commanding. They were formal, old-fashioned, and uncertain:

> It is unbearable for me to see the brave and loyal fighting men of Japan disarmed. It is equally unbearable that others who have rendered me devoted service should now be punished as instigators of the war. Nevertheless, the time has come to bear the unbearable. . . . I swallow my tears and accept the Allied proclamation.[2]

The emperor had surrendered in the holy war. The twenty-four-year-old navy officer from the prominent family was spared. He was relieved of duty, but now forced into another fight: surviving the chaos of a desperately poor economy that had been destroyed by Allied bombs and by the megalomania of Japan's imperial government. Akio Morita put down his sword and stared ahead. With no mission, he did not know where he would go next or what he would do. If the emperor no longer had any power, a young physicist certainly did not.

How remarkable to think, then, that within fifteen years, Akio would lead his country and ultimately the world on a mission to the electronic frontier, empowering individuals to choose their own music, television, and games. When Akio turned off the radio on August 9, 1945, it might have been the last day that all Japanese listened to and marched to the same drummer.

THE EARLY YEARS

Akio Morita may not have been destined for greatness, but it would have been a big disappointment to his ancestors if he had ended up taking orders from someone else who held the title CEO. As the firstborn son of a family that had been making sake and soy sauce for hundreds of years, Akio was trained to take charge from the day of his birth in January 1921. Even when Akio was in grade school, his father would haul him to business meetings and demonstrate how to count inventory and, most important, exude confidence when dealing with subordinates. The Morita family (the name meant "prosperous rice field") lived in privilege, with a tennis court, luxury automobiles, servants, and neighbors like the Toyodas (founders of the Toyota Motor Company). With a smile quicker and his eyes a shade lighter than most Japanese, Akio seemed to glow with promise and confidence.

Akio's family straddled two battling eras: the age of the shoguns and modernity. In the late nineteenth century, Japan itself had lurched from a closed society, angry at barbaric westerners, to the era of the Meiji Restoration. In just a few years, the reigning motto of Japan switched from the xenophobic battle cry *Sonno joi,* meaning "Revere the emperor! Expel the barbarians!" to the all-embracing *Bummei kaika,* meaning "Civilization and enlightenment!" In the 1870s, Emperor Meiji sent delegations to Washington, D.C., and Paris to bring back the latest ideas on law, policy, and fashion. Japanese officials arrived in the West wearing robes, but returned to Tokyo in top hats. By the 1890s, a Japanese school team (named Ichiro) began trouncing American sportsmen in Yokohama in a series of baseball games. Ichiro won nine of ten games, outscoring the Americans 230–64.[3] The American team usually had the home-field advantage, playing in a private park where Japanese men were banned.

The Morita family struggled with the opposing tugs of tradition and modern times. Akio's mother, Shuko, always wore a kimono, yet she asserted her opinions freely. To toughen his mind, Akio's parents sent him to a highly disciplined school, which provided no heat in winter and forbade students from wearing an extra layer of clothing. Yet, his mother bought him a western mattress instead of a traditional tatami mat. Though his parents did not know it, the family was grooming Akio to lead an East–West fusion.

Akio's grandfather had nearly bankrupted the family business by "investing" in ancient Asian crafts, like tea-ceremony ceramics. Yet, this same grandfather led Akio to a movie theater to see *King Kong.* Talkie movies had just emerged from Hollywood, and Akio's grandfather likely took him to see the 1928 smash hit *The Singing Fool,* starring Al Jolson. In that movie, Jolson thrice sings a sentimental song called "Sonny Boy." The phrase "sonny boy" stayed on Morita's mind.

Akio's mother adored Western music and would sit with Akio as together they hand-cranked the old Victrola to play records by Enrico Caruso and violinist Efrem Zimbalist. Somehow Caruso's soaring tenor pierced through the old mechanical box with greater fidelity than other singers' voices. While Shuko listened for the trills and the wails in Caruso's voice, Akio sat with his head tilted like the dog in the Victrola ad who hears "His Master's Voice." Akio did not feel strongly about the musical composition per se, but he felt passionate about the sound mechanism. How did the Victrola work? Why did the records sound scratchy? Why did some recordings have a higher ratio of music to hiss? How could they stop the hissing? When Akio reached junior high school, his father surprised the family and brought home an electric phonograph, a pricey privilege. For the price of two Electrolas, you could almost buy a car. His father did not buy it because he cared about Caruso, but because he thought that listening to the scratchy, hand-cranked Victrola would damage Akio's hearing.

"I will never forget the fantastic sound. . . . I was absolutely astounded," Morita said.[4] He and his mother carefully placed Ravel's *Boléro,* Mozart, Beethoven, Bach, and Brahms on the turntable and marveled at American ingenuity. The mesmerizing, nearly hissless melodies hooked Morita. Electronics became his obsession. While other teenagers grew obsessed with collecting stamps or chasing girls, Akio would devote all his after-school hours to building electric radios and other devices. He subscribed to a new Japanese magazine called *Wireless and Experiments,* and followed the diagrams in foreign magazines as well. He took apart every appliance he could find. Akio could usually figure out how to get them back together again. After years of learning and tinkering, he finally figured out how to make a crude recording of his own voice.

Like so many obsessed boys, Akio could not be bothered with the pedestrian interests of his teachers. Who cared about history and geography when you were discovering the secret of a sapphire phonograph needle? He cared only about science, and within science, mostly about the physics of sound. He nearly flunked out of school, until his parents forced him to buckle down with private tutors. He entered high school with the distinction of earning the lowest possible grades. Of course, Akio would specialize in physics. His father was disappointed. Remember, Akio was supposed to be preparing to run a respected sake business. He should have been specializing in economics or perhaps the chemistry of brewing rice and soybeans. The physics of music was a reasonable hobby, but not a profession.

Akio resisted his father's urgings and stuck to science. On the morning of December 8, 1941, he sat up in his bed listening to a radio that he had constructed himself. He had equipped the radio with an alarm clock that woke him faithfully at six o'clock. The voice of the newsreader shook the small radio. The news bulletin was shocking, unnerving, and exciting. The Japanese had executed a successful surprise attack on Pearl Harbor. The reporter described plumes of smoke over the U.S. Navy base. Akio might have been filled with pride, but the pride turned to worry. He knew technology. The Americans were far ahead in avionics, automobiles, and electronics. How could Japan possibly compete against a brilliant power like the U.S.? Though Japanese propagandists began to fill the airwaves with news of the conquests of the Philippines and Hong Kong, Akio could not join in the militaristic spirit of imperial Japan. He would hear Tokyo Rose on his homemade radio, but he could not believe that she would prevail over Bing Crosby.

WARTIME SERVICE

Of all the Asian words that have crept into the American vocabulary, from "karate" to "futon," the last one you would apply to Akio Morita's wartime service would be "gung ho."[5] By entering the service as a physics researcher, Akio assumed he would be assigned a high-tech position. Instead, he was sent to a factory where he tediously hand-filed steel parts. After a few weeks of dreary menial labor, someone figured out that it might help the Japanese war effort if they took him off the assembly line. Soon he was in a laboratory with other brilliant researchers trying to design night-vision glasses and heat-seeking weapons. They never succeeded in developing the heat-seeking missile. (It would be another decade before America succeeded in launching the Sidewinder missile.)

Akio's own autobiography credits his navy service with teaching him to be a "wheeler-dealer."[6] Though he personally did not devise any scientific breakthroughs, he did figure out how to get stationed at a beachfront country house far from the action, close to a hotel that the navy had commandeered. He arranged for his family's soybean company to ship valuable soybean paste and miso in containers marked "For Naval Use" to his team. They traded these precious commodities for other desirables. Akio had his own logical and sardonic view of air-raid sirens. Whenever an air-raid alert sounded, other military battalions would jump out of bed, jump into uniform, and man the fire pumps. Akio had a different view. He told his men to stay in bed, figuring, *If they hit us, we'll be dead anyway.* I don't know whether Akio Morita ever saw the 1960s television show *McHale's Navy,* but he would have fit in quite well.

A WAR BRIDE

Besides learning to be savvy and shrewd with his superiors, Akio Morita gained something else from the war: the most valuable relationship of his life. He met in the research lab a thick-fingered, bespectacled man who sounded, not like the blue-blooded Morita, but like a blue-collar workingman in urban Tokyo. Yet behind the thick glasses and the gruff accent was a mind that twinkled with scientific genius. Masaru Ibuka was just as fascinated by physics as Akio. And he was even more inventive about applying his passion. As a boy he had been notorious for taking apart toys and appliances. "Masaru's here, better hide the toys and clocks!" his family would exclaim. He would lick a sound cylinder to feel how smooth and well engineered it was, his eyes flashing in delight.[7] Ibuka was thirteen years older than Akio. By 1933 he had already achieved fame and earned the accolade "genius inventor" by winning a gold prize at the Paris world's fair for an invention he called "the dancing neon" (which used sound waves to control long-distance light signals). Akio was mesmerized by Ibuka's ingenuity. One day Lieutenant Morita visited the laboratory where Ibuka was designing a powerful new amplifier, which allowed low-flying airplanes to detect Allied submarines coursing 100 feet below the surface by measuring the slightest disturbance in the Earth's magnetic field. Properly tuned, the amplifier could detect tiny frequencies of just a few cycles per second. Akio opened the door to the lab and saw Ibuka surrounded by girls from a nearby music academy. Ibuka correctly conjectured that the girls' highly trained ears would allow them to fit the oscillation of his transmitters to the pitch of a one-thousand cycle tuning fork.

Despite his genius for science, Ibuka was never meant to be a CEO. Yes, he could pick apart and understand any technology, but he lacked the knack and shrewdness for understanding and commanding people. He even failed the entrance exam to get a job at Toshiba's forerunner, Shibaura. Though Ibuka appeared like the proverbial absentminded professor, Akio saw in him the perfect partner. For the rest of their lives, they enjoyed nothing more than sitting on the floor together and tinkering with toys. When Akio would visit FAO Schwarz in New York, he would come back with two of everything, one for him, one for Ibuka. Ibuka's son later said, "They were closer than lovers, even Mrs. Morita felt that. They were bound together by a tie so tight that it was more like love than friendship. The connection was so deep that not even their wives could break into it when they were together."[8]

PEACE BREAKS OUT

Over half of Tokyo's land was burning, simmering, or too emptied of kindling even to fuel a fire. The Meiji Shrine and the cathedral and temples of the Tokugawa family had been pulverized by air raids. Even the imperial palace smoldered. As the surrender took effect and General MacArthur landed in the city, workers were dumping tons of cinders into Tokyo's canals.[9] There was no gasoline available, and the few working vehicles had been converted to burn charcoal or wood instead. It was not a promising place to launch a new business.

Like a character in *Slaughterhouse-Five,* Masaru Ibuka (not yet in partnership with Akio Morita) led a few employees into a burned-out, cracked-up department store, where they tried to figure out how to turn their intellectual capital into money. The site was so dingy and damaged that policemen frequently busted in to accuse them of trespassing or squatting. Other than undertakers, who were thriving, what kind of business could survive amid the rubble, in a city that resembled the year 1745 more than 1945? Though Ibuka was trained in advanced electronics and physics, he even considered such low-tech ideas as baking sweet bean cakes or even opening up a miniature golf course. Finally, they agreed on a simple electrical device, a rice cooker. Rice is so important to the Japanese that the word for cooked rice, *meshi,* means "meal." Ibuka went to work on a clever design in which the rice itself would turn off the cooker as it absorbed the water. Unfortunately, the quality and texture of Japanese rice varied so greatly that Ibuka's mechanism seldom worked well. The cooked rice was either too soggy or too dry. No Japanese consumer could afford to waste a cup of rice on a newfangled contraption. Ibuka's pockets got emptier and his staff more restless.

The next project, a device to convert AM radios to shortwave radios, was more successful and sold under the company name, Tokyo Telecommunications Research Institute. During the war, Japanese military police had ripped out the shortwave wires in radios, fearing that citizens would tune in to Allied propaganda. Ibuka knew how to restore the shortwave capability by installing a single vacuum tube. He sent his employees on a mission to scrounge up tubes on the black market that he would then clean up and install. Ibuka's lucky break came when an acquaintance at the *Asahi Shimbun,* Japan's biggest newspaper, wrote a glowing article about Ibuka's efforts, even stating that Ibuka was providing this service just from charitable motives. The article assured readers that Ibuka's rebuilt radio would put consumers in a great position once private broadcasting resumed.

Akio Morita read this article and rushed to join Ibuka's enterprise. He learned a lesson from the article and never forgot the value of media buzz. If the *Asahi Shimbun* had ignored Ibuka's tinkering, the business might have floundered and ultimately failed. Instead, the media attention generated customers and calls from would-be suppliers. Akio learned that positive media buzz cut a doubly favorable path for a business: First, by goosing demand, it allowed a business to charge more for its product. Second, it created competition among suppliers, which pushed down the price of inputs. Each blade of the scissors cut in favor of the business. Each side contributed to higher revenues and profit margins. For the rest of his career, Akio would pursue media contacts, which would occasionally annoy colleagues and competitors. The most dangerous place to be was standing between Akio and a television camera. As his career continued, did Akio turn into a showboat? Perhaps, but his showboating helped the bottom line. Media buzz became, and has since remained, a keen marketing tactic. During the 1979 summer launch of the blazingly successful Walkman, Akio sent free Walkman units to television, movie, and recording stars. Sure enough, magazines like *People* were soon printing photos of celebrities bopping to tunes on their revolutionary portable tape player.

Two obstacles blocked Akio's entry to Ibuka's factory. First, to make ends meet after the war, Akio had taken a job with his old professor, teaching physics at a technology institute. He needed a proper excuse to quit or else he would be committing a terrible insult to the professor. Luckily, General MacArthur provided the excuse for him. The occupation forces had imposed a purge from the schools, declaring that former military officers would not be permitted to spoil young Japanese minds and twist them back toward militarism. Akio's superiors at the technology school did not care a bit about the decree and were hardly worried about Akio's military past. But since Akio wanted to lose his teaching job, he pretended to be so gravely worried about the decree that he got the dean nervous enough to let him go. By the time Akio was done exaggerating his anxieties, the dean probably thought that Admiral Nimitz was sailing his battleship to the campus to arrest the physically unimposing Akio Morita.

Second, and far more intimidating, Akio had to confront his father and explain why his firstborn son was going to be the first in fifteen generations to leave the esteemed Morita sake and soy dynasty in order to pursue rice cookers and cheap radios. Akio would not make the trip alone. In accordance with Japanese tradition, Ibuka, too, owed Morita-sama an explanation, much like a young man asking a father for his daughter's hand in marriage. Luckily for Ibuka and Akio, they were joined by Ibuka's father-in-law who had held senior positions in the Japanese government.

The three men traveled at night on rickety rails to the Morita home far southwest of Tokyo in Kosugaya. With destruction all about, they bounced up and down while fetid air blew in through broken windows. They were not sure whether they would be asking the patriarch for permission, a blessing, or a badly needed loan for the infant business. After many hours of a bumpy and nerve-racking ride, they arrived at the Morita estate, which, despite the war, appeared a sanctuary enjoying its own separate peace. Even as most Japanese scavenged for scallions and diluted their rice with potato meal, the Morita family served warm bread, jams, and tea. The family still had sake, though the government had been rationing it for years and desperate black marketeers were routinely diluting it with water and even formaldehyde. Judging by the Morita family, however, the war had not wiped out all of civilized bourgeois society. As the visitors munched on the welcoming meal, Morita-sama was waiting for them to drop their bombshell. He knew why they had come, and for years he had observed Akio's passion for science and his boredom with staples like sake and soy. Ibuka presented his business ideas and tried to convince Morita-sama that Akio was a crucial partner who could accomplish great things. Morita-sama stood his ground and reminded the men that they were asking him to allow Akio to break a three-hundred-year-old tradition. How much must Japanese elders surrender in order to accommodate the modern world?

Then Akio's father dropped his own bombshell. He would not shackle his son to the family businesses. He looked at Akio with resignation and said, "You are going to do what you like best." [10] Then he smiled as Akio and his partners sat gaping. But before they could say much more, Morita-sama dropped yet another surprise. Not only would he approve Akio's break with tradition, but also he would lend them money for their new enterprise. A series of loans from the Morita family soon added up to about $60,000 (in today's dollars) and made the Morita family the largest shareholder in the newly named Tokyo Telecommunications Engineering Corporation, or Totsuko. In retrospect, it was an awesome investment, ultimately generating billions of dollars of wealth for the family.

BACK TO THE DUMP

Akio and his partners rode back on the train with some money in their pockets. Soon after they arrived back in Tokyo, they discovered they were homeless. In August 1946, the department store where Ibuka had started his business had decided to renovate. Most insulting, the owners were renovating to make room for a dance hall for the occupation troops. Back in Great Britain, American soldiers were famously decried for being "overpaid, oversexed, and over here." In Japan, male resentment toward their brawnier Yankee occupiers was less comical.

Nonetheless, Akio tried to learn from the setback. Although the dance hall was intended for occupation soldiers and their dates, Akio noticed that their music was sweeping Japan. The imperial government had banned American jazz and swing music during the war. That was one reason the army ripped the wires out of household radios, while neighborhood associations called Tonarigumi would snoop on suspicious families who tapped their feet in jitterbug time. But as soon as the emperor surrendered, Tommy Dorsey, Harry James, and Frank Sinatra became stars in the Land of the Rising Sun. Louis Armstrong's cornet sounded on radios, helping to inspire "J-Pop," homegrown Japanese music with a Western flair. In 1948, *Down Beat* magazine reported from Japan that jazz had "swept over this country like wildfire since the end of the war."[11] Akio did not focus on this phenomenon just because he liked to tap his feet. He detected a *commercial* movement, too. All of Japan was undergoing a transformation. And this transformation would generate a huge demand for sound, that is, record players, radios, and anything else he and Ibuka could come up with. But there were two obstacles: they needed supplies and, quite simply, a place to work.

Kicked out of the department store, Akio and Ibuka had no time to

sulk. The dank and damaged department store was hardly a modern factory. They immediately began looking for another location and settled
upon a hovel near the harbor. The roof leaked, requiring workers to keep
umbrellas under their desks. Akio recalled that to reach his "office," he
had to duck under the neighbors' clotheslines, often festooned with baby
diapers. Those relatives who visited him thought he had gone under-
ground, literally and figuratively, as an anarchist. Instead he became a
black marketeer. Of course, everyone shopped and sold in the black market, as Japan had reverted to a barter state. Akio and Ibuka were the only
members of the company who had driver's licenses, so they pooled their
funds to buy a beat-up Datsun truck that they had to hand-crank to start.
Together, these august executives would scour the streets looking for supplies—metals, wires, coils—and then hand-crank their truck back under
the neighbors' clotheslines and into the leaky hovel. They might as well
have been riding a Fred Flintstone car in Bedrock.

The engineers at Totsuko were forced to jury-rig their own equipment. They ransacked for vacuum tubes, found motorcycle springs in the
ruins and turned them into screwdrivers, and tore out telephone cables
from junkyards and used them for electrical wiring.

INDEPENDENCE DAY

Akio and Ibuka could have led an easier life if they had acted a little more
Japanese. The two men refused to join big Japanese corporations and refused to bow to anybody else's consensus. Instead, they launched their
own enterprise independent of the reigning giants. Before World War II,
three major "money clans," or *zaibatsu,* dominated Japanese industry:
Mitsubishi, Mitsui, and Sumitomo. After the war, General MacArthur
tried to shake up these behemoths. Nonetheless, these three firms, along
with Sanwa, Fuji, and Dai-Ichi, outlived the 1947 Anti-Monopoly Law
and morphed into six primary *keiretsu.* A *keiretsu* is an interlocking family
of companies that buy from, supply, and lend to one another.[12] Even today, about half of Japan's top companies belong to one of the six major
keiretsu. For example, the old Fuji *keiretsu* today includes Sapporo beer,
Nissan cars, and Canon copiers.

If Akio and Ibuka had simply rushed into the arms of a *keiretsu,* they might have avoided scavenging for spare parts, begging for supplies, and ducking under clotheslines. But the men knew there was a tremendous upside to independence. By staying independent, they could act more nimbly and more creatively, thereby allowing Sony (as they officially named the corporation in 1958) to leapfrog its more powerful competitors. After serving in the imperial armed forces, perhaps the two men just got tired of taking orders.

While Ibuka immersed himself in the sometimes soggy laboratory, Akio began to plot out business missions for Totsuko. He was not prepared, but he quickly learned lessons and led Totsuko toward solvency and then prosperity.

AKIO LEARNS ABOUT CONSUMERS

If the fans don't come out to the ball park,
you can't stop them.
—YOGI BERRA

In 1949, Akio thought he could sell Japanese families a tape recorder that weighed one hundred pounds and cost more than one year's salary. He had a lot to learn. He naively thought that the tape recorder would be seen as very valuable simply because his team had worked to the point of exhaustion to make it. But Japanese consumers who were deciding how to spend their scarce yen replied, "Who cares how much time you put in? We don't want it." To economists, young Akio sounds as if he were intoning Karl Marx's "labor theory of value," which was firmly rebutted by the Victorian economist Alfred Marshall.[13] Labor is useless if it is wasted on unwanted goods. For Akio, the mystery was to figure out who would value the recorder.

Before revealing the answer to Akio's mystery, it is worth taking a moment to see how resourceful Akio and Ibuka were in building their tape recorder. While visiting NHK (the Japanese broadcasting service) in the late 1940s, Ibuka noticed an American-made tape recorder and was stunned by its performance. Japanese engineers had heard about magnetic tapes used by German propagandists and by American firms (the tapes were often made by Minnesota Mining and Manufacturing—now 3M and known for Post-its), but the engineers had not actually heard the tapes perform. Magnetic tape appeared a miraculous invention. This may be hard to fathom today, considering that CDs, DVDs, and iPods have made tapes so obsolete that cassettes and, heaven forfend, eight-track tapes are the butt of jokes along with shag carpeting and mullet haircuts. Akio and Ibuka could not figure out how to produce magnetic tape, especially since postwar Japan lacked plastic. They sat on the floor cutting strips of cellophane with hand-held razor blades, but the cellophane quickly stretched and clogged up their crude recording mechanism. What other material could they try? They cut up fine paper with the razor blades, ground up magnets into a powder, and then tried to pulverize the magnets into the paper strips. No luck. Finally, their precocious researcher Nobutoshi Kihara read in a book about magnets that if you burned oxalic ferrite, it would turn into ferric oxide, a magnetized material.

Morita toured the back rooms of wholesalers until he found oxalic ferrite powder. Now what? The magnet book did not exactly explain how to convert it to ferric oxide. They swiped a frying pan from a kitchen and sautéed the powder, which then turned from yellow to brown to black. That was too much cooking! Anyone who had seen magnetic tape knew that it was brown, not black. They cooked up another batch, but quickly doused it with water after it turned brown, in order to stop the chemical reaction. So now they had a magnetic material but still no way to coat the tape. They tried gum and even a paste made from valuable sticky rice. They had better luck when they mixed the brown stuff with a clear lacquer, which provided the stickiness they needed. Finally, they needed a tool to apply the sticky magnetized ingredient to the paper. An airbrush proved too powerful for the delicate work. They tried numerous paintbrushes, finally choosing one with soft bristles from the underbelly of a badger. So, with a recipe that sounded like it came from the witches of *Macbeth*—did they try eye of newt and wool of bat?—Morita and his teammates ultimately created what they called "talking paper," a working magnetic tape. Minnesota Mining and Manufacturing obviously used a far more advanced technique than frying pans and badger bellies. Nonetheless, the experience boosted Morita's confidence in their ingenuity.

And for all the trial-and-error work with razor blades and frying pans, he got the last laugh when, fifteen years later, IBM chose to rely on Sony magnetic tape for its data storage. The prize for innovation does not always go to the guys with the most money. The billions of dollars jangling in the pockets of Google's and eBay's founders attest to that, even as they competed against General Electric and other well-funded behemoths.

One last note on the frying pans and innovation: 6,700 miles away, during this same period in the late 1940s, one of our other great CEOs, Estée Lauder, was literally boiling pots with her recipes for facial creams. Two people who would someday be worth billions of dollars began by standing in front of a hot stove and refusing to turn off the heat until they had found their recipe for success.

After all of Estée's boiling, she had smooth emollients that she could package attractively in three-ounce jars. When Akio and his team finished cooking and assembling, they had a hundred-pound tape recorder. Who could possibly afford the contraption? Akio surely had the determination. Like a door-to-door salesman, he cold-called, hot-tipped, and hopscotched across Tokyo, lugging the beast in and out of his Datsun truck and demonstrating the magical recording device. Businesses and households enjoyed the novelty, but virtually no one reached into his billfold when Akio finished speaking, singing, and tap-dancing before the microphone. The tape player might have taken ten thousand man-hours to develop and build, but if no one wanted it, it had no value. This was a searing lesson that Akio would never forget. Even today, I come across new products that make little economic sense, except as a oneshot novelty. Late-night television ads for plastic exercise steps come to mind. What's wrong with walking up your own steps? Are there that many apartment or ranch house dwellers really yearning for a set of steps? In Japan the rush into high-tech gadgets has been more reckless and irrational than in just about any other country. A Japanese inventor named Kenji Kawakami recently coined the word *chindogu* to mean a useless invention that at first appears to be a plausible gadget, for example, "Walk 'n' Wash" ankle-attachable laundry tanks, which let you wash your socks while getting your daily exercise, or slippers for cats so they can help dust the floor while they chase yarn balls.[14] Unless they become comical fads like pet rocks, these products can never hope to reward their manufacturers.

We must give Akio Morita credit, though. After failing to sell any tape recorders, he could have melted them down for scrap and tried to reverse the ferric oxide back into oxalic ferrite. Instead, he took a stroll around town. He passed an antiques dealer and witnessed a customer purchasing an old vase. Akio himself did not care much for antiques, though his father and grandfather had amassed a vast collection.[15] At first he felt insulted. How could someone pay scarce yen for a dusty old vase, yet customers scoffed at his nifty tape recorder? But Akio realized that the vase, though it was low-technology and not very useful except to display flowers, had value simply because that man was willing to pay for it. The value came, not from the labor, not from some scientific calculation of its intrinsic appeal, but from the supply and demand in the marketplace. His tape recorder might have some value—but only if he could find customers who placed value on it. That was the mystery he had to solve. Akio had to discover whether the tape recorder was worthless or whether he had been wasting his time trying to sell to the wrong target audience.

Who was the target audience for an expensive tape recorder that weighed as much as a young woman? Remember, Ray Kroc tripped upon the McDonald brothers because they ordered eight Multimixers, while most small burger joints could not be bothered with a machine that could make five milk shakes at once. Akio and his partners realized that a struggling salaryman in Japan could not afford their tape recorder. The sheer heft of the device screamed the word "institutional," not "family." It looked like something that belonged in an office, not a living room. But what kind of office? Who really needed to record voices? And if they did, who had the money to invest? The answer: Japanese courts. After the war, Japan suffered a shortage of court stenographers, since so many stenography schools had closed down when students were pushed into the war effort. Writing Japanese is tremendously complex and, as I discovered while doing business with Japanese colleagues, can confound and embarrass even native Japanese. You can eat a great dinner in Kyoto and your host can add up the tab, but do not ask him to read from the check. Japanese includes Chinese kanji symbols, as well as two different sets of symbols representing syllables. One prewar study found that even literate Japanese soldiers had forgotten most of the kanji symbols they learned in school.[16] And among those symbols they could read, they could not necessarily remember how to write them without being given some clues. Understandably, then, Japanese courts could not quickly deputize citizens and expect them to perform as stenographers, able to flawlessly transcribe complex discussions in real time.

Using an introduction from Ibuka's famous father-in-law, former education minister Tamon Maeda, Akio marched into the Japanese Supreme Court to demonstrate what they called Model G, for "government." This time, instead of bemused and befuddled looks from workingmen who thought the tape recorder was a toy to empty their too-thin wallets, Akio saw the looks of overworked bureaucrats who urgently needed help. Model G instantly gained Totsuko twenty orders from the Supreme Court, which, unlike households, had the funding to support the stenography pool. Akio had finally figured out he needed what we economists call "effective demand": a desire to buy coupled with the money to back it up.

Were there any other institutions that could use a tape recorder? Just as the occupation forces had shaken up the legal system, they had also stirred up the schools, which had been insular in attitude, imperialistic in ethos, and focused mostly on rote memorization. The U.S. Education Mission cut out the emperor-worshipping morals courses and emphasized audiovisual tools rather than the abacus. In the U.S., this was the beginning of the "golden age of filmstrips." [17] Teachers would turn off the lights, flip on the gunmetal Bell & Howell projector, and mesmerize the kids with corny, clunky strips of plastic that taught everything from how to wash out head lice to why you cannot eat your math teacher's pi. The U.S. began to export these films both to teach foreigners about America and to help modernize postwar Japan. A 1949 film called *People Are Working the World Over* portrayed the fictitious Okamoto family paying a "cow tax" and eating rice out of a big bucket they shared. Akio and his partners noticed one big problem in the American scheme: the voices and text were in English only. Ibuka's father-in-law figured out that the schools, like the courts, had funding for special projects. So Akio once again marched into the fray, toting his tape recorders and explaining to school principals and teachers that they could record a Japanese sound track to accompany the American filmstrips. With the revenue from the court stenography business, Totsuko was able to invest in shrinking the machines down to just thirty pounds. They called it Model H, and it, too, found plenty of happy buyers.

Again Totsuko followed up by reinvesting its profits and shrinking the machine. In 1951, it introduced the twenty-pound Model M, which could be carried by a shoulder strap. News reporters soon began toting around the Model M to grab quick interviews from newsmakers and men in the street. The recorders were later nicknamed Densuke, after a fictional comic strip news reporter, and Densuke became the generic term for a portable tape recorder. In the 1954 classic *Godzilla*, a reporter carries a Densuke through trampled Tokyo.

Many years after dragging his original hundred-pound recorder around in his Datsun, Akio triumphantly proclaimed that the "market research is all in my head! You see, we *create* markets."[18] But before he learned to create a market by unveiling totally new products, he first had to learn to identify a willing audience. Back in 1946, he was like a farmer trying to plant a young orange tree in Cleveland. It might have been a nice tree, but a successful orange farmer would need to find a more fertile, less frosty field. So did Akio with his recorder. By 1950 he had figured out how to distinguish a promising target audience from one that would merely shrug and turn away. His fields started to look fertile indeed.

NOT INVENTED HERE

Confucius had a lenient view of intellectual property theft. To steal a book was an "elegant offense." He admitted that he "transmitted" but did not "create" new knowledge.[19] This Confucian perspective raises a touchy point with Japanese inventors, namely, the charge that they merely copy and improve, rather than invent whole new technologies. The Japanese word for "learn" (*manabu*) derives from the word for "imitate" (*manebu*). This chapter is not the place to stage that debate, though I would argue that Japanese inventors have become more and more daring over the decades. Today, Japan files twice as many patents as the U.S., mostly in electronics (and with a few in medicine, pharmaceuticals, and agriculture).[20] When Toyota unveiled the Lexus in 1989, it may have copied the lines of a Mercedes S–class, but it also reinvented the luxury car market and set a standard that the more expensive Mercedes has struggled to meet. Infiniti's raging Q-45 engine embarrassed BMW into offering an eight-cylinder engine for its sedans. And, no surprise to auto buyers, Lexus sits on top of global quality ratings, while Mercedes and BMW put out almost twice as many defects per car.[21] When you humiliate your elder competitors, you must be doing something more than mimicry. When I was a kid, before Lexus came along, we used to joke about Japanese cars and refer to the Toyota as the "Corroded." Toyota got the last laugh.

Totsuko could have taken the mimicry route and tried to copy American electronics goods, as it did with magnetic tape. Or the young company could have driven in the opposite direction and posted a sign denouncing any product that was "not invented here." Over the course of his career as CEO, Akio Morita tried to navigate between the two posts, improving on the breakthroughs of others, while often staking out totally new ground. He took great pride in helping to demonstrate Japan's prowess as a technology power. When Akio traveled to Germany as a young man, a waiter in Dusseldorf pointed out that the tiny umbrella in Akio's cocktail was made in Japan. Embarrassed, Akio swore to himself that he would help lead Japan out of trinkets and into the most sophisticated devices.

Consider the transistor. In 1947 at Bell Labs in New Jersey, John Bardeen, Walter Brattain, and William Shockley (who would later become infamous for his controversial comments about IQ) invented the first transistor, which regulated electricity flow and acted as a switch for electronic signals. Bell Labs and its parent, Western Electric, figured that this solid-state device might be very valuable for hearing aids. Akio and Ibuka had no idea what they could do with the transistor, but they also had no interest in hearing aids. In Japan, deafness carried a stigma, and hearing aids would only call attention to one's affliction. At this time, high-fidelity sound was the rage, as consumers tuned in to FM radio, listened to 33 rpm vinyl records, and boosted their loudspeakers with tweeters and woofers to more faithfully represent low and high frequencies. Audiophiles would sit in darkened rooms, close the doors, and listen to lifelike recordings of locomotives roaring by and airplanes screeching to a halt.

Could transistors replace vacuum tubes in radios? Akio and Ibuka wondered. If so, they could miniaturize the radios and make them more portable because they would get by on smaller batteries. The experts at Bell and at Japan's Ministry for International Trade and Industry (MITI) answered with a loud, high-fidelity "No!" When Bell scoffed at the idea, it was like "the voice of God" saying no, recalled one of Akio's scientists. MITI planners laughed them out of the room.[22] Akio negotiated with Western Electric for a license so Totsuko could pursue its harebrained transistor ideas, but MITI used its bureaucratic powers to block Akio from wiring the $25,000 license fee to the United States. Surely, MITI believed, a sketchy new company like Totsuko had no business competing with the Americans or even with established Japanese firms like Matsushita. After six months of lobbying and cajoling, MITI finally relented, and two years later Totsuko had figured out how to conquer the transistor and produce a miniaturized radio.

Akio was not surprised at their technological success. Japan is good at "small": small homes, small lunch boxes, folding fans, scrolling art, all make up Japanese culture. A three-line haiku can touch a nerve more deeply than six volumes of prose. In 1955, Totsuko sold its first transistor radio, which was nicknamed the UN radio because it resembled the New York building. Unfortunately, the original model warped and nearly melted in the hundred-degree heat of Tokyo's summer of '55.

But Akio had set an even more ambitious goal than a portable transistor radio; he wanted a "pocketable" radio that would fit in a shirt. By 1957, the company released the TR-63, a technological and marketing marvel. The sales price was 13,800 yen, equal to a month's salary for an average worker. Coincidentally, Victor Records had released a hit parodying the life of a workingman, entitled "Thirteen Thousand Eight Hundred Yen." Victor advertised the song by dropping flyers that looked like 10,000-yen notes from airplanes. Radio dealers pasted these notes to their storefronts, promoting the TR-63. But the song crossed international boundaries, too. In order to beat the Christmas rush in the U.S., Akio chartered a JAL cargo jet and packed it with pocketable radios, which sold for $39.95. Between the Orient and the Occident, Totsuko sold 1.5 million radios. With such momentum, the company had left its ramshackle hovel far behind.

With this success, Akio also proved he could think outside the box, or the pocket. He later admitted that he shaved the truth about the

TR–63. In 1957 his engineers had not completely solved the miniaturization process, so the slim radio was still slightly larger than a businessman's shirt pocket. No problem, Akio figured. He ordered special shirts for his salesmen that had pockets just a tad larger than normal!

THE NAME IS THE BRAND

Besides being nearly pocketable, Totsuko's radios featured one other innovation: the brand name Sony. This was a long way from Tokyo Tsushin Kogyo, or the shortened Totsuko. By the mid-1950s, Akio and Ibuka had been to the U.S. often enough to realize that Americans did not have a clue how to pronounce Japanese names. They could say "Hirohito," but only because war correspondents like Edward R. Murrow had repeated his name so many times. This problem persists even today. I have a cousin in New York who worked for Midori, the liqueur company. When a Japanese businessman would be assigned to New York, she would give him an Americanized nickname. She had a sense of humor, so she would choose playful names. If an executive came over with the name Motoshi, she would print business cards for him that said "Moishe." One guy showed up with hair slicked forward over his forehead like a ledge. She called him "Cliff," and he was flattered to be compared to Cliff Robertson.

Akio knew that Totsuko needed a catchier name that translated well or, even better, would not need translation. In New York, he had seen the RCA Building and had admired the name recognition for the three-letter networks owned by RCA, NBC, and CBS. He considered TTK, but that sounded too much like a Japanese railroad named TKK. Maybe letters were not the answer. How about a sound? After all, Akio had been fascinated by sound since he was a youngster. After tearing through dictionaries searching for bright, upbeat words, Akio and Ibuka came across *sonus,* the Latin word for "sound." Akio pushed for the name Sony, which blended *sonus* with the common American expression "sonny boy." Totsuko was a young, friendly company devoted to sound. Why did they choose Sony instead of Sonny? The double *n* would have been pronounced by Japanese as *sohn-nee,* which means a money loser. General

Motors committed such a blunder when it tried to sell the Chevy Nova in Mexico, despite *no va* being Spanish for "doesn't go."

The name Sony fit beautifully, especially since Americans, Europeans, and Japanese could all pronounce it. Moreover, *the brand name would be the same as the corporate name;* Sony would save on advertising costs. (In comparison, the Matsushita Company had to pay double to advertise its Panasonic brand.)

Choosing Sony was, of course, a brilliant idea. Naturally, the traditionalists hated it. It was a dishonor to choose a name that could not be represented with a Chinese kanji symbol, argued one of Totsuko's old advisers who had once served in the emperor's household. But Akio carried on and began appending the Sony name everywhere. He realized it was a success when a Japanese chocolate company started to use the same name. Since Akio had no confidence in the quality of the chocolate—and he was quite certain chocolate was not pocketable—he filed a lawsuit and prevented the incursion. Akio maintained that a trademark and a company name are not just clever gimmicks—they carry responsibility and guarantee the quality of the product. During this same era, Texaco service stations were using a catchy jingle with the same message: "You can trust your car to the man who wears the star, the big, bright Texaco star."

Akio did not trust anyone else to uphold the Sony brand and was willing to lose money to keep control. Shortly before the pocketable radio conquered the U.S., he was in New York trying to drum up sales for his tape recorders, microphones, and the first transistor radio. He heard a lot of nos from New Yorkers. In the Eisenhower era, Americans were moving into bigger houses and driving bigger cars. Smaller was out. However, a buyer from the prestigious Bulova watch company happened to admire the little radio. "We'll take one hundred thousand units," he casually said. One hundred thousand? Sony could not churn out that many unless it massively expanded its hiring and buying of parts. But how could it turn down the deal? This was a make-or-break opportunity. And Akio's arms and feet were tired of traipsing around New York with briefcases of samples. He was ready to do what any sane entrepreneur would: take the offer and then figure out how to finish the job!

Then the Bulova buyer added one minor point: Sony would stamp the radios with the Bulova label. Again, any levelheaded entrepreneur would have said, "Of course." One hundred thousand orders by a prestige buyer would catapult Sony into the major leagues and guarantee that it would never move back to a hovel located beyond the diapered clothe-lines. In fact, all of the senior managers and board members back in Tokyo directed Akio to say yes. They agreed with the Bulova man who told Akio, "Our company is a famous brand name that has taken over fifty years to establish. Nobody has ever heard of your brand name. Why not take advantage of ours?"[23] Sony's official history suggests that Akio and the board debated over a pay telephone, until he ran out of coins in New York and won the argument. Considering Akio's ego and foresight, I imagine he deliberately ran out of money and decided to declare himself the winner. In any event, he turned down the Bulova offer and later de-clared it the best decision he ever made. In future years, Sony would leap far ahead of Bulova in surveys of the most admired brand names. In 1990, the Landor survey ranked Sony number two in the world in overall name-brand power, behind only Coca-Cola. Sony benefited from a side effect of increasing globalization: brands that might once have taken many decades to establish could now gain prominence more quickly. The trend has accelerated: in eighteen months, YouTube catapulted from nothing to a billion-dollar name. I am not surprised by Sony's jump over Bulova, in particular. I have traveled to and from New York's La Guardia Airport on hundreds of occasions. The Bulova Building, a grace-ful art deco construction from the 1950s, sits just outside the airport. Most times I have passed the massive clock adorning the front, the time has been off by at least fifteen minutes, mostly late.

GET ON THE GROUND AND GET DIRTY

"I hear hard work never killed anyone, but I figured why take a chance."
    Akio Morita never heard that old saw and would not have believed it. We have already seen Akio trudging or driving a hand-cranked truck through Tokyo, trying to persuade others to believe in Sony's wares and refusing to give up when others scoffed. Though he was raised by his fa-ther to reign over the family business like an imperial prince, Akio learned how to look like a leader while still getting his hands dirty. In 1960, Sony

had a dispute with a low-end U.S. marketing company that was advertising television sets without Sony's permission, even before Sony agreed to use them as a distributor. As a result of this dispute, Akio insisted on buying back the company's inventory of Sonys. And so, on a frozen February morning in the SoHo neighborhood of Manhattan, Akio and a few other employees stood in front of a borrowed warehouse in buttoned-up winter coats. They were anxiously waiting. Finally, truck after truck began to ride toward them on the icy streets. When the trucks skidded to a halt, Akio and the others opened their back doors and revealed thirty thousand boxes, each containing a neatly packed radio. From midmorning throughout the day and night, until four the following morning, Akio and his crew carried the thirty thousand boxes into the cold warehouse. Around dawn, as they sat huddled in front of a coffeemaker, one of them tripped a burglar alarm. Security guards poured into the warehouse and saw the dirty, weary Akio and his team. They obviously looked like thieves. The security guards rounded them up and began calling the police to arrest Akio, whose English was not so fluent under stress. Before the guards sent for the paddy wagon, however, one of the suspect men proved that he knew the combination to the warehouse safe and, therefore, must have legitimate access.[24]

It turns out that Sony already had a history with thievery in New York. In January 1958, the *New York Times* and local radio stations announced that four thousand Sony pocketable radios had been stolen from a different warehouse. While this was distressing, it was also quite wonderful because the media reported that the thieves stole only the Sonys and did not touch the stacks of radios made by Sony's competitors. If thieves preferred your brand, what better endorsement could you get?

Shortly after Akio's warehouse bust in 1960, Sony began working on its initial public offering in the United States. Akio again demonstrated his tireless work ethic. Each evening after normal New York hours, he would to go the Nomura Securities office, watch Sony's stock trade on the Tokyo exchange, and strategize with the Nomura advisers. Because of the time difference, he would return to his New York apartment around 2:30 a.m. Because his apartment was located across the street from the Gaslight Club on East Fifty-sixth Street, the doorman was convinced that Akio spent every evening drinking at the club until closing time.

I thought about Akio's conviction and leadership several years ago when I was sitting on an American Airlines jet in Dallas. The flight was delayed, but the pilot did not tell us why. As I was reading the in-flight magazine, I recognized that the passenger across from me in the first-class cabin was Donald Carty, then CEO of the airline. The magazine featured an article by him and his photograph. Clearly, he was not happy about the delay. He called over the flight attendant and mumbled something. After about twenty minutes, he stood up, grabbed his bag, and left—without saying good-bye, without introducing himself to the passengers, without solving or explaining the delay. I was not impressed. What kind of leadership was this? What would he have done if thirty thousand radios showed up at his warehouse on a bitter February morning?

Akio was a hands-on character, always cradling a device or toy in his hands. He imagined that others enjoyed the same, which led him to open a showroom in Tokyo's flashy Ginza district. The store, the brand, the name, were lit up in neon. Akio had taken home movies of Broadway and showed them to his board, arguing that Sony needed the panache, or at least the glitz, of the famous Broadway advertising symbols, like the famous Camel smoker who blew real smoke rings from his cigarette.

Akio was after bigger game than Ginza. Throughout the 1950s, Akio tried to motivate and direct Sony into generating at least 50 percent of its revenues from outside Japan. That is why the 1957 airlift of TR-63s was so momentous. After Akio successfully led Sony to issue shares on the New York Stock Exchange in 1961, he led the charge to open a showroom in New York. Just as Estée Lauder had prowled Saks, looking for her chance to open on Fifth Avenue, so had Akio gazed up at Saks, Bergdorf, and Tiffany, dreaming of his place along the boulevard. In 1962, at Fifth Avenue and Forty-seventh Street, he cut the ribbon for the showroom and then unfurled a Japanese flag; it was the first time the flag had flown in New York City since before World War II.

He was not finished. He would move to New York and lead Sony of America. His colleagues in Tokyo thought it was a reckless error. What kind of CEO leaves the home office? According to the official Sony history books, he responded, "We may be acting a little prematurely. But a business that doesn't take advantage of its opportunities doesn't deserve to be called an enterprise. We may be overextending ourselves, but the time to act is now. We at Sony don't believe in shying away from the hardship that comes along with a good opportunity."

Akio's wife and children were not surprised that he came up with such a bold and nutty scheme as to move the family to a new continent. Neither Yoshiko nor his three young children spoke English. Apparently, their eight-year-old son thought Americans spoke Japanese, since he saw so many American television shows dubbed into Japanese. Akio wondered how best to mollify their worries, then he promised to bring them to Disneyland first. It seemed to work for a while, but in the end, his children knew that their father was not just the boss of Sony, but also the authority at home.

Akio was of the sink-or-swim mentality when it came to children. He immediately enrolled his boys in an American summer camp in Maine, where they would have to adapt or, well, drown. Eventually the boys became popular with the American kids, and in school, they were known for bringing cool electronics presents to birthday parties. Yoshiko also was known for her party prowess and soon became one of New York City's great hostesses. She kept detailed cards on file identifying famous celebrity guests by their tastes and preferences. According to her notes, the pianist Andre Watts was a mama's boy, and his mother did not like fish. Leonard Bernstein wolfed down sushi with one hand while holding a chopstick like a baton.[25] Yoshiko did more than arrange dinner parties, however. Unlike most traditional Japanese husbands, Akio wanted his wife to have a driver's license, which gave her some independence. It also allowed her to drive Sony employees around town when necessary. Akio recalled occasions when Yoshiko would drive engineers all around the suburbs of New York so they could check the reception on Sony's new FM radios.

The point here is that Akio jumped into the U.S. market without reserve. If Sony was going to win over Americans, Akio and the Sony brand would have to live and breathe like Americans. Akio later opened a Sony base in Rancho Bernardo, California, which today makes Vaio laptops and serves as an engineering hub for the company. Akio was nervous about the quality of U.S. workmanship when the Rancho Bernardo site opened in 1972. In the beginning, American plant workers were merely reassembling television sets that had already been assembled, adjusted, and disassembled in Japan. Management was not altogether certain they could do that simple trick.[26] To demonstrate the importance of quality, Sony deliberately rigged the Rancho Bernardo assembly line to make mistakes, thereby showing the employees how their potential mistakes could ruin a television set. Even in Japan, Akio forced all his new engineers to work on the assembly line so they could understand the risks inherent in the manufacturing process.

Compare Akio's aggressive attitude with those American executives who thought they would successfully export to Japan without at all adapting to Japanese tastes. For example, many American car companies refused to offer steering columns on the right side of the vehicle. Did they expect the Japanese to drive backward looking over their shoulders?

Akio felt so strongly about winning in the brutally competitive American marketplace that in 1966, Sony placed a classified advertisement in a Tokyo newspaper: "Wanted: Japanese men up to thirty years of age who can PICK A FIGHT in English!"

Akio was a globalist, though, not just a Japanese eager to win in America. He pursued open markets everywhere. He even sought to energize and globalize Tokyo's restaurant culture by personally arranging for the legendary Maxim's de Paris restaurant to come to Tokyo. In retrospect, without Akio Morita, I doubt that Tokyo chefs would have developed into the innovative "Iron Chefs" of today.

FIND YOUR MENTORS

Akio Morita did not have all the answers, and he certainly did not start his career with many at all. When he began traveling to New York in the 1950s, he was really quite green. He stayed in flea-ridden motels near Times Square, sneaked into automats for dinner, and even did his laundry in the sink. He was limited by Totsuko's budget and by MITI, which restricted Japanese businessmen from spending more than $500 per trip abroad. But a Hawaiian-born Japanese American named Yoshinobu "Doc" Kagawa, who had served in Japan as a lawyer for the occupation forces, convinced Akio to step out of the fleabags and the Horn &

Hardart's and into better hotels and restaurants. If Akio (and Sony) was going to project an air of progress and know-how, Akio should not smell like a tuna sandwich. Besides, he was more likely to make business contacts while staying at a more posh address than Forty-second and Ninth.

In New York, Akio befriended a variety of mostly Jewish businessmen who served as his Sherpas as he explored New York's retail culture: Adolph Gross, a cigar-chomping manufacturer's rep; Gross's lawyer, Edward Rosiny, who would become Sony's best U.S. negotiator and Akio's tutor in legal affairs; and Irving Sagor, an accountant who became CFO for Sony of America. These men would meet with Akio over matzo ball soup and plan Sony's expansion into the U.S. market. This experience seemed to turn Akio into a philo-Semite, as he kept a soft spot for Jewish businessmen and said he identified most with Tevye from *Fiddler on the Roof*. He even arranged for a Tokyo production of *Fiddler*. Throughout the 1980s and 1990s, Sony's executive ranks were dotted with Jewish businessmen, including several division presidents and the chief executive of Sony of America, Michael Schulhof.

A later president of Sony, Nobuyuki Idei, observed that Akio "seemed less like a Japanese than an American from the east coast. He had the air of a New York businessman. . . . One would think he might have been an American in a previous lifetime."[27] Imagine, that statement about a man who just a few years before was ducking to his office beneath ropes hanging with damp laundry!

THE MISSION

Akio Morita, as CEO of Sony, had a more challenging mission than many other CEOs. Most important, he constantly had to define his mission. What was Sony, anyhow? The CEO of Schwinn bicycles knew that three years in the future, say, he was going to be selling bikes. The CEO of Prudential knew he would be selling insurance. Sony was different. As technology sped ahead, how did the CEO of Sony know what he would be selling three years ahead? Sony was really a brand built around a talented group of engineers and scientists and that was plowing about 6–10 percent of sales into research and development. In three years' time, they might or might not be making televisions, or stereos, or telephones. Sony's mission was a fast-moving target. Akio's job was to stay ahead of the target.

The best example, of course, is the Sony Walkman. Before the Sony Walkman shook up the music world in 1979, nobody was banging on Sony's door asking for a little cassette player that could be connected to one's ears. But Akio had been to the beach with his children often enough to be offended by the lousy music blaring from bulky boom boxes, which offended his ears and his sense of aesthetics. Why couldn't everyone listen to his own music and create his own sound track for his life? Around the same time Sony engineers had hooked up a big cassette player with large earphones for Ibuka to take on long airplane rides. Morita tried out Ibuka's cumbersome set, called his staff together, and told them that they must shrink it, improve it, and sell it as the next Sony megahit. He was taking Sony on the road to glory again.

Naturally, his senior staff was shocked and appalled. First of all, Sony had no market research. Second, the device relied on earphones—didn't Akio know that earphones and headphones were taboo in Japan because they were identified with deafness? Third, the device could only play cassettes. Who would buy a player that did not offer recording capability? Akio replied by reminding the skeptics that people bought car stereos that could not record. Then he put another obstacle in front on them: the player would be cheap enough for teenagers to buy. To seasoned engineers, this was blasphemy. Akio did not care. Faced with doubters in the engineering, marketing, and accounting departments, he announced that he would resign if thirty thousand units did not sell quickly.

With his pride balancing on a tightrope, Akio jumped into every part of the rollout, from fine-tuning the shape to choosing the advertising slogans. He demanded a summer launch, remembering the boom boxes on the beach. The project was behind schedule. May and then June 1979 passed without a final product. Finally, on July 17, 1979, Sony began to ship the Walkman, along with posters featuring the slogan "Why man learned to walk." It was an immediate dud. For its first month, the boom boxes flew off the shelves and the Walkman stayed put. Then in August, something began to stir. Word of mouth and sexy advertising started to draw young people into the stores. By the end of the summer, Sony's thirty-thousand-unit inventory was exhausted, they doubled up the assembly line, and the Walkman raced into electronics history. By 1986, it had also raced into the *Oxford English Dictionary,* despite endless meetings at Sony over whether the word "Walkman" was ungrammatical. Akio kept his job.

While the U.S. automobile industry has been plagued by bad management, occasionally an executive comes along who throws himself into the breach, rolls up his sleeves, and guides his employees toward success. In the early 1990s, Chrysler president Bob Lutz looked at his lineup and declared the cars boxy, boring, and out-of-date. The company hardly had a pulse.[28] The hard-charging former Marine fighter pilot shook up the engineering team until it came up with models that splashed across the front pages: the 400-horsepower Dodge Viper, the Dodge Ram pickup, and the LH sedan series, nicknamed "Last Hope." I remember speaking to Lutz on the lawn of the White House just before he unveiled the LHs. He was chomping on a cigar, ready to chomp on the competition. Over the next few years, Chrysler raced from "footnote to first-in-class" among American automakers.[29] In 2002, Lutz joined General Motors as vice chairman, where battling the bureaucracy requires even more skills than those provided in the Marines' training manual.

HITS AND MISSES: CAN SONY COME BACK?

The Walkman was a mind-boggling victory, as was the Trinitron television picture tube, the first compact CD player, and a number of other category killers. Akio Morita endured a few big losses along the way, most notably the war between Betamax and VHS. People who remember the late 1970s remember that Sony's Betamax technology produced a far sharper picture than VHS tapes. Even today, professional cameramen prefer Beta to fuzzy VHS images. Nonetheless, VHS clobbered Beta in living rooms. Why? Three reasons conspired against Sony: First, Beta was more expensive to produce, partly because VHS was a cruder, simpler technology. Second, VHS tapes could record movie-length programs, while Beta tapes could not. Third, a number of Sony's competitors—JVC, Matsushita, Sharp, Hitachi, and Sanyo—simultaneously adopted the VHS format. Sony quickly lost the battle, as consumers preferred the cheaper, longer-playing format.

Despite the commercial debacle, I should note that Sony did win an important victory for home consumers. When Hollywood studios discovered that Sony was introducing a recording system, they filed federal lawsuits to block Sony from selling the Betamax. The Motion Picture Industry Association called Betamax a parasite and an abomination. How dare Sony empower Americans to record broadcast programs! Hollywood was following a long tradition of trying to control the spread of culture, a tradition that began with the pope denouncing the Gutenberg Bibles (which cut out his priests and monkish middlemen). Lucky for consumers, Sony won the suit against Universal Studios and its coplaintiffs, or else the VHS and the recordable CD and DVD business would have been aborted.

Sony's other troublesome endeavor came during Akio's final years in the early 1990s, when Sony bought Columbia Pictures and paid a ridiculous amount of money for two Hollywood producers to run the studio. The episode, chronicled in a book entitled *Hit and Run: How Jon Peters and Peter Guber Took Sony for a Ride in Hollywood,*[30] reminds me of Ernest Hemingway's warning to authors whose books are desired by Hollywood: Go to the Nevada border, throw your book over the border fence, and then spend the money they throw back. Remember, don't go past the fence!

In the past few years, Sony has slipped further from the glittering days of Akio Morita. According to Interbrand, a global consulting firm that provides advice on brand management, Sony's brand value has been sliding since 2000, with Samsung actually leapfrogging it in 2005. In 2006, the fear of exploding laptops forced Sony to recall eight million batteries. Moreover, Sony has lost market share in televisions, digital music, and other key areas. It is a dangerous and embarrassing situation. Remember, Sony historically grabbed an extra slice of profit by charging more than competitors. Customers paid up because of Sony's perceived style, innovation, and panache. As a result, the company always rested on the precipice of a perception cliff. If today Sony decided to gain market share by slashing prices, it would tarnish the premium image of the brand and perhaps do more harm.

Some blame Sony's problems on the MBAs that Sony started hiring in the 1990s who relied on sheer data to decide what markets Sony should enter.[31] But that just begs the question: Why would you let a bunch of pinheads run your company? I would diagnose the sickness with three words under the acronym ADD: attitude, drift, and distraction. Sony's attitude has been a frustrating combination of hubris and defeatism. Akio Morita certainly swaggered in 1955 when he turned down Bulova's offer to buy one hundred thousand radios. He would occasionally take a verbal swipe at a competing company. But he never demeaned his customers! Since Akio's death, Sony has often been on the wrong side of the democratic revolution that Akio led. Akio made it possible for everyone to have his own personal sound track. He plunged Sony into the development of small headphones so that life would be more convenient. Today's economy relies more and more on individuals creating their own businesses from their own laptops. Anyone can write and publish a book, launch a retail sales company, or upload her own comic rap video to the Internet and watch the electrons fly. Chris Anderson's *The Long Tail* describes some goofy amateur comedians who score their way to *Saturday Night Live* through a bad homemade white-boy rap video rhyming "You kissed Shannen Doherty" and "I majored in pottery." MIT professor Eric von Hippel has argued that customers invent the newest products, from surgical instruments to kite-surfing kits.[32] What has Sony done lately to help the "new producers"? Apple led the charge to link home computers to home video. In contrast, the proprietary memory stick in a Sony camera turns customers away because they worry about compatibility. Is Sony the incompatible partner in the customer relationship? Whose side is Sony on?

Sony is nervy when it should not be, but it has lost its nerve when it should flash more confidence. Sony's current CEO, Howard Stringer, is smart, charming, and aware of Sony's challenges. Yet, I was disappointed last year to hear him effectively concede defeat to Apple in the iPod revolution. Now, I think the iPod and iTunes are awesome, paradigm-shattering achievements. The earplugs are so cool they attract thieves, leading *PC* magazine to nickname the color "mug-me white." [33] But does Sony really think that they cannot be improved or beaten . . . ever? Even in five hundred years, will people still be using those white earplugs and the iPod wheel? How about in five years?

Sony has suffered from "style drift" and "distraction" as well. In the world of investment fund management, we accuse a portfolio manager of style drift when he begins to trade differently than he promised—a large-cap stock investor starts betting on IPOs, for example. Sony, too, has drifted all over, a multinational octopus with no control of its own tentacles. In contrast, Samsung has stuck to hardware, producing flat-panel televisions, wireless telephones, and other tangible products. There is nothing wrong with Sony's forays into software, except when its drift into software cripples its ability to fight on the hardware front. Because of Sony's missteps on flat-panel televisions, it now must buy flat-panel inputs from Samsung.

Why did Sony not develop the iPod and iTunes before Apple? I suspect that Sony's focus on record sales and film-studio revenues frightened it away from a headlong plunge into the kind of democratic downloading that Apple promotes. How ironic! Akio Morita battled lawsuits from Hollywood executives who argued that the Betamax and the VHS would rip off studios, even if they empowered consumers. Sony should have been on the customer's side of that argument again. But instead it was distracted and torn by its fear that iPods and iTunes would rob it of record sales revenues.

Can Sony turn around? Of course. First of all, product cycles have shrunk. The bell is constantly ringing for a new round of a new fight. For example, cell-phone owners typically keep their telephones for just seventeen months. Twenty years ago telephone customers kept their telephones for twenty years! Electronics makers now have innumerable opportunities to get back into the ring. In the cell-phone arena, LG came almost from nowhere (actually Korea) with its "Life's Good" advertisement and convenient handsets. For all my complaints about Sony, I am writing this book on a sleek, superlightweight Sony Vaio. I remain a fan of Sony's past and believe it has the resources to power forward again. But Sony needs to reassess and restate its mission. Toshiba and Panasonic used to cringe in fear that whatever they came up with, Sony could make smaller, more powerful, and more stylish. Is Sony still devoted to that? Do not dismiss style. According to surveys, most people choose their cell phones on the basis of style, not the features or battery life. Think about how style made some of the great icons of today and yesterday: the 1955 Chevy Bel Air, Frank Gehry's Guggenheim in Bilbao, and the Herman Miller Aeron chair. Oh, yes, the Walkman from 1979, too.

Naturally, style does not suffice. Performance must excel. Akio Morita demanded that Sony lead the way on both fronts. Of course, it is a brutal business. But Akio did not hand-crank a truck and lug hundred-pound prototypes around war-ravaged Tokyo so that his successors could whine about the weight of their troubles in today's competitive economy.

LAST DAYS

During his last years of running Sony, Akio Morita starred in a television advertisement, but not for Sony. It was one of those American Express ads, in which he asked, "Do you know me?" Until Akio came along, Japanese executives seemed faceless and interchangeable to Americans. A poll of Americans once showed that the most famous Japanese was Bruce Lee. Never mind that Lee was from Hong Kong. Akio shredded the standard script for the stern, mechanical Japanese CEO.

Unfortunately, Akio Morita suffered a debilitating stroke in 1993 after a game of tennis. Robbed of speech, he lived another six years mostly in seclusion, with occasional visits from his old friend Ibuka, also wheelchair-bound and in poor health.

Looking back, perhaps the most striking facet in Akio's career success is this: He started as a kind of prince, serving his patriarchal father and, in wartime, his emperor. But in his mind he held an unshakable belief that technology would make the world more democratic. When government bureaucrats on high, and even his own board of directors, shouted "No!" Akio insisted that everyone could have his own personal sound track, everyone could have a television, and everyone could record music and television for his personal use. No mandarin should force everyone to march to the beat of the same drummer. With Akio Morita's story we see how, as world economies develop technologically, they empower more and more people. Here was a man who emerged from an ancient, insular Japanese society, but never smiled so broadly as when he saw an American, a Frenchman, or a Finn boogie down the street as his own individual tune played on his Sony Walkman.

8

Walt Disney: Disney

The Imagination Machine

I only hope that we don't lose sight of one thing—
that it was all started by a mouse.

—WALT DISNEY

Hollywood usually doesn't get it right. The famed screenwriter William Goldman revealed Hollywood's dirty little secret: "Nobody knows anything." Two examples may help. Paramount Pictures once looked at a screen test of an unknown actor and reported, "Can't sing. Can't act. Slightly balding. Also dances." The name on that screen test? Fred Astaire.

A few years earlier, Hollywood bungled even worse. Gossipy producers shared the rap on a young farm boy named Walter Elias Disney. Sure, the kid had ambition. After all, he'd worked on the railroad to make his way from Chicago to Los Angeles. But according to the wags at the Beverly Hills Hotel, the kid just did not have much talent for drawing cartoons. While the brothers Warner, Samuel Goldwyn, and Louis B. Mayer were lighting up theaters with the brightest stars in the universe—Douglas Fairbanks, Charlie Chaplin, and Gloria Swanson—this kid was wasting his time working on a sketch of a rabbit. *A rabbit?* Wait a minute! Didn't Disney tell us it all started with a mouse? It turns out that the old fable maker was misleading us about his career. You see, long before there was a mouse, there was a rabbit you've probably never heard of. Yet, we cannot understand the multibillion-dollar global entertainment conglomerate named Disney without first focusing on a homely rabbit.

"Oswald the Rabbit" is like Citizen Kane's sled named "Rosebud"— the shadowy figure that explains it all: Disney's quest for utter control, his urge to vertically integrate, and his endless striving to launch another spin-off. By doodling a rabbit, Disney showed others how to put the *business* in show business.

IN THE BEGINNING . . .

Walt Disney built one of the most durable firms in American economic history. The firm is so ingrained in our culture that in 1993 Disney actually found buyers for one-hundred-year bonds, known as "Sleeping Beauties." Yet, Walt himself did not come from such stable stock. His father, Elias, could not keep a job. He was a preacher, a construction worker, a carpenter, a mailman, and apparently, a pretty lousy farmer. He was, however, an attentive and stern parent who believed in thrift and despised swearing. As a preacher, Elias interpreted the holy scripture very strictly. For example, he refused to put fertilizer on his fields because he believed that "putting fertilizer on plants was just the same as giving whiskey to a man—he felt better for a little while, but then he was worse off than he was before."[1] So instead of a Garden of Eden, Elias ended up with his own personal dust bowl.

As severe as Elias was, his parents had set even more severe and somber standards. Their Congregationalist church forbade dancing. Not only did they frown on secular music, they literally smashed a fiddle to bits over Elias's head when they found out he was sneaking off to a dance hall to play.

As Elias moved from job to job, his wife, Flora, and his three sons and one daughter would pack their bags and move too. Walt was born December 5, 1901, in Chicago, but his father soon took the family to a small farm in Marceline, Missouri. They stayed only a few years, yet Marceline became the "home plate" in Walt's itinerant youth. While his older brothers Roy, Herbert, and Ray sweated in the fields, young Walt learned how to swim in creeks, ride hogs, and generally live the life of Tom Sawyer. When Walt was old enough to make some money with a newspaper route, Elias made sure there was no kidding around. Unlike other boys, Walt was not permitted to toss the papers from a bicycle; he had to dismount and carefully place the papers on the front porch.[2] Frankly, I cannot imagine why. When I had a newspaper route, I tossed the papers from my Schwinn—except on wintry days, when my brother would take me in his car. He would tear through the neighborhood in his Ford Pinto at thirty miles per hour (its top speed) while I hurled the papers out the window and watched them skid across the icy lawns. Sometimes the papers would land in the vicinity of the porch.

To Walt, Marceline *was* Main Street, USA, now memorialized as the nostalgic early-twentieth-century town that welcomes visitors to Disneyland and Walt Disney World. In fact, along Main Street, Walt honored his father with a fictitious second-story shop, featuring the following window sign: *Elias Disney—Contractor—est. 1895.* Walt might not always have been so grateful to Elias. Perhaps it was the memory of that fiddle thumping against his head, but Elias had a wicked temper. According to Walt, "My dad was the kind of guy who'd pick up anything near him. . . . He'd pick up a saw and try to hit you with the broad side of the saw. He'd pick up a hammer, you know, and hit you with the handle."[3] This home was hardly the happiest place on earth. Young Walt showed an early flair for acting, and Elias did his best to beat it out of him. Nor was Elias a charming conversationalist. His discussions with Walt resemble the father-son exchange in Ring Lardner's story "The Young Immigrants:"

"Are you lost, Daddy?" I asked tenderly.
"Shut up," he explained.

To Elias's displeasure, Walt wanted to draw, to act, and to jump onto any stage, even as a young boy. In school he frustrated his art teacher by drawing flowers with human faces and arms, ignoring the real flowers sitting in vases as "models."[4] In a precursor to Disneyland's famed animatronic Abe Lincoln, in sixth grade Walt showed up for Lincoln's birthday dressed and bearded like the late president. Walt's austere, sometimes hard-fisted upbringing, could have been a recipe for a bitter rebellion. Yet, Walt embraced these early years and learned not only to look back nostalgically, but also to get half the world to look at this era wearing his rose-colored glasses. Though foul-tempered, Elias never used foul language. Walt recalled that his father's cussing amounted to mostly "consarnits" and "great Scott." In retrospect Elias sounds like the G-rated Grumpy from *Snow White and the Seven Dwarfs*. Despite Elias, Walt grew up to be an affectionate man, often draping his arms on the shoulders of others. Though he also grew up to be a tough and sometimes surly boss, he maintained a charming "Call me Walt" simplicity. His wife, Lillian, confessed that when Walt danced, she would watch his lips count, "One, two, three."

It seems that Walt learned early on how to nurture creativity despite a hard-hearted environment. This was perfect training for Hollywood. Walt Disney was destined to invent Fantasyland.

After failing to raise many crops in Marceline, Elias dragged the family to Kansas City, where Walt got his first chance to sneak away from Elias's sight. He spent the summer of 1917 riding the rails for the Santa Fe Railroad, hawking peanuts, popcorn, and Cracker Jack. Always a showman, Disney enjoyed wearing the blue uniforms and flashy gold buttons. The experience turned Walt into a train nut, a tendency which would show up much later in his career. During the 1940s, when the pressure of union organizers and collapsing revenues badly frayed his nerves, he retreated to the backyard of his home and actually put together a half-mile miniature railroad.[5] This, of course, inspired the trains at the Disney parks. And the uniform he wore as a teenager on the Santa Fe Railroad inspired the conductors' uniforms for the Disney theme park trains. We see a recurrent theme in Walt's life: when faced with adversity, he managed to save his sanity by plucking from his mind his rosy-colored memories.

Like Ray Kroc, Disney's travels sometimes brought him to exotic locations. A train passenger recommended an inn during their overnight stay in Pueblo, Colorado. When the young man sat down for a beer he noticed some couples coming close to coupling in public. "Well, I was pretty naïve, but I soon caught on to where in the hell I was," he recalled. A bordello! So Disney guzzled his beer and jumped back on the train to safety.[6]

Walt's next summer job required some inventiveness. The family had moved to Chicago. He was turned down by the post office because, at sixteen, lanky Walt looked about fourteen. A master of disguise, he returned to the personnel office wearing a different kind of hat and makeup (not the Lincoln costume). He added ten years to his application and, sure enough, got the job from the same man who had turned him down earlier.

But even riding the rails and touring the city as a mail carrier felt limiting to young Walt. The headlines of the newspapers screamed about war in Europe, and Walt watched as doughboys packed up their old kit bags and marched onto ships that steamed "over there." They included his three brothers. He wanted to see the action, not stay at home and hand out envelopes for the post office. But once again his age worked against him. After the Army and Navy said no, he even tried to persuade the Canadian armed forces to take him. He had no choice. He had to lie. But instead of donning makeup and a costume, he convinced his mother to lie about his age on an application for the Red Cross Ambulance Corps. Walt was so desperate to go, Flora believed that he would simply smuggle himself to Europe if she did not comply with his scheme. For two seemingly contradictory reasons, they both risked a beating from Elias. First, Elias had explosive fists. Second, his politics leaned toward pacificism and socialism!

By the time Disney arrived in France, the armistice had been signed, but he did manage to spend ten months shuttling dignitaries around Europe, including the eleven-year-old son of General George Pershing. Unlike the experience of so many other World War I soldiers and volunteers, serving abroad did not slow down Disney's march toward a career in cartoons. He painted fake decorations on uniforms, granting his colleagues military "promotions." To Walt, the Ambulance Corps was just another animation cel for his sketches. Most World War I ambulances looked a drab green, with a red and white cross. Not Disney's. He painted his with original cartoon characters. Then he and a friend from Georgia came up with a novel idea to make some money. They began collecting German army helmets, painting them with camouflage, and beating them with rocks. For the pièce de résistance, they would fire bullets into the helmets, creating "authentic" battered war relics. Today's critics who complain that

Disneyland is too commercial should remember that Walt Disney's first effort was to commercialize a world war!

A few years ago when I visited Beijing, I saw a storefront window with a ghastly coat on display. It was fake fur dyed with a glowing, fluorescent Mickey Mouse image. I thought that the Disney management would be infuriated to see such a crass knockoff of the Disney brand. But considering Walt's behavior in war-torn France, it might be tough to feel so indignant about Chinese entrepreneurs taking liberties.

If Disney could make a living as a cartoonist and fantasist amid war ruins, he certainly felt confident he could do it upon returning to the United States. So he left the family in Chicago and took his pencils to Kansas City, where he found work with an advertising agency that specialized in farm equipment. No doubt Disney brought a special flair to ad campaigns for corn seed and tools for removing manure. The job did not last long, but Disney soon struck up a lifelong relationship with a funny man with the remarkable name Ubbe Ert Iwwerks. The very name sounds like a joke—a court transcript of a stuttering burp—but Iwwerks had the wit to carry it off. Iwwerks's face resembled those wacky photos of Albert Einstein, with frizzy hair and arched eyebrows. According to Chuck Jones, the esteemed director of Bugs Bunny and Daffy Duck, Iwwerks was "screwy" spelled backward. Disney thought that Iwwerks had a genius for cartooning that exceeded even his own. Together with Iwwerks and a few other young cartoonists, Disney formed Laugh-O-Gram Films.

Disney launched Laugh-O-Gram with two principles in mind: First, he did not want to be anybody's employee. After serving his father and U.S. Army officers, he had answered to enough ham-handed bosses. Second, Disney wanted to leapfrog current technology. During the early 1920s, one-minute animated advertising films looked basically like crude paper dolls with pins stuck in the limbs. Half a century before Bill Gates and Steve Jobs tinkered in their garages, Walt Disney dragged a stop-action camera into his garage and started experimenting with more sophisticated drawings. The results were stunning. Because the figures looked like more than paper cut-outs, the characters could have some personality. The audiences began to care about them. In 1922 Disney released a very contemporary, six-minute long "Little Red Riding Hood."

In the film, the grandma goes to the movies and the girl is rescued by an airplane pilot. And Disney's wolf does not look like a taxidermy specimen from the Museum of Natural History. The villain stands on two legs and wears a top hat and tailcoat.

With the backing of the Newman Theater chain in Kansas City, Disney collected $15,000 from local investors. He attracted more illustrators who were young, gifted, and filled with the rambunctious energy of a litter of pups. They created cartoons and newsreels and even tried to meet their payroll and rent costs by taking baby pictures. At one point Disney's business depended on cashing a $500 check he received for producing a film on dental hygiene. Along the way, Disney came up with yet another startling breakthrough: putting a human actor in a cartoon setting. In 1923, Laugh-O-Gram issued *Alice's Wonderland*. In the film a six-year old actress asks Disney, Iwwerks, and others to draw her some cartoons. Soon she is jumping into the story and dancing as a band of cats plays their instruments. To appreciate Disney's innovation, remember that sixty-five years later filmgoers actually gasped at the brilliant *Who Framed Roger Rabbit?* (produced by a Walt Disney Company affiliate), in which a detective played by a real-life Bob Hoskins skids in and out of Toontown. Of course, the Oscar-winning *Who Framed Roger Rabbit?* raked in $350 million, not just because of its visuals but also because of its script, too. At one point, the curvaceous femme fatale cartoon, Jessica Rabbit (voice by Kathleen Turner) says, "I'm not bad; I'm just drawn that way." Similar techniques were used in 1945 when Gene Kelly danced with Jerry the mouse (of Tom and Jerry fame) in *Anchors Aweigh* and in *Mary Poppins* in 1964, when Dick van Dyke challenged cartoon penguin waiters to a dance contest.

Disney's Laugh-O-Gram company got laughs and applause. What it did not get was enough money to pay for salaries and office space. The young pups broke up, and Disney started staring at train schedules and maps. In the prior few years he had been to Germany, France, and Chicago. Penniless and unemployed, there was just one place he needed to go now. He located Hollywood on the map. Now he needed to locate some money to pay for a ticket. An up-and-coming producer could not ride the train hobo-style. He darted around Kansas City taking moving pictures of babies. Then he hawked the films to the proud parents. With just enough cash to buy a one-way ticket, he hopped aboard the Atchison, Topeka & Santa Fe.

When the train pulled into Union Station in Los Angeles, Disney stepped off with no money, no job, and just a head full of cartoon sketches. Hollywood could be a nasty place to do business. As Woody Allen said, it's worse than dog eat dog. It's "dog won't return other dog's phone call." Luckily, Walt had an uncle with an extra bed and who was not demanding rent. Walt's brother Roy was also in town, but as a patient in the veterans hospital.

For his first job, Disney got hired as an extra in a western. Though it was being filmed in a desert location, his debut was rained out, and the studio replaced him with another nobody. "That was the end of my career as an actor," he said.

The studios were not exactly leaping at the chance to work with a skinny kid from Kansas City. Turned down by every moviemaker in town, Disney assessed his strengths. He was not a sharp manager of money. He was not a terribly gifted manager of people. But he did have an awe-inspiring imagination. Remember, this was the Lincoln-impersonating kid who tried to fool the military with makeup and a costume. How could he turn that "gift" into a job? He would harness his imagination to persuade people he was a coveted talent who already had a job!

What was the first thing a big executive needed? Stationery and a calling card. Flashy paper was no obstacle for a cartoonist like Disney. Soon he fired off a missive to his New York distributor that sounded as if it could have come down from Mount Olympus or even Cecil B. DeMille's desk. He announced he was launching his new studio in Los Angeles to produce a "new and novel series of cartoons." Moreover, he claimed to have taken with him a "select number" of staff.[7]

The missive did not bother revealing that the "select number" was zero. But it did the trick and attracted orders for six new Alice cartoons. Now that Walt had a commitment based on his fictitious studio, he had to create a real one quickly. With $500 borrowed from his landlord uncle, he ran into his brother's hospital room and begged hardheaded Roy to join the business, which Walt had already called Disney Bros. Studio. The $500 got them a rental space in the back of an office, a camera, and two female employees at $15 per week. Just imagine the conversation between the bare-bones but ambitious brothers: You need a table to work on? Stack up some cans and boxes. You're hungry? Pop open a can of peas and let the table tilt for a while. Roy and Walt had always been lean in physique, but their budget reinforced their biology. They worked late into the night, churning out one Alice cartoon each month. To stretch out their meager capital, the brothers rented a cheap one-room apartment. When they felt like splurging, they would wander into a local cafeteria and order a meat plate and a vegetable dish. Then they would split them at the table.

"We cooked, ate, and slept in that one room, and had to walk about a mile before we reached the bathroom," Walt remembered. "And yet when I think back, we had a grand time in those days."[8] The female employees made the times a little grander. One of them, the daughter of an Idaho blacksmith, painted and inked very efficiently. Lillian Marie Bounds was also efficient with money. She even agreed not to cash her paycheck when she heard that the Disney brothers were running low on dollar bills. Walt fell in love with this talented and understanding midwesterner and married her two years later.

After six Alice pictures, Walt and Roy realized they needed more hands and more paintbrushes. So Walt called back to Kansas City for Ubbe Ert Iwwerks. By now Iwwerks had changed his name, presumably to make it easier to pronounce. While during the 1920s European new-comers like Greta Gustafsson chose shorter, simpler names like Garbo, Iwwerks merely changed his name to Ub Iwerks. Still, nobody could fig-ure out how to pronounce it. Soon after the new and improved Iwerks arrived, Disney persuaded four more of his old Laugh-O-Gram col-leagues to hop on the train to Hollywood. With all this manpower, the Alice stories started rolling off the desks as if they were assembly lines. By 1926, Disney Bros. sold twenty-six Alice shorts, enough to help pay for a new studio built on an empty lot on Hyperion Avenue.

THE RISE AND FALL OF THE RABBIT

It all began not with a mouse, but with a rabbit and an outrage. By 1927, the world had seen quite enough of Alice, and Disney and his producers, Margaret Winkler and her husband, Charles Mintz, had encouraged Disney to come up with a new character. Disney developed a jaunty, self-confident leading "man" named Oswald the Lucky Rabbit. Benefiting from Iwerks's eye for mechanical detail, Oswald could interact with unique characters whose limbs could be used for just about anything. In one movie, playful Oswald turns a milk cow's teat into a working faucet. In another, *Poor Papa,* Oswald must deal with the reputation of rabbits for excessive fertility. A stork swoops down on Oswald, again and again and again, each time dropping off yet another baby. How can Oswald stop the continual flow of babies? Films like *The Mechanical Cow* and *Trolley Troubles* pleased audiences and generated strong cash flow. During the late 1920s, Oswald was famous, a Buster Keaton of celluloid.

With cash in the bank and his confidence almost as high as Oswald's, Disney and his wife boarded the train for New York to negotiate with Mintz for higher fees. Mintz not only rejected the plea for a raise but also actually threatened to slash Disney's pay by 20 percent. Disney was stunned. At first he scoffed. What leverage could Mintz hold in this bargaining? After all, Mintz was just a distributor. Then the second blow struck. Mintz announced that he had already signed up several of Disney's best animators—stolen them away! Among them were a few of Disney's original teammates from Kansas City. Just as Disney caught his breath, a final blow knocked the air out of him: Mintz declared that Disney had no rights to Oswald, a Disney creation! According to Mintz, Disney had unknowingly signed over the rights to Universal Studios. Disney was a mere employee, fireable at will.

Disney had seen the trenches of World War I Europe, the poverty of a failed farm, and the bankruptcy of his Laugh-O-Gram business. But he was not prepared for the raw swindling and intellectual property thievery he faced in Mintz's office. This was not just a matter of money to Disney. Oswald was his and Iwerks's creation. Oswald did not fly in hanging from a stork's beak; he came directly out of their imaginations. By swiping Disney's staff and, more important, his ideas, Mintz had virtually perpetrated an involuntary lobotomy. Disney later described his "cutthroat" encounters, where producers put "a knife in your back" while "laughing and having a drink with you."[9] The Emmy Award–winning writer and producer Steve Bochco (*NYPD Blue* and *L.A. Law*) explained why Hollywood executives always touch your body when they speak to you. They are gauging how soft you are before they eat you.

Disney was so horrified by the Mintz smashup that he tried to shield Roy from the truth. Before stepping onto the train for the long ride back to the West Coast, Walt sent Roy a Western Union telegram:

"LEAVING TONITE STOPPING OVER KC ARRIVE HOME SUNDAY
MORNING SEVEN THIRTY DON'T WORRY EVERYTHING
OK WILL GIVE DETAILS WHEN ARRIVE—WALT."

Despite Disney's rage, I would argue that Mintz's knife and the theft of Oswald *made* Disney. If Disney had achieved the modest raise he was looking for and if Mintz and his partners at Universal Studios had complied with Disney's requests for better cameras and technological enhancements, Walt Disney might have ended up as a very well compensated and highly decorated studio executive. But there would not have been Walt Disney Studios, Disneyland, and today's $72 billion market capitalization. How so? Of course, Disney was very ambitious, but he did not keep hanging up "Disney" shingles in Kansas City and Los Angeles because he was an incorrigible egotist who refused to answer to superiors. He hung up shingles when no one else would hire him to do what he wanted to do. Remember, he borrowed $500 from Uncle Robert because hanging around the major studios applying for work got him nowhere in 1923. Mintz's manhandling of Disney and Oswald convinced Disney of two key tenets that guided him for the rest of his life: (1) work for yourself and (2) fight to own the rights to unique, proprietary products. At various instances during his career, he was willing to accept less compensation in order to retain his freedom.[10] Like Ray Kroc, Disney had little taste for get-rich-quick schemes. From the moment he left Mintz's office, he turned into a builder, not the kind of man to cash out of an enterprise. After the debacle with Charles Mintz, he was more determined than ever to rebuild his business and his reputation.

Oh, there was just one more little thing that came from Oswald's kidnapping: Mickey Mouse. Before we get to that matter, let me tell you about a coda to the Oswald story. For nearly eighty years, the Disney "family" held a grudge against Mintz and Universal Studios. Finally, in February 2006, they had the chance to rescue Oswald from what is now called NBC Universal. ABC (a Disney property) sportscaster Al Michaels wanted to jump from ABC to NBC Sports to rejoin football giant John Madden. But Michaels needed Disney to release him from his employment contract. Disney demanded a price from NBC Universal. That price included the release of Oswald. In effect, Michaels was traded for an eighty-year-old rabbit. When the trade was announced, Walt's daughter Diana Disney Miller applauded Disney chairman Bob Iger for his dealmaking.

And Al Michaels noted that he would live forever as the answer to a trivia question.

FROM OSWALD TO MICKEY

What do you do when someone steals from you and you cannot report him to the police? Walt boarded the train back to Los Angeles seething. He felt robbed of his employees and of the best idea he'd ever had. Of course, Oswald was not simply an idea. Oswald was a steady stream of money, the meal ticket that took Walt and Roy away from canned peas and blue-plate specials at the cafeteria. With Lillian by his side, Walt sat on the train, grabbed some paper, and began to sketch. He needed a new character. Walt thought about all the animals in his film studio's celluloid menagerie: the rabbit, the chicken, the duck, the mechanical cow. Disney folklore suggests that while riding the train, he thought back to his office in Kansas City, where little mice used to race across his desk. Unlike most of us, apparently, Disney enjoyed that kind of company. He used to keep them in cages and take them out to play. So on the train, Disney began to sketch the head, the ears, the plump body. He added color. He considered the name Mortimer, but then yielded to Lillian's view that Mortimer sounded too formal. I could go on and on about the creative process that inspired Mickey Mouse. But, at the end of the day, there is one salient point: Mickey Mouse is a dead ringer for Oswald the Rabbit! If you rounded Oswald's ears and stuffed his belly with ten pounds of chocolate fudge, you, too, could come up with Mickey Mouse. They both shared that slick black widow's peak that was unequaled until Richard Nixon came on the scene. Disney figured out how to keep the form of Oswald, even while Mintz kept the darn rabbit itself.

But Disney was not willing to stop with just an Oswald look-alike. He needed Mickey to surpass Oswald, since Mintz and his minions would be producing more Oswald movies. This would be a head-to-head competition between the two varmints. But how could Disney one-up his own creation? Here is where Disney's genius came through and where he made a lasting contribution to the business and economics of marketing. While other cartoonists drew characters and then crossed their fingers, hoping that audiences found them interesting, Disney first tried to analyze the *audience*. Then he designed the cartoons to appeal to the needs of the audience. If Mickey Mouse was going to topple Oswald, Mickey must possess a deeper personality that could resonate with the dreams and conflicts facing moviegoers and readers. Long before political hacks started testing their candidates by using "focus groups," Walt Disney was taking Mickey Mouse to focus groups. He would bring preliminary prints of Mickey's escapades to a theater in Glendale, a suburb of Los Angeles. Then he would sit in the back and take notes on the reaction, not just of the children, but of the *adults*. He was trying to understand what he called the "Mickey Mouse audience." Like a Jungian analyst, Disney realized that Mickey could represent universal symbols and appeal to the "primitive remnants of something in every world-wracked human being which makes us play with children's toys . . . the Mickey in us."[11] By the way, this was several years before Carl Jung wrote *The Archetypes and the Collective Unconscious*. Whenever a Procter & Gamble researcher spreads some scented lotion on the hands of a focus group, he is just following in the footsteps of Mickey Mouse. Eventually Disney's Story Department produced serious, detailed character analyses for its stable of stars. Donald Duck was "vain, cocky and boastful. . . . The duck never compromises. Regardless of the odds against him."[12]

How else could Disney deepen the connection with the audience? Disney realized that he needed to tap into the zeitgeist, the spirit of the times. Mickey would not live in some unclocked, uncalendared haze. It was the Roaring Twenties; stocks were flying, and flappers were letting loose. In olden days a "glimpse of stocking was looked on as something shocking," but in the late 1920s, Cole Porter reported that "anything goes." Mickey would not be a party pooper. Shedding stilted Victorian manners, he would kiss his girlfriend in public view. In *Traffic Troubles,* he would romance his sweetheart in his automobile. Mickey was a cheerleader for the Jazz Age. And he wore good clothes for a mouse, occasionally outdoing a Gatsby.

Walt Disney figured out how to bring the front pages onto the screen without making Mickey quickly passé. If Charles Lindbergh's flight across the Atlantic captivated Americans, then Mickey would star in *Plane Crazy.* When the Great Depression crippled the country and made it tough for families to buy movie tickets, Mickey Mouse was on their side, not the plutocrats.' In a movie called *Moving Day* (1936), Mickey confounds the vulgar repo man who demands the rent and their furniture. Disney thought it was a perfect time to release an updated fairy-tale movie based on King Midas. In *The Golden Touch,* everything turns to hamburger. Mickey might have timeless appeal, but Disney knew that audiences needed to feel a connection; he had to be of their age. The ability to be timeless and relevant is a gift of staggering and rare importance. Walt Disney shared with Ronald Reagan a talent for conjuring up the nostalgic memories of Americana and using them to inspire the people of his day.

Disney's experience yields a valuable lesson for the entertainment industry. A few years ago, a musical was being developed on the West Coast that hoped to reach Broadway someday. It was called *Jersey Boys* and was about Frankie Valli and the Four Seasons, whose heyday was in the 1960s. Now, back in 2004, the theater world was suffering from too many so-called catalog musicals. Shows based on hits of the Beach Boys (*Good Vibrations*) and Elvis (*All Shook Up*) busted like broken bulbs on abandoned Broadway marquees. The critics were aiming their poisoned pens at any producer who dared to show up with hits from the 1960s. And yet I thought that *Jersey Boys* would light up the town. Why? Believe it or not, it was not the music that sold me. I did not care so much that Frankie Valli's piercing falsetto had sold millions. That was forty years ago! The boys and girls who bopped to "Big Girls Don't Cry" were grandmas and grandpas now. You have heard the expression "Here today, gone tomorrow." These days it is "Here today, gone today." I agreed to back *Jersey*

Boys as a coproducer because it tapped into the zeitgeist, much as Disney did. First of all, Jersey was hot, and Italians from Jersey were the hottest. The HBO hit *The Sopranos* inspired tours of Italian neighborhoods where the fictional Tony Soprano held court. Second, the show's director, Des McAnuff, used huge, blown-up comic strips to illustrate scenes, cartoons that looked like Roy Lichtenstein paintings. Lichtenstein's works were breaking records at Sotheby's. Third, certain scenes celebrated cars. What kinds of cars had been racking up tremendous prices at auctions? You guessed it, 1960s muscle cars, the kind that Frankie Valli's fans would drool over. Finally, the script (cowritten by Woody Allen's former writing partner Marshall Brickman) was far wittier and more poignant than any of the failed catalog musicals. In the end, I put up my money because the show encapsulated an era without looking stodgy. It was the lesson of Walt Disney and Mickey Mouse.

When motion pictures first began sweeping the country, President Woodrow Wilson said that movie technology was like "writing history with lightning." But in October 1927, that lightning was matched with thunder: Al Jolson's *Jazz Singer* burst out, and mass audiences saw the vaudevillian dancing and crooning—at the same time! The talkie was born. But the talkie led to all sorts of trouble, especially for strapping leading men who turned out to have lisps, Germanic accents, or whiny, high-pitched voices that sounded like they belonged to svelte leading ladies.

Earlier in this chapter we saw how Disney felt compelled to stay at least one step ahead of his competitors technologically. There was no doubt in Disney's mind: Mickey must speak. In fact, it would be a disaster if Oswald spoke first. Disney was quite happy to provide the squeaky voice himself. There was only one problem: the soon-to-be-released Mickey feature, *Steamboat Willie,* had already been completed as a silent film. Disney slammed on the brakes and searched for a company that could provide sound for the approximately twenty thousand frames. Walt had planned on selling the silent *Steamboat Willie* to a distributor for $3,000—though he would certainly keep all rights to Mickey. But now he realized he would have to spend many times that amount to get Mickey singing and talking. Disney traveled back to New York and settled in the studio with musicians who had a terrible time keeping up with

Mickey and his boat. After numerous tries and about $15,000, finally the music and dialogue accompanied the mouse.

The mouse roared. Or at least the audience did, when *Steamboat Willie* premiered at New York's Colony Theater on November 28, 1928. Disney aficionados still consider this Mickey's birth date. Presumably, Oswald and Charles Mintz spent that evening quietly.

Over the next few years, Mickeymania swept the country. Fans across the globe from Franklin Roosevelt to Mussolini applauded his antics in the films that followed. The phrase "What, no Mickey Mouse?" became a hit song and a common expression for any disappointment. Each country seemed to come up with a nickname for Mickey: In Italy he was "Topolino" (little mouse), in Sweden "Musse Pigg," and in Spain "Raton Mickey."

Distributors started pursuing Disney, waving big checks, but Disney wanted to make sure he stayed independent. He signed a long-term deal with a Hollywood hustler named Pat Powers, who had a sound system called Cinephone. The Powers Motion Picture Company would take 10 percent of the gross, and Disney would rent the Cinephone system for his new talkies.

Though Disney retained all control of Mickey Mouse, as each new film debuted, he noticed that the revenues passed through Powers's filter more slowly, with less and less money dribbling out. In late 1929 Roy headed for New York to sort out the financial confusion. The report was not good. "That Powers is a crook," Roy told Walt. At first Walt defended Powers, retorting to Roy, "You just don't believe in people." [13]

Fearing a rerun of his disastrous confrontation with Charles Mintz, Walt headed back to New York to discuss finances with Powers. He was right to be fearful. Powers was staging a coup d'état. He first announced that he was stealing away Ub Iwerks and setting up for Iwerks an independent studio to compete with Disney. Powers was sure that Iwerks was the real genius behind Disney and that Walt was merely a broker. Figuring that Disney was just a shell, he offered to buy the studio and give Walt a nice weekly salary. With memories of Mintz bouncing around in his brain, Disney tore up Power's proposal and stormed out. He would not surrender Mickey Mouse to anyone, no matter how generous the terms or nefarious the blackmail.

Incidentally, Iwerks gave up a 20 percent ownership in the Disney studio in order to jump in bed with Powers. His heirs may be kicking at his grave because that 20 percent would be worth billions more than the shares in the Iwerks Studio, which evaporated in 1936.

Walt and Roy went back to the drawing board, hired more animators, and got to work on a fictitious story about a good person sucked into a world of evil. To Walt, his encounters with the wheelers and dealers of the motion picture industry may have inspired his next big triumph, the first full-color, full-length feature film, *Snow White*. The kid from the small farm in Missouri felt like Snow White whenever he had to sit down at a table with another producer, distributor, or financier. He called them wolves and leeches. Next time you see *Snow White* and cringe as the hideous witch entices Snow White by dangling a highly polished, highly poisoned apple, imagine Charles Mintz and Pat Powers offering Walt Disney a sweet distribution deal.

Why did Walt bother with a full-length film instead of churning out successful shorts? Two reasons. First, he was ambitious and eager to gain the respect of big studio moguls. Second, he was a shrewd manager, despite his down-home country manner. Movie theaters were starting to cut back on cartoon shorts in order to squeeze in double features. While Mickey was hugely popular, Popeye, Felix the Cat, and other characters were always vying to overtake Mickey's standing. But if he could produce a complete feature, Disney could dominate the marquee. This was a huge and treacherous leap, requiring hundreds of new animators. Disney did not just want an extralong cartoon; he also wanted to produce a brilliant, captivating drama. As busloads of workers scurried about the studio, the budget started growing from just $250,000 to $1.5 million. Disney's creditors started worrying, and, of course, the frugal Roy grew more nervous by the day. When Roy first screened *Snow White* before its official release, he anonymously filled out an audience survey form: "Walt, stick to the shorts!" Of course, Walt would not listen. Even Walt's wife, Lillian, warned him to veer off of this dangerous path. Finally, as the budget busted the adding machines, Walt mortgaged his house to come up with extra money. How could Walt ever recoup this money on a cartoon that all of Hollywood was calling "Disney's Folly"? Some cartoon! Every frame of *Snow White* received special attention, pushing the limits of current technology.

Sometimes the animators were forced to rely on the oldest technologies. At an early preview, Walt decided that the Snow White character herself looked, well, too snowy and pale-faced. He called up the Inking and Painting Department. What could they do? This was fifty years before computer-generated fine-tuning. Today, simply pressing a button could transform Snow White from a pale-faced to a sunburned princess. The women in the department fell back on old technology, namely, the rouge in their personal makeup compacts. They carefully and consistently smudged rouge on all of the cells. If Walt had not hired any women, for generations of children, Snow White would have looked like an anemic.

When *Snow White* opened in Hollywood, Cary Grant, Charlie Chaplin, Jack Benny, and numerous A-list stars strutted across the red carpet to see the show. Meanwhile, the Disney bank account was an even brighter shade of red. Walt was not sure how much the audience liked the movie until the very end. Snow White lay in a coffin, asleep in suspended animation. He looked around the theater and heard noises. They were weeping! To Disney, that was the happiest sound on earth. The cynical, crusty Hollywood crowd was so drawn into the story that it had been mesmerized by a cartoon fairy tale.

Cured of her complexion defects, Snow White "killed," raking in nearly $600 million (in 2000 dollars), breaking all box-office records for that time.[14] It is still the highest-grossing animated film of all time. The movie was so widely admired for its colorful animation that in 1938 the Metropolitan Museum of Art actually displayed a watercolor from the movie. (If that shocked the highbrows, they probably experienced heart attacks when the Guggenheim exhibited motorcycles in 1998.) The hundreds of thousands of cels that make up the film are routinely auctioned for over $5,000 each. In 1939 Walt Disney won a special Oscar for *Snow White,* awarded by Shirley Temple. The girl starlet presented Disney with one regular-sized Oscar and seven tiny models. With the momentum and money of *Snow White* propelling his studio into the 1940s, Disney soon conquered the box office again with *Pinocchio, Dumbo,* and *Bambi.*

During the 1930s and early 1940s, Disney expanded his repertoire, not just artistically but financially. He hired more staff, built a $3 million studio campus in Burbank, and held his first public stock offering. While

Yankee Stadium was called the "House That Ruth Built," Walt called Burbank the "House That Snow White Built." But Walt did not invest in Burbank simply to replicate Snow White. Unlike Hollywood honchos today, he had little interest in sequels. Though his movies all had that "Disney touch," none of them were cookie-cutter deals. Each had its own budget and financial profile. After investing huge sums in *Pinocchio,* which involved very complicated scenes (in small Italian towns and inside the mouth of Monstro, the whale), Disney knew he needed to scale back. Therefore, he designed *Dumbo* to be a more modest, less splashy story. His animators finished the project in record time, and the movie earned quick profits. In between major releases, the studio churned out numerous shorts starring Mickey and the gang. They cost about $50,000 each and generally earned more than twice that in revenues. Roy Disney, always the more practical and money conscious, preferred these quick hits to the more speculative full-length features.

AND NOW A COMMERCIAL BREAK

Walt Disney's movies were stunning innovations. But Disney did not fool himself into thinking he was a creative genius like Shakespeare or Picasso. Since every major film could potentially bankrupt his studio, he knew that he also had to focus on making money—or else he would be tossed out of the turbulent industry. So he perfected the link between creativity and money. For generations naive professors have fooled naive freshmen into seeing artists as pure creative forces, divorced from their pocketbooks. They teach that artists have a unique insight into the human condition and that they should not be spoiled by crass commerce. Yet history screams, "Bunk!" Shakespeare filled the Globe with plays that thrilled the masses, with drama and lascivious double entendres. Picasso knew darn well the value of his art, once purportedly buying a car in exchange for a pencil sketch done in the showroom of an auto dealer. A companion asked, "Don't you feel guilty about getting a car for two minutes of scribbling?" Picasso answered, "That two minutes took me sixty years." Even the socialist George Bernard Shaw recognized his pocketbook priorities when he tried to work on a Hollywood screenplay. He told movie mogul

Sam Goldwyn, "The trouble, Mr. Goldwyn, is that you are only interested in art, and I am only interested in money."

Let us examine how Walt Disney cleverly closed the gap between art and commerce. Following the Baby Ruth candy bar in the 1920s (which the Curtiss Candy Company suspiciously claimed was not named for Babe Ruth) came the Oswald Rabbit bar. To raise some money for *Steamboat Willie,* Disney had licensed Mickey's face for a pencil tablet.[15] Though Walt did not invent the idea of Mickey Mouse Clubs, he backed them with enthusiasm in the early 1930s, publishing newsletters and offering buttons, pencil boxes, and a theme song. Twenty years before the perky Annette Funicello showed up on television, half a million kids were already members of the club. And the merchandise? It was cradle-to-grave coverage, with over a hundred manufacturers from around the world cranking out baby rattles, bedsheets, cups, soaps, and probably canes, too. With $100 million in sales, Disney had trouble keeping track of Disneyware, though the studio negotiated a wide range of commissions from 0.5 percent to 10 percent.[16] Fans bought millions of Mickey ice-cream cones during their first month available. Of course, nothing took off like the iconic Mickey Mouse wristwatch, which managed to bring whimsy to the era of the Great Depression. By the late 1930s, Donald Duck began to surpass Mickey. Perhaps his feisty, surlier moods better matched the country's frustrations. In any event, Donald began to appear on watches, popcorn, and even orange juice. I must confess that I once ate at the French restaurant at Epcot and tried to order "Donald Duck à la orange." The fake French waiter was very snooty about it.

Disney's innovations did not stop at merchandising the characters on the screen. We must give him credit for teaching the business world the importance of speed, too. While other companies might have produced toys based on popular characters, Disney pressed to get those toys and gadgets out sooner—before the characters burst onto the big screen. Before *Snow White* and *Pinocchio* opened, department stores flooded newspapers with advertisements enticing kids to play with Snow White dolls and eat their peanut butter sandwiches off Dopey plates. Who was this Jiminy Cricket on the milk glasses? parents asked. They would soon find out.

I did not realize the power of Disney's speed until 1995, when my then-two-year-old daughter uttered her first multisyllabic words. She was toddling into a Target store and saw a poster for a movie that had not yet been released to the public. She pointed her finger and said quite clearly, "Poca-lady." Weeks before the movie hit the big screen, kids like mine were learning all about Pocahontas. Of course, we ended up buying her an Indian princess costume.

By forcing his merchandising chief, Herbert Kamen, to focus on speed, Disney created a kind of self-reinforcing turbocharger for his revenues. Parents snatched up the goodies, which built up more pressure to see the movies. The kids demanded to see the movies, and then after the show, the parents would snap up even more goodies. Finally, with more revenues in its coffers, Disney could afford to produce ever more impressive works. So successful and encompassing was this cycle that it revolutionized the link between a brand and a product. Previously, a manufacturer would have to build up a brand name by first delivering an unknown product to the stores and then advertising. Now—as long as the product had Mickey's, or Donald's, or Jiminy's face on it—the product was instantaneously well-known *before* it hit the shelves.

Disney's focus on speed persists today and has even intensified. Nowadays, speed is crucial in selling DVDs and video games. According to the Ditan Corporation, which manages inventory for many of the leading software firms, about 40 percent of the revenues come in the first three days! An overwhelming proportion of new video games, for example John Madden's NFL football series from Electronic Arts, are released on Tuesdays and bought by young men. Suppliers and companies that manage video game inventory like Ditan absolutely must have the games on the shelves when the doors open on Tuesday morning. The video game *Sudden Death* will describe any deliveryman who stops too long for a cup of coffee on the way to Wal-Mart on a Tuesday morning.

Even where Disney had no commercial tie-in, firms often profited as "free riders." Economists call a firm a free rider if it benefits from another firm's activities but does not pay for their benefit. This can also be called a "positive externality." When *Snow White* displayed a long scene with the princess washing her clothes, soap sellers rejoiced, and the trade journal *Soap* featured an article entitled "Walt Disney Puts Soap in the Movies."[17] I suppose hygiene was not so important until Snow White came along.

We economists also discuss negative externalities; for example, the cruise ship industry worries that movies like *The Poseidon Adventure* will scare away customers.

Of course, more recently, Hollywood has tried to wipe out free riders by auctioning off "product placement." If you see a can of Coca-Cola in a Tom Cruise movie, there is a very good chance that Coke paid a price. These deals are now done very early. Today the screenplay analysts at Creative Artists Agency—the most powerful talent agency in Beverly Hills—examine screenplays to see which ones best lend themselves to product placements.

When Disney's television efforts took off in the 1950s and 1960s, the coonskin-capped Daniel Boone and Davy Crockett became the leading action heroes among young boys. The price of raccoon pelts shot up twentyfold. Furriers rejoiced, and when they ran out of raccoon, some of them painted stripes on rodents. Never to miss an angle, Disney commissioned a theme song for Davy Crockett, which shot to the top of the hit parade and has earned royalties ever since. As a young boy, I watched reruns of the Boone and Crockett shows. To this day, I have trouble remembering the difference between the Kentuckian and the Tennessean, since actor Fess Parker played both of them and seemed to be wearing the same cap! Parker, who now operates a successful hotel and winery in Santa Barbara, California, suddenly became so popular that, as with Elvis and the Beatles, girls and boys chased him around as if he were holding the winning ticket to a billion-dollar lottery.

Disney's flurry of merchandising set the scene for today's scramble for consumer dollars. Marketing managers today yearn to spur "viral marketing," a cheap frenzy of consumers spreading their consumption views across their networks. Just flip your history book back to the 1930s and ask: What in the world were all those hyperactive Mickey Mouse Club members squawking about in the early 1930s?

THE MARCH ON MICKEY'S HOUSE

In addition to American fans, Mickey, Donald, Goofy, and the rest of the gang had converted children all around the world to be Disneyphiles.

Fans beyond U.S. borders generated almost half of the studio's revenues. But while Walt Disney entered the 1940s full speed ahead, Hirohito's airplanes and Hitler's tanks suddenly plunged him into the most difficult business period of his career. The Pinocchio story was based in Italy, but when Disney released his version in 1940, Europe was overrun by Nazi conquerors and Mussolini's troops.[18] Soldiers in jackboots kicked shut the doors to foreign markets, and Disney's revenues began to plunge. Although Burbank was thousands of miles from any bombs or rifle shots, shortly after the Japanese attacked Pearl Harbor on December 7, 1941, five hundred American troops marched through the gates of the Disney Studios and took over. The troops had two missions. First, they were protecting a nearby Lockheed aircraft plant. Second, they turned the Disney fantasy machine into a war machine, producing everything from military logos to training films. Disney designed a logo for the Navy's torpedo boats, also known as mosquito boats. It was a menacing mosquito straddling a torpedo. Dumbo showed up on air squadrons riding bombs and saying, "We never miss."

Over 90 percent of Disney's film production in 1942 was devoted to the war, and the Navy pressed the studio to churn out six times as much feet of film as it had in peacetime. Though Walt Disney was a patriot and proud that his company could serve the military, even he was startled when an old Navy commander camped out in his personal suite for months and, perhaps thinking he was on the front lines at Guadalcanal, actually began washing his socks in a bucket while Walt tried to conduct production meetings. The Department of War harnessed Disney's talent to produce films with such eye-catching titles as *Hookworm, How Disease Travels,* and *Cleanliness Brings Health.* Needless to say, Disney's typical fans did not race to buy tickets. With fifteen hundred people on the payroll, the studio soon found itself over $4 million in debt. While Walt understood the need to sacrifice, occasionally the U.S. government seemed less than grateful. In one notorious example, the U.S. Treasury commandeered Donald Duck to appear in a film warning Americans to pay taxes on time, called *The New Spirit.* Treasury Secretary Henry Morgenthau actually complained to Walt about Donald's performance. Walt Disney blew up: "I've given you Donald Duck. . . . That's like MGM giving you Clark Gable!" Despite Donald's apparently flawed acting, tens of millions of Americans saw the film, with a Gallup poll showing that 37 percent were more willing to pay taxes.

Disney felt squeezed, not just by the War Department, but his own employees, when the unions called an acrimonious strike in 1941, complaining of erratic pay. Disney was made distraught by what he saw as yet another betrayal, similar to those perpetrated by Mintz, Powers, and Iwerks. He actually had to cross picket lines manned by his own animators. Most painful of all, they marched with signs depicting his cherished cartoon characters denouncing him. It must have been anguishing to see Goofy call you a "scab."

Between the costs of the war and the costs of a union deal, Disney's finances faded further away from prosperity. After the war, in 1946, he was forced to sell preferred stock and to lay off about one-third of his fifteen hundred employees. Through this period he constantly fought with his brother and trusted advisers. Walt Disney, the master of fantasy and escapism, had trouble coping. He snapped at his staff and felt as if his spirits were snapping. It was a dark period on the Burbank campus. He lurched between insomnia, prowling the hallways ready to pounce, and at the other extreme, retreating to his home.

REBIRTH IN ANAHEIM

After World War II, Walt began tinkering with a new hobby that would ultimately save his sanity and save his company. The distant sound of the Santa Fe train had echoed in his mind since the time he was a child. Now an accomplished but terribly stressed adult, he gazed at his backyard and decided he could cut down some trees and make room for a train. In 1947, he told his sister Ruth, "I bought myself a birthday/Christmas present . . . an electric train. You probably can't understand how much I wanted one when I was a kid, but I've got one now." It is hard to believe that this manufacturer of fantasy had denied himself a toy until he was in his mid-forties. Of course, this was hardly a Lionel starter set. Walt ultimately built a half-mile loop with a 120-foot tunnel under Lillian's garden. The trains were one-eighth the size of real trains. At some point, Walt called his Prop Department, asking it to deliver one-eighth-size humans to ride the trains. "I need passengers to make it look right," he said. The prop manager snapped to attention and assured his boss that they would try. Only after hanging up the phone did the prop chief realize Walt was joking. Even the Seven Dwarfs would have exceeded the one-eighth requirement.[19]

Walt's miniature train, a project he latched onto during a dark period for his studio, helped inspire the idea for Disneyland. Quite often inspiration strikes when a person is floundering in the dumps. In 2005 Steve Jobs delivered a remarkable commencement speech at Stanford. According to Jobs, the Apple revolution would not have taken place had he not tumbled onto hard times.

> I didn't have a dorm room, so I slept on the floor in friends' rooms, I returned Coke bottles for the 5¢ deposits to buy food with, and I would walk the 7 miles across town every Sunday night to get one good meal a week at the Hare Krishna temple.... Because I had dropped out [of Reed College] ... I decided to take a calligraphy class.... It was beautiful, historical, artistically subtle in a way that science can't capture.... None of this had even a hope of any practical application in my life. But ten years later, when we were designing the first Macintosh computer, it all came back to me.... It was the first computer with beautiful typography. If I had never dropped in on that single course in college, the Mac would have never had multiple typefaces or proportionally spaced fonts.[20]

Of course, Disneyland derives not just from the fact that Walt and his studio were struggling with cash flow issues in the 1940s. Disneyland also derives from Walt's devotion to his daughters, Sharon and Diane. He was a playful, attentive father who designed his family home to have a soda fountain in the playroom. According to Sharon, "He'd go out there and make these weird concoctions that nobody would eat."[21] With his children, he had visited amusement parks around the world and mostly found them dingy and staffed by toothless carnies who would be happy to swipe a quarter from a kid. He admired Tivoli Gardens in Copenhagen and wondered whether he could design an even better park, filled with the fantasies his animator geniuses had put on film.

CEOS SHOULD NOT BE SNOBS

Walt's ultimate success with Disneyland brings us to another lesson: The CEO should not be a snob (though Estée Lauder had no trouble going after the pocketbooks of snobs). The revival of Disney's studio business and the stunning launch of Disneyland in the 1950s were powered by television. If Walt had been snobbish about a new medium called television, Disneyland would not have been an international smash, and his films would have limped along underfinanced.

Fred Allen, a huge radio star in the 1940s, quipped that television was called a medium because "nothing is well done." But Disney proved him wrong. From a pure business point of view, Walt showed utter genius in figuring out how to cross-promote his television work and his new theme park. During the early 1950s, most television programs were simply trying to squeeze old radio shows through a cathode-ray gun. Shows starring Jack Benny and George Burns even ran concurrently on television and radio. And many of the television writers and performers who had transferred their skills from radio had actually started in vaudeville in the 1920s, simply migrating their routines from live theaters to studios.

But Walt saw something new and fresh in television. While other film studio heads quaked in fear that television would steal their audiences, Walt realized that television could excite people into attending his movies. Furthermore, instead of delivering his productions "on spec," he could negotiate up-front fees from the networks or from corporate sponsors to defray costs. In 1950, Walt delivered a Christmas special for NBC television called *One Hour in Wonderland,* which Coca-Cola paid $125,000 to sponsor. The show resembled a party in Walt's office, hosted by Edgar Bergen and Charlie McCarthy, the ventriloquist and his dummy. Like other television personalities, Bergen and McCarthy had first been *radio* stars. A ventriloquist on radio? That is like listening to a tap dancer on your iPod. It could be Savion Glover—or maybe it is just some guy smacking a spoon on a table. If you ever see old video clips of Edgar Bergen, his lips move as if he is, well, trying to talk without moving his lips.

In any event, the real innovation of the 1950 Christmas special was the five-minute preview of Disney's yet-to-be-released *Alice in Wonderland.* Disney was pleased and stunned by how the television preview energized children around the country and got them buzzing about the upcoming movie. As soon as the preview clip ended, children begged their parents to see the movie. And the parents bombarded Disney Studios with a pointed, urgent question: "When can I buy tickets?"

Disney revealed, "I am a great believer in the TV medium to sell pictures. . . . Gallup found that our Christmas show sent the [audience] penetration way up. We plan to use TV for point of sale."[22] While others quickly denounced the television wasteland, Walt became television's biggest advocate: "It appeals to people of all ages and all classes. It is the most intimate medium of communication yet developed."[23] Even after just one television program, though, Walt wanted to push the medium toward better technology. Just as he had in the 1920s leapfrogged the crude pin-limbed cartoon paper dolls, Walt decided to drive past the grainy kinescopes and demanded that his shows be recorded on film. Kinescopes were made by aiming a camera at a television monitor and recording the image off the monitor's screen while a live program was being aired. It was a fuzzy, distorted second-generation print that made reruns frustrating and unappealing to watch. It also meant that only viewers who lived in the same time zone as the original studio would see a clear shot. The move from crude kinescopes to film helped define the long-term winners and losers in television. Generations have roared over *I Love Lucy* for two reasons. First, it is very funny. Second, it is very clear. Desi Arnaz in 1951 devised a method to record and broadcast on brilliant, cloudless film. Disney had similarly high standards. In comparison, the vast catalog of fuzzy kinescopes that dominated television in the 1950s seem unwatchable to modern audiences.

Walt shrewdly agreed with Desi Arnaz and Lucille Ball on another count: he demanded ownership of his television work. He would live the rest of his professional life as if Oswald the Rabbit were standing on his shoulder whispering in his ear. He reportedly turned down millions of dollars from the television networks who begged to buy and then broadcast his films.

Following the success of the 1950 Christmas special, Walt signed on to do a 1951 special, but this time his name would be in the title. Johnson & Johnson paid $250,000 to sponsor *The Walt Disney Christmas Special,* which highlighted a preview of Walt's next big project, *Peter Pan.* Once again the children started begging, and Walt could see advance ticket sales building into a mountain of revenue.

But Walt had another obvious priority beyond Christmas specials and ticket sales, namely, Disneyland, his plan for a revolutionary theme park, featuring pirates, adventures, fairy-tale princesses, and his own memories of Marceline, Missouri. It sounded great to him. Unfortunately, brother Roy thought it would be a great way to lose a fortune, bankrupt a company, and turn a happy band of public shareholders into an army of litigants. Bank lending officers shared Roy's view. So Walt did the natural thing, natural from the mind of Walt Disney. He sold his vacation home in Palm Springs, borrowed on his life insurance, took out loans from his own employees, and formed an independent company later called WED Enterprises (for Walter Elias Disney). But he still did not have enough money to fund a $17 million spectacle. Where could he get the money? He looked no further than his black-and-white television for the answer.

Walt and Roy traveled to New York in 1953, carrying with them a painting of the imagined theme park for Anaheim, California. They made appointments at the two major networks, CBS and NBC, and were eager to negotiate a television deal in exchange for theme park financing. The suits at CBS and NBC said they were very enthusiastic. And then they said no. They could get along quite nicely without a risky deal. The Disneys trudged over to ABC, then the weakest network, a minor player that seldom hosted a hit show. But it turned out that ABC needed Disney as much as Disney needed ABC. ABC agreed to pay $500,000 in cash and guarantee $4.5 million in loans, in exchange for a one-third ownership position in what would be Disneyland (in 1960, ABC sold back that stake for about $7.5 million). Under the historic deal, Disney would also produce a weekly program. What would they call the show? What name would serve Walt's interest in cross-promoting film, television, and his theme park? The choice was obvious. In the fall of 1954, ABC aired *Disneyland,* which reinvented the network as a place for the young and ambitious. For the first time, ABC actually had a show in the top ten and was able to attract more talent and advertising attention.

Walt shrewdly used *Disneyland* to excite the public about Anaheim. Just as the theme park would be separated into Frontierland, Adventureland, Fantasyland, and Tomorrowland, so would the television show.

Viewers would watch a clip about, say, Tom Sawyer and then hear about how they would someday be able to hop onto a real raft that would take them to Tom Sawyer's island. In addition to these entertaining and enticing tidbits, the *Disneyland* television show let viewers gaze through the back door of the studios and the upcoming theme park. The show provided a kind of backstage tour, even broadcasting screen tests. This too was an innovative idea. The producer Mike Todd once advised, "Never let the audience backstage." Like magicians, most producers agreed with Todd and lived in fear that the audience would be turned off by the banal reality behind "movie magic." Disney did not. He figured that if audiences could see film professionals at work, they would be even more thrilled to see the final version. Following Disney's lead, in 1964, Universal Studios created its highly successful Hollywood studio tour.

Disneyland, the television show, did almost as well as Disneyland the theme park, trouncing CBS and NBC combined in major cities and earning Emmy Awards from the critics. Arthur Godfrey used to "own" Wednesday nights for his variety show on CBS. Then *Disneyland* came along and took Paul Bunyan's ax to Godfrey's ratings. Godfrey mused, "I love Disney. I wish I didn't have to work Wednesday night and could stay home to watch his show." [24]

Television did not just make Disney. Disney made television. I would argue that Walt Disney provided the single biggest boost to television makers by promoting color television sets at a time when an overwhelming number of Americans were just delighted with black and white. As always, Walt was looking for the cutting edge in technology. By the mid-1950s, black-and-white television reminded him of the kinescopes he disdained in the early 1950s and the simplistic cartoons he snubbed in the 1920s. Color was the key. As we saw in our chapter on David Sarnoff, Disney divorced from ABC and jumped to NBC, which through its parent, RCA, had the edge in color broadcasting. In 1955, NBC had already broadcast a live performance of the ballet *Sleeping Beauty.* If NBC could successfully promote Tchaikovsky, it could do wonders for Walt Disney. Once again, Disney and the network chose an obvious but highly effective name for the show: *Walt Disney's Wonderful World of Color,* which debuted in 1961 and sent families rushing to their local RCA Victor dealers for color sets. By the spring of 1962, RCA announced a 166 percent leap in color television sales, while corporate earnings roared. Any kid in the 1960s felt pretty dreary on Sunday nights if he watched the *Wonderful World of Color* in drab black and white. It was like taking a kid to Baskin-Robbins and telling him he could order only vanilla. Oh, the show had a second corporate sponsor who also enjoyed the rush to color our world. The company was Eastman Kodak. It really is hard to find an angle that slipped past Walt Disney.

ANAHEIM/MARCELINE

With the momentum of the films and a hot television show, the Disneyland theme park was of course a huge hit, and the doubters, including Roy, had to shred some of their old memos. Roy always acted like Apollo to Walt's Dionysus, trying to impose logic and structure on Walt's outrageous but glorious imagination.[25] For a few moments on opening day, July 17, 1955, Roy might have felt vindicated. With ABC's cameras rolling (the broadcast was cohosted by a movie has-been named Ronald Reagan), the park seemed jinxed. The summer heat melted the asphalt into a gooey quicksand for shoes, a gas leak shut down Tomorrowland, counterfeiters had sold fake tickets, and the few working bathrooms and drinking fountains could not accommodate the thirsty and bladder-bloated guests. To entice the folks back home, Disney and ABC had their cameras shift away from the debacles and instead focus on Disney employees and their families, who were told to wave and smile madly, even as they found themselves locked up in cattle cars on the Disneyland railway and marooned on Tom Sawyer's island. Walt and his staff referred to July 17 as Black Sunday. I suspect that Disneyland's opening day was jinxed by angry and aggrieved mice. During the construction of the park, a color-blind contractor bulldozed all of the orange trees, including many that were tagged to stay. The fallen trees yielded an infestation of mice. Then the contractors unleashed cats to fight the mice. How could the home of Mickey Mouse begin by sending cats on a mouse hunt?

After the jittery Black Sunday, the park began to prosper, attracting a million visitors in its first six months. By the 1980s, Disneyland brought in over ten million and faced serious competition only from Disney

World, the Orlando version. Walt's nostalgic depiction of Main Street, USA not only put visitors in a friendly mood, even after they fought traffic on Interstate 5, but it also put them in the mood for shopping! After all, Main Street, USA was not just a series of facades—it was a sequence of stores, selling Disney-branded merchandise. Disney has also used corporate partners to underwrite some of the stores, with varying degrees of success. Personally, I still think Disney is struggling with food merchants. The Carnation Café, located on Main Street since 1955, offers family fare and an attractive "painter's palette" for kids, featuring peanut butter, marshmallows, grapes, etc. But outside of this location on Main Street, I do not think either company has yet figured out how to build on this relationship. Across the street is Hills Brothers Coffee, which, last I checked, served a steely old brew. It turns out that Walt's taste in food spanned the spectrum from hash to chili. He was far happier with diner fare than with sophisticated dishes. He was not the type to worry which fork to use with the salad. In 2005, an older Hispanic man came out of the Carnation Café wearing a chef's outfit. I noticed that his name tag said "1955." He told me he was there on opening day. "Did you meet Walt?" I asked. "Of course," the man said. "He was here early every day, inspecting everything. I was so scared I hid behind the big soup pots."

Despite my quibbling about the food, it is clear that at the end of a long day, as a daily parade sweeps down Main Street, Disneyland guests pour into the gift shops, leaving the park with great big bags of merchandise, much of it high-quality clothing. The visitors are very tired, but very satisfied, too. Walt believed in value-plussing, that is, making sure that customers felt they received *more* than their money's worth. He insisted that Disneyland create what we economists call "consumer surplus," that is, an extra amount of value that the consumer would actually have paid even more to receive. As of this writing, a ticket to Disneyland costs an adult $63. While that may sound like a lot, an adult will pay $57 to walk through the gates at nearby Legoland, which is open fewer hours and offers very few attractions for kids older than ten years of age. No wonder the gates at Disneyland are packed with willing customers, while Legoland seldom hits its capacity.

In the 1950s, the combination of Disneyland, hit television shows, and blockbuster movies like *Peter Pan* and *Lady and the Tramp* propelled revenues like the launch of the Space Mountain ride. During that decade, revenues multiplied eightfold to over $58 million, and profits almost quintupled. Disney's enterprises were so captivating, they were an antidote to the panic that struck America when the Soviet Union successfully launched the Sputnik satellite. So what if the Soviets are ahead in space; we have Disney. A Russian propagandist even tried to debunk Disneyland, claiming that Disney actually kept real tribal Indians as prisoners in Frontierland! Suddenly, balmy Anaheim was Siberia. Despite the bad press in Moscow, in 1959, Nikita Khrushchev flailed at his aides for scheduling a meeting with Nixon instead of going to Disneyland.

WHAT IS AOL?

The Las Vegas magician David Copperfield thought he had the greatest disappearing act since Harry Houdini. Then in 2000 America Online and Time Warner decided to merge. Those two companies figured out how to wipe away $220 billion in shareholder value. Copperfield merely made an elephant disappear.

Back in 2000, of course, no one knew exactly where the Internet was heading or whether anyone would ever make any money investing in Internet media stocks. AOL CEO Steve Case, Time Warner CEO Gerald Levin, and a cast of outsized characters like Ted Turner suddenly turned up to announce their blockbuster news. How much homework did everyone do to make sure this secret deal would work? About three days.[26] I bet Copperfield spends a lot more time breaking in a new elephant.

When the AOL–Time Warner merger was announced, I was sitting in a studio in Washington, D.C., being interviewed by ABC television's legendary White House correspondent, Sam Donaldson. Neither of us felt confident about the merger, yet neither of us felt confident that we had much of a clue. Where was the synergy between the two giants, the Internet king and Time Warner, the cable and magazine king? Surely, I suggested to Sam, if Tom Cruise came out with a Warner Bros. movie, AOL could blast a sneak preview to the computer screens of its thirty million subscribers. AOL subscribers might feel that they had the inside scoop on some cool *Mission Impossible* car-crash scene. But then I wondered, *Why would Time Warner want to limit the sneak preview just to AOL customers? It wants to entice everybody on the planet, doesn't it? And why would AOL want to limit such sneak previews to Warner Bros. Pictures? Wouldn't it want sneak previews from Sony Pictures, too?* In other words, I had trouble seeing how this blockbuster deal would create proprietary value.

Walt Disney would have objected to the deal on numerous counts. In fact, according to the lessons of Walt Disney, the AOL–Time Warner debacle neatly shows how to ruin value. First of all, Walt proved throughout his career that he was willing to invest to stay in the technological lead. At the time of the merger, AOL was stuck in ancient history, using slow dial-up telephone technology, while millions of Americans were signing up with cable companies and for DSL lines. AOL even seemed to deny that it was stuck until it embraced Time Warner, which had cable access. This, despite a litany of customer blackouts and billing debacles at AOL. Even today, one wonders why AOL, which calls itself the best online community builder in the world, did not come up with MySpace or Facebook or YouTube, or any number of other communities that are spreading from teenager to teenager faster than acne. (Of course, one might ask whether during the 1990s, Disney Studios' falling behind the computer animators at Pixar, producers of such hits as *Toy Story, Monsters, Inc.,* and *The Incredibles,* ultimately led to Disney's purchase of Pixar in 2006.)

Compare AOL's and Time Warner's lethargy to Walt in the early 1920s, tinkering in his garage, borrowing a stop-action camera, trying to devise a better way to make cartoons, rather than manipulating paper dolls. Then remember Walt investing huge sums in *Steamboat Willie*—he was unwilling to give even Al Jolson much of a lead in talkies. During the television era, Walt insisted on film, then jumped to NBC because he needed to see his cartoons in living color. When Walt needed better cartoonists, he started an art school on his campus and attracted Salvador Dali, Grant Wood (of *American Gothic* fame), and the great Russian filmmaker Sergei Eisenstein. For his risky musical extravaganza *Fantasia,* he attracted Igor Stravinsky, George Balanchine, and, of course, Mickey's co-star in the movie, Leopold Stokowski. Walt was no highbrow—he once said a sculpture tribute to him looked like a "burnt turkey"—but he knew that the greatest intellects and imaginationists of the century could enhance Disney's offerings.

Walt also would have deplored the lack of leadership at AOL and Time Warner. Who was in charge? It was hard to say when the deal was hatched so secretively. It seemed that Levin controlled the levers. Case admitted, "I probably wasn't the right guy to be the chairman of a company with 90,000 employees.... In retrospect, none of us were the right guys."[27] No wonder Case sold about $100 million of stock shortly after the merger. Again, compare this to Walt Disney mortgaging his home and borrowing to pursue Disneyland and ambitious film projects. The sometimes rocky relationship between Roy and Walt ensured that Walt's seemingly outlandish dreams had regular meetings with a balance sheet and an adding machine (and a subtracting machine). The cash-outs by AOL–Time Warner executives did not seem to involve much leadership, except leading shareholders to the slaughterhouse as share prices fell 70 percent.[28] Walt Disney died a very wealthy man, but he did not plunder from his shareholders along the way. Remember, his reigning symbols were a mouse and a duck, not a pig and a wolf.

FINAL DAYS

Walt lived long enough to see Julie Andrews mesmerize audiences as Mary Poppins. Walt had personally negotiated (for almost twenty years!) with the prickly author P. L. Travers, who always seemed grumpy about the movie even after it broke box-office records. The Disney merchandising team was smart enough to line up the National Sugar Company to promote the song "A Spoonful of Sugar." *Mary Poppins* was the first movie I ever saw. Now as a parent, I enjoy taking my kids to the city of London to see where Mr. Banks worked and where the old lady "Feed[s] the Birds." Around the same time that *Mary Poppins* triumphed, Walt saw his idea for the 1964 world's fair enchant the most jaded New Yorkers. It was a stunning boat ride around the world accompanied by the hypnotic tune "It's a Small World."

In 1965, Walt secretly bought up twenty-seven thousand acres of swampland in Orlando, Florida. He was concerned that real estate speculators would sniff out a big deal and drive up prices. He and Roy nimbly orchestrated the deals just in time, and they set the stage for Walt Disney

World, which opened in 1971. Unfortunately, Walt passed away in 1966, a victim of lung cancer.

It would be easy to wrap Walt Disney's image up in the American flag and say he was an American saint who only brought joy to children. Was he Mother Teresa? Hell no! He did bring lots of joy to children, but creating joy in children often meant bringing some tears to his staff. He worked hard and was quick to rip into the inferior work of another cartoonist. No doubt he was sometimes unfair and short-tempered. But he never cheated his chief clients—the children in the audience. Nor did he ever rip off his shareholders. No, he was not Mother Teresa or even Mary Poppins. But the refracted light of America's great creative geniuses, Thomas Edison and Ben Franklin, certainly shone more than a few rays upon him.

Despite a hard and humbling youth and the harsh discipline of a father who could not keep a job, Walt Disney knew, like Edison and Franklin, that he was destined to become a symbol. During the 1920s, while struggling for an advertising agency, Disney was asked by Ubbe Iwwerks to join in a poker game. Walt declined. He said he was too busy toiling on some sketches. A little later, Iwwerks snuck behind his partner. Those sketches? Walt was actually practicing his signature, that simple yet stylish script that instantly tells adults and children that creative fun waits just around the corner, just after the commercial break.

9

Sam Walton: Wal-Mart

A Penny Saved Is a Billion Earned

Bentonville, Arkansas, the headquarters of Wal-Mart, is about the most powerful place in the world today, except for cities with either a stock exchange or a standing army. One man built up this powerhouse, starting with a truck with bald tires. Sam Walton turned his most outstanding personal trait into a conquering business strategy: the man who would make billions out of selling goods cheaply was one cheap so-and-so himself. The CEO and eight of his staffers once shared a room in a dumpy Chicago motel. In 1985, *Forbes* named him the richest man in America with $2.8 billion. After appearing on the front cover, Walton changed. He started doubling up in motel rooms. He still drove his red pickup truck, flew a used putt-putt prop plane, and dragged his bird dogs to work each morning around four o'clock. He needed a cup of coffee at that hour, but he did not get upset if he spilled some brew on his truck's torn and tattered seats.

This humble retailer from Arkansas broke the mold of the clichéd robber baron. He did not amass billions of dollars by cornering the market, ripping off consumers, or violating antitrust rules.[1] Sam Walton grew rich, not by picking customers' pockets, but by stuffing dollars into their pockets and saving them money. It was not easy to get rich on the cheap. Here is a simple way to compare Walton's business plan to those of Sony's

Akio Morita and McDonald's Ray Kroc, two other CEOs in this book who also sold directly to the public:

1. Morita pushed Sony to sell *better* products for *more* money.
2. Kroc led McDonald's to sell *better* products for *less* money.
3. Walton drove Wal-Mart to sell the exact *same* products for *less* money.

Customers crammed into Wal-Marts to buy Crest toothpaste, Oreo cookies, and Fruit Of The Loom underwear for less. Unlike Morita and Kroc, Walton did not control the boxes on the shelf. He could not save money by designing a cheaper tube, charging more for a mintier taste, or making toothbrush bristles vibrate. How could a kid raised in the Great Depression who had to borrow from his father-in-law just to open a five-and-dime shop figure out how to clobber JC Penney, Kmart, and Woolworth? The answer is simple to state and hard to achieve. Thrifty Sam Walton guarded his customers' pockets as closely as his own. The competition did not.

In 1971, mighty Sears collected revenues of nearly $10 billion, two hundred times the size of Sam's revenues that year. What did Sears do with its profits? It built a 110-story monument to itself in downtown Chicago, costing $200 million. From the moment Sears's officers moved into their penthouse suites, market share began to drop. Sears had to mortgage its own building and moved out of the tower in 1995. What did Sam Walton do when he needed a new office for his director of distribution? He punched a hole in a wall and created an attic office above a neighboring shoe store. And what did he buy when his stores passed $10 billion? A new pair of jeans—from Wal-Mart—for about $5.

Sam Walton teaches us about thrift, modesty, and hometown values. But he was more than a walking, talking homily. He taught lessons about supply-chain management that are still the marvel of the savviest business school professor. And unlike many tenured professors who lecture from old notes, Sam Walton woke up early each morning to keep learning and keep improving his ideas and methods. With his limitless energy and spunky spirit, he was convinced that his old pickup truck could stay ahead of his competitors in their million-dollar Gulfstream jets.

THE EARLY YEARS

Sam Walton was born in a farmhouse in Kingfisher, Oklahoma, on March 29, 1918. He could have grown up an Okie trapped in the dust bowl and the Great Depression. John Steinbeck's Tom Joad starts in Oklahoma and ends up escaping with his family to California, where he organizes unions. Why didn't Sam turn into Tom Joad, instead of a billionaire who confounded union organizers? Like so many Okies, Sam's father, Thomas, worked hard tilling land that was settled under the Homestead Act. Like so many Okies, Thomas failed. Instead of loading up the truck and rolling farther west like the Joads, Thomas Walton signed up to work for his half brother, a mortgage agent in Missouri.[2] If Thomas and his wife, Nan, had turned left, rather than right toward Missouri, Wal-Mart might never have happened. Sam was just five when the family left Oklahoma, first for Springfield, and then in his teenage years for Columbia.

Sam did not have much in common with his father, whom he described as lacking the ambition to start a business.[3] Moreover, Thomas did not believe in taking on debt. Avoiding debt might have been wise of Thomas in the pre–Depression years, but Sam thought his father too risk-averse. Later in his career, as his stores were taking off, Sam's daughter Alice cried to her friend: "I don't know what we're going to do. My daddy owes so much money, and he won't quit opening stores."[4]

Sam did admire certain traits of Thomas. His father was an enthusiastic wheeler-dealer who would trade for horses, mules, cattle, and cars. Sam never knew what his father would come home with or without. Thomas was also a sharp-eyed negotiator who had an instinct for the other guy's breaking point. He would haggle and dicker until one second before his counterpart would storm off in a huff. Sam did not think that he inherited this talent, but he insisted that the buyers who worked for him display such skills.

Sam spent some time with his father's business and found it heart-wrenching. As a mortgage agent in the 1930s, Sam's father repossessed hundreds of farms. Sam learned it was a whole lot better to create wealth than to search for survivors in an economic wreck.

If Sam had one personal regret about his growing up in the Walton household, it was this: his parents constantly squabbled with each other, creating turmoil for Sam and his younger brother Bud. Sam's mother may have been more of a role model than Thomas. Nan pursued inventive business ideas. When Sam was in high school, Nan decided to start a dairy business with Sam. He would milk the cows, she would bottle it, and then he would deliver it after his football practice. Best of all, she skimmed the cream and turned it into ice cream.

Sam was a popular kid, and though he claimed not to be a gifted athlete, he managed to lead Hickman High School in Columbia to state championships in basketball and football. He was a wiry kid of average height with a sharp beak. Sam quarterbacked the football team, which never lost a game. Though Sam claimed he was not a great student either, he managed to make the honor roll and was named "Most Versatile Boy" and president of the student council. How did he do it? He got up earlier and stayed later than anybody else: competitive juices flowed through his blood. As a child he bet his Boy Scout friends that he would achieve Eagle Scout rank before they did. He won. At age thirteen, he became the youngest Eagle Scout in the history of Missouri.

Here is a good test to see if a child is CEO material: give him a newspaper route and then watch. Most children will hurl the morning paper from their bicycle, throw down the empty satchel, and then head for their next activity. Sam Walton, like David Sarnoff, figured out how to turn the paper route into a business, farming out new routes to other youngsters, drawing up a payroll, and building market share. Nothing was a throwaway job for Sam. He kept his paper route through high school and college, earning over $4,000 a year, a hefty paycheck in the late 1930s.

At the University of Missouri, Columbia, Sam, who studied economics and joined the ROTC, developed a discipline that he would later teach to Wal-Mart employees. He discovered a breathtakingly simple "secret" to campus popularity: say hello to people walking down the sidewalk before they spoke to you. He soon knew the name of every janitor, and every student knew him. At Wal-Mart, he called this the "Ten-Foot Rule," the outer limit of what you might call the "radius of friendliness." Before long, Sam was featured in a fraternity magazine under the headline "Hustler Walton." In the profile the word "hustler" was a compliment, not the name of a pool-hall shark or a magazine.

If Sam had more money, he might have followed his dream and attended the Wharton School of Business after graduating college in 1940. But if he had had the money in 1940, would he still have ended up as America's richest man in 1985? Sam turned his charm and energy into job offers from JC Penney and Sears. He went for the "cash," that is James Cash Penney, and reported to Des Moines, Iowa, for management training, at a monthly salary of $75. The founder and legend himself showed Sam how to wrap a gift package. Sam watched the tycoon's hands manage to wrap the box using less paper and string than Sam thought possible. A Woody Allen character, on his deathbed, delivered a vital piece of advice to his huddled and perplexed children: "Save string." It might not have worked in the comedy sketch, but it worked well enough for JC Penney.

Sam was even more inspired by a JC Penney manager and trainer named Duncan Majors, who hosted his staff at his home every Sunday to talk and teach business over Ping-Pong and cards. Those Sundays taught Sam that any future employee of his would have to work on weekends, too. For most people, weekend work depleted morale. Sam thought the opposite and tried to persuade Wal-Mart managers that weekend meetings boosted spirits. In his Wal-Mart years, Sam would arrive at 4 a.m. on Sundays, check the sales data, duck out for church, throw money on the collection plate, and then dart back to the office. While his wife, Helen, expressed dismay about forcing employees to work weekends, one of Sam's confidants said her admonishments "went in one ear and out the other."[5] His weekend imperative created an easy dividing line to separate the managers he wanted to keep from those who should move on to more cushy storefronts.

With gold stars and letters pinned to his chest for sports, academics, and ROTC, in 1942, self-confident Sam figured he would go to war and earn stars from the U.S. military. His brother Bud served as a Navy bomber pilot, helping to liberate Okinawa. But for the first time, Sam failed in something he wanted to do. It was not for lack of trying or talent. Army doctors informed him that he had a minor heart defect. There would be no combat, no heroism, no sacrifice for his country. He watched other boys march off to Europe and the Pacific. Yes, some would die; but the boys who stayed home suffered with a stigma they could not easily shake. Instead of taking orders from Eisenhower or Nimitz, Sam spent dreary days at a gunpowder plant near Tulsa and guarding POWs in California. The effervescent boy who had bounded up and down basketball courts and football fields was now a young adult, dragged down by his physical predicament. At the same time, he faced an emotional trauma: after bickering for year, his parents separated, scarring even his memories of childhood. The country was at war, Sam could not help, and he could hardly confide in his troubled parents.

After months of gloom, he pulled out of this glum phase when he met his future wife, Helen Alice Robson, while bowling near Tulsa. Helen was the daughter of L. S. Robson, a prominent lawyer and banker who would become a role model for Sam. Robson was "one of the most persuasive individuals I had ever met.... I said to myself: maybe I will be as successful as he is someday," Sam later wrote.[6] For about two years, they moved around the country, as the Army shifted Sam from one dull job to another. Helen was pretty, affluent, and levelheaded. She knew how to nurture Sam's ambitions, but she had the backbone to rein him in, too. Here are two examples of her good sense. Sam wanted to own his own retail store, but Helen insisted on two criteria. First, she did not want to live in the same town as her prominent father, for that would overshadow Sam. Second, she told Sam that she did not want to live in a big city. After moving with him sixteen times in two years, she knew what kind of life she wanted for her family. It was not in Chicago or other retail capitals. She believed in small-town commerce. This turned out to be the secret of Sam's success. Had he launched his retail career in Chicago, Wal-Mart would not have come to be.

FIRST TRY

Sam and Helen ended up in a little Arkansas town called Newport, surrounded by more livestock than people. After the Great Depression, the average person owned few more assets than the average hog anyway. Per capita income was just a few hundred dollars per year. But twenty-seven-year-old Sam took pride in his five-thousand-square-foot Ben Franklin variety store overlooking the railroad tracks near the town square. As a Ben Franklin franchisee, Sam eagerly attended training school in Arkadelphia, where he learned of nifty accounting tools like "Beat Yesterday's" books, which allowed a franchisee to compare this year's sales to last year's on a day-by-day basis. He felt exhilarated to lead his own team for the first time since he stopped playing basketball. The exhilaration wore off when he realized that he had been suckered into the deal. The prior franchisee had done a miserable job, had turned off customers, and had turned in sales numbers less than half the level of the competing store across the street, a Sterling variety store. Even worse, Sam learned that the franchisee nut, 5 percent of revenues, was far above what anyone had ever been buffaloed into paying. Furthermore, the Ben Franklin group required him to buy 80 percent of his merchandise from it. He had signed not just a contract, but also a vise. Helen was pregnant, and Sam had too much pride to back out of the deal. He was stuck in a town of five thousand mostly low-income people, wondering how he could get some cash into his cash registers.

Sam had to escape the vise. He could not survive simply by selling the same old merchandise at the same price as his predecessor. In this vise, he taught himself lessons that would revolutionize retail stores. Sam needed more stuff on the shelf at lower prices. He began checking out other stores and suppliers and learned that he could access merchandise at prices 25 percent less than what Ben Franklin was charging him. Though Sam's franchise contract required that he buy 80 percent, he looked for wiggle room and defined "80 percent" rather loosely. (Remember how one of the secrets of Ray Kroc's success was not exploiting his franchisees.) At first, suppliers refused to sell to him, fearing that Ben Franklin would retaliate. So he would drive his rickety car to offbeat manufacturers in Tennessee or even New York City, dragging a trailer behind him. He would fill the trailer with shirts, panties, kitchen gadgets, anything that he could buy low, stack high, and sell cheap. He sometimes took circuitous dirt roads to avoid weighing stations that would cost him precious dollars. The supply-chain revolution, which fills bookshelves at business schools, began with a rickety car weaving its way around the South and East, looking as sophisticated as a swap meet at a dog track.

KNOW YOUR COMPETITOR BETTER THAN
HE KNOWS HIMSELF

Sam's greatest asset was his unstoppable drive to learn from everybody. He began to chat up customers and competitors. He spent as much time across the street at the Sterling store as he did at his own Ben Franklin. He took notes on the prices, the displays, and the signage. His competitive juices overflowed. Remember, this was the boy who never lost a football game. He overheard that the Sterling store had run out of a popular new line of rayon panties for ladies, which sold for 30¢ a pair. Sam jumped into his car and raced to Sterling's distributor in Little Rock. He snatched up all the remaining panties, leaving the Sterling manager pantyless. When he heard that the Sterling owner was thinking of buying out the lease from the Kroger grocery store next door, Sam rushed over to Hot Springs and begged the landlady to lease him the space. She did, and Sam got to expand rather than Sterling.

Sam never stopped visiting his competitors. He even had the nerve to interrogate their clerks, without necessarily revealing his identity: "How often do you reorder? If you order on Tuesday, when do they deliver?" Even after he launched Wal-Mart in 1962, Sam could be found crawling on his hands and knees, sliding back the panels under the display racks of other people's stores, counting their shirts and checking sizes. He carried a blue spiral notebook and recorded his observations. His staffers picked up on his methods and sometimes crawled through the trash of their competitors looking for price tags.[7] Once while Sam was speaking into a tape recorder at a Price Club warehouse in San Diego, a hulking security guard abducted him and confiscated his tape. Sam, somewhat sheepishly, wrote a letter to founder Sol Price's son asking for his tape back.

Sam liked to visit with customers, too, always asking for their advice. He could not afford fancy marketing, so he appealed to customers like a barker at a county fair. He rolled a buttery-smelling popcorn machine onto the sidewalk to draw people from across the street. As discussed in the chapter on Estee Lauder, today, the Cinnabon company entices mall shoppers by pumping intoxicating aromas into the air. With the success of his popcorn machine, Sam convinced the local bank to lend him $1,800 for a soft-serve ice cream machine, another novelty for Newport. (In a little bit of sibling antagonism, Sam made his brother Bud clean the machine, though Bud hated dairy foods. When they were children, Sam used to squirt him while milking the cows.) After just a year in Newport, running his first store, revenues jumped by 45 percent. The newcomer with the popcorn and ice-cream concessions quickly jumped into community affairs, heading up the chamber of commerce and helping to lead the Rotary Club and the local Presbyterian church. The glum memories of his World War II wandering had faded away. Within five years, he had almost quadrupled his sales and built the most successful variety store in Arkansas and in any bordering state.

But just as Sam looked like the prince of Newport, the wheels flew off his popcorn stand and disaster struck. Remember the deal he was suckered into when he opened the Newport store? He had not read the fine print. His five-year lease did not grant him the right to renew. The landlord of the Ben Franklin store admired Sam's success so much that he decided to give his son a crack at it. He figured now that Sam had done all the hard work to prove the high value of the property, it was the perfect launching pad for his own son. Sam and Helen were crushed. Sam felt betrayed, belittled, and "sick to my stomach. I couldn't believe it was happening to me. It really was like a nightmare."[8] He felt like an "exile," forced to pack his bags in search of another start. Newport was their home; they were raising three children. It's tougher to start anew when you have debts and children and are leaving behind a store whose floorboards were stained with your sweat.

In the chapter of Walt Disney I discussed the terrible emotional blow Disney felt when he discovered that he did not hold the contractual rights to his first cartoon creation, Oswald the Rabbit, and could not stop Universal Studios from swiping him. Newport was Sam's Oswald. And Wal-Mart would be his Mickey Mouse.

BENTONVILLE BOUND

Bentonville, Arkansas, may feel like the middle of nowhere, but it's the center of the universe for those folks trying to stretch the spare change in their purses. Wal-Mart's revenues make up about 2 percent of U.S. gross domestic product. Retail suppliers around the world love and hate Bentonville, headquarters of Wal-Mart. They love the idea of getting their stuff onto the thousands of miles of Wal-Mart's shelves. They hate the idea of going to the former two-horse town, which even today does not offer many more amenities than when Sam arrived in 1950. They especially hate the process of sitting down in a stark conference room at Wal-Mart and trying to negotiate with the most famous tightwads in American history.

Bentonville did not wow the Waltons when they first saw it. Helen called it a "sad-looking town" with just three thousand people and some chickens. In comparison, the dreary military postings she had endured did not look so bad. But Sam found two things to like. First, good bird hunting (not the chickens). Second, a humble store on the town square that had some potential. It was so humble that it had earned about one-tenth as much money as the Newport store he had left behind. Sam would learn from his mistakes, though. He signed a ninety-nine-year lease. And he avoided the viselike contract he'd had with the Ben Franklin suppliers. Here he could invent the discount store, which he called Walton's Five and Dime. Of course there had been five-and-dime stores long before Sam Walton. Back in 1931 Tin Pan Alley songster Harry Warren had a huge hit with his song "I Found a Million Dollar Baby in a Five and Ten Cent Store." But in the 1950s, Sam began rapidly introducing innovations that allowed customers to get bargains and the owner to get rich.

Self-Service

In 1950, most variety stores looked like Sam Drucker's general store on the television sitcoms *Green Acres* and *Petticoat Junction*. The goods were kept behind counters and so were the cashiers. Shoppers did not have much access to the shelves. In many stores, they would pay for, say, shirts at one counter and soap at another. Sam Walton decided to give the shoppers more room and to centralize the cashiers in one part of the store. By putting the cashiers together, he gave shoppers more time to shop and let them spend less time standing in line. No longer isolated, cashiers also felt less tempted to dip into the till. Self-service boosted sales and cut "shrinkage," that is, theft. Walton's Five and Dime was not literally the first "self-service" variety store in America. It was the third—Sam slept on an overnight bus from Bentonville to Minnesota in order to take notes on numbers one and two.

Novel Goods and Knockoffs

By definition, a five-and-dime store cannot pay top dollar. Sam would search out novel goods, buy them cheap, and then surround them with festive balloons. With great fanfare, he sold bins of zori sandals until nearly everybody in landlocked Bentonville was walking around like an L.A. beachcomber. When the hula hoop craze struck, he realized that his store could not afford the real deal from Wham-O. So he and a colleague secured plastic hose of the same diameter from a factory and started fusing together fake hula hoops in an attic. They sold a ton. Even his advertisements were knockoffs! Rather than hire a graphic artist for newspapers and flyers, Sam would sit on the floor with a stack of old newspapers and attack them with a pair of scissors, cutting out pictures from another store's ads. If Sam had cases of, for instance, Pennzoil motor oil on hand, he would cut out a picture of a Pennzoil can and paste it on a paper. Then he would scribble his price next to it. He turned "cut and paste" into a tactic that would have incited Madison Avenue executives to attack him with pitchforks—had they been paying any attention to this hick in the Ozarks.

Sam would go anywhere to learn about making his stores better or to access better or cheaper products. The man willing to ride an overnight bus to Minnesota before the days of reliable heaters was the right man to lead retailers into the globalized economy. He opened stores in Fayetteville, Arkansas, and then outside of Kansas City. In 1957, he bought himself a putt-putt airplane that could go only one hundred miles per hour and had once lost engine power while circling Fort Smith, Arkansas. He got a deal on the plane. Bud hated the plane, convinced that Sam was already the "world's worst driver" on land. To say the least, the plane was not the extravagance of an egotistic CEO. Sam flew himself around the South and Midwest to identify promising locations for his stores. From the sky, he could spot new housing developments, roads, and utility lines. He would get excited when he spotted new terrain and a Caterpillar earthmover. Once he was circling Cullman, Alabama, when he spied some chicken coops and rolling hills: "This is it!" he announced. "It looks just like northwest Arkansas." [9] During his career, Sam would buy eighteen airplanes—none of them new. Let the Sears guys pay for depreciation on a new plane. Of course, he knew Sears men would never buy a cheap propeller job.

WAL-MART RISES

By the late 1950s, Sam was operating a string of small and successful five-and-dimes. But a new phrase began creeping into his vocabulary: "discount store." He jumped in his sensible 1953 Plymouth and drove around the country inspecting big stores that were cropping up just outside of large cities: Two Guys, Korvette, Zayre, and Fed-Mart, Sol Price's store. He began to map out a whole new strategy that baffled his bankers and changed the world. The strategy had three key insights.

Small Towns Are a Sweet Spot

Each time that Sam drove his Plymouth and trailer of goods through the countryside looking for bargains, he noticed that he had more company on the road. The number of cars in the U.S. had exploded after World War II, which later inspired President Eisenhower's Federal-Aid Highway Act of 1956.[10] More cars and highways inspired new shopping centers outside of the downtown areas, with their numbers multiplying from eight at the end of World War II to nearly four thousand in 1960. He noticed, however, that the big players in retail discounting avoided small towns. Sam lived in what coastal snobs call flyover country. He spotted a billion-dollar opportunity. Nobody was interested in building big stores to serve his kind of customer. But big stores could thrive in small towns if they attracted other folks to hop in their cars and drive over from another small town. Just as Ray Kroc saw McDonald's beating out White Castle because

America's car culture gave people an excuse to drive a few miles, Sam saw that cheap prices could get shoppers to rev up their engines, too. It took decades for major retailers to catch on. Their New York–based management teams scoffed at Sam, as if they were watching comedian Jeff Foxworthy tell redneck jokes: "You might be a redneck if you think a quarter horse is a ride out in front of Wal-Mart; you might be a redneck if the biggest city you've ever been to is Wal-Mart." Sam Walton snickered at the city-slicker retailers.

Scissors Economy

In my 1999 book *Market Shock,* I introduced the term "scissors economy" to describe how middlemen were being snipped out of nearly every transaction. Do you really need a stockbroker? Or a travel agent? The scissors economy drives down prices for consumers. Sam understood the scissors economy and had a very sharp blade. In 1962, he created the sixteen-thousand-square-foot Wal-Mart in Bentonville and basically forbade middlemen from walking through the doors. He purchased straight from the manufacturer and was able to slash prices by 25–50 percent. He even economized on the name, choosing "Wal-Mart" in part because it had just seven letters, which required less neon than "Walton's 5-10." Sam admitted he was also influenced by Sol Price's succinct "Fed-Mart" name.[11] He also posted signs that said "We Sell for Less" and "Satisfaction Guaranteed."

The big-city folk thought the idea was preposterous, while a prominent southern retailer thought he was a "bush-league variety store merchant who possessed neither the finances nor the experience necessary."[12] Even Sam's own brother Bud initially refused to invest, finally coughing up about 3 percent of the funds needed. Through the years, Bud played the sober-minded, straight-man accountant role that Roy Disney did for Walt, consistently trying to rein in expectations and fanciful plans. (Recall that Roy Disney opposed Disneyland itself.) With few investors available, Sam and Helen Walton decided to gamble with the deed to their house and anything else they could get a lien on. It proved to be a pretty good bet.

Small-town folks began to flood into the store, realizing that by stretching their dollars, Sam was lifting their standard of living. Obviously he did not do this because he wanted to be the Albert Schweitzer of Arkansas. It was in his own self-interest. But as Adam Smith taught, "It is not from the benevolence of the butcher, the brewer, or the baker, that we can expect our dinner, but from their regard to their own interest."[13] No one left Wal-Mart with an empty cart, and in its first year, Wal-Mart's cash registers rang to the tune of $1 million.

In 1964, Sam opened his second store, a concrete barn next to a former cattle corral. One of Wal-Mart's future CEOs, David Glass, drove to the opening and observed "the worst retail store I had ever seen. Sam brought a couple of trucks of watermelons in and stacked them on the sidewalk. He had a donkey ride out in the parking lot. It was about 115 degrees, and the watermelons began to pop, and the donkey began to do what donkeys do, and it all mixed together and ran all over the parking lot. And when you went inside the store, the mess just continued, having been tracked all over the floor."[14]

Despite the stench and the businessman's sullied view, the folks loved it anyway and snapped up socks, shirts, and lightbulbs for 20 percent less than they had ever paid before. Sam refused to let anyone beat him on price. Kmart came to Little Rock; Sam dropped the price of Crest toothpaste to just 6¢ a tube. With "everyday low prices," Wal-Mart did not have to waste much money advertising. Word of mouth did the trick. Even in the 1990s—long after Sam stopped cutting and pasting his own ads—Wal-Mart still spent at least 2 percent less than competitors on marketing.[15] His managers opted for splashy, homegrown gimmicks like shopping cart bingo, a mound of hay for kids to jump into, and a shopping cart drill team in Nebraska. When Sam opened his third store, he slashed the price of antifreeze to $1 a gallon and watched as a massive crowd poured through the doors, frightening the fire department, which closed the doors, as if containing a riot. The cashiers were overwhelmed, and Sam took out a tackle box to help make change.

Sam helped create the scissors economy both by snipping out the middleman and by snipping excess fat from every other place. He hired buyers who were so frugal, they probably wore shoes with the socks sewn into them. Sam trained them to negotiate, not only on store products, but also on the cost of temporary services, electricity, and drug-screening services. Sam refused to meet with the CEO of Procter & Gamble because Sam refused to spring for the hotel, which would cost over $100 per night. The P&G CEO called Sam and fibbed, telling him that he had found a $59-a-night joint. In truth, P&G secretly picked up half of Sam's bill.[16]

Control the Supply Chain

Sam also applied his scissors to the supply chain, inspecting every link that connected the shopper to the manufacturer. He hung out with the truckers in the back lot, bringing them doughnuts at dawn. From them he learned about delivery snags, backups, and even the morale of managers. Since his profits depended on selling so much stuff and rapidly turning it over, Sam decided he did not want to depend on someone else's delivery schedule. Other stores waited for a manufacturer's truck to pull in. Sam wanted his own trucks. He had loaded and driven enough delivery trucks to see that vehicles dedicated to Wal-Mart would haul more speedily and have no other priority than to serve his customers. How else could he know that a delivery truck was not first stopping at Kmart? Or taking a midafternoon break at a saloon or truck stop? In 2006, Wal-Mart announced it would double the fuel efficiency of its trucks, by investing in lower-friction axles and tires, for example.[17] Sam Walton built massive warehouses to serve his stores. After the 1973 oil crisis, he insisted that no store be built more than twelve hours from a warehouse. Competing retailers built warehouses near existing stores. Sam turned the logic on its head. He grew so focused on the supply chain that he would build a giant warehouse, then plant stores around it. He refused to build any stores that would start out inefficient. He avoided rushing into cities, instead opting for a shrewder strategy. He bought suburban properties in a ring outside of the cities, figuring that populations would eventually push out to him. "Sooey! Come and get it!" he cried to the city slickers who had snubbed him. His supply-chain model chopped out inefficient inventory space. While other stores used up to 25 percent of their floor space to stack stuff that the customer never saw, Sam's inventories took up just 10 percent.

His ratio of sales to floor space clobbered those of Sears and Penney, even though they sold more expensive stuff. Today, Wal-Mart's distribution centers exceed one million square feet, large enough for twenty football fields. Wal-Mart's ratio of sales per square foot equals $438, about 20 percent more than that of the admirable and attractive Nordstrom.[18] There is no room for a tuxedoed pianist at Wal-Mart.

TECHNO-RETAILER

My first day on my first job, my boss gave me a gun. Now, I would like to swagger and sound like Clint Eastwood protecting the common folk, but I have to admit it was a plastic labeling gun. I worked in a supermarket, and my job was to squeeze the trigger so the gun would spit out "$.49" stickers on the yogurt containers. Nobody does that anymore. Bar codes and scanners do it. Likewise, we would occasionally close the doors and hang in the window a sign that now belongs in the Smithsonian: "Closed for Inventory." We liked it because we would get paid double time on a Sunday to count toothpaste tubes. Nobody does that anymore either. Sam Walton did more to cut out label guns and "Closed for Inventory" signs than anyone else in America.

Sam was hardly a computer whiz, and he sure fought his vice presidents when they wanted to buy supercomputers at retail prices. Nonetheless, he led the charge into UPC scanners and bar codes to make his warehouses and stores more efficient. He authorized a central control system in Bentonville that allowed him to maintain consistent temperatures in Wal-Marts across the country. In 1985, Wal-Mart inaugurated a Hughes satellite, which allowed Sam to speak to all of his thousands of employees simultaneously. The McKinsey Company consulting firm estimated that innovations at Wal-Mart alone contributed over 10 percent of the productivity burst in the U.S. economy in the 1990s.[19] In the post–Sam Walton years, Wal-Mart has stayed on the cutting edge. In 2005, the company ordered its suppliers to begin placing radio frequency ID (RFID) tags on their goods, which would enable Wal-Mart to reduce inventory further. Using RFID antennas, "smart shelves" would automatically reorder a box of detergent when a customer tosses one into his cart.

MANAGEMENT STYLE

Former employees have characterized Sam's style in numerous ways, including management by "walking round," "flying around," and "looking
over your shoulder." Though he would visit stores, demand to see the financial books, and peer into every aspect of the store's business, managers
did not see him as a brutish autocrat. He liked informality and liked to be
called Sam. Those who were intimidated called him "Mr. Sam." Like
Thomas Watson Sr., he liked pep rallies, and he wrote a monthly column
for the *Wal-Mart World* newspaper. He would hop onto a table and lead
cheers, often at the expense of competitors: "We've got what it takes to
be number one. So watch out Kmart, here we come!" In 1984, he dared
his team to achieve an 8 percent profit level. After they beat the mark, he
fulfilled his end of the deal by doing a hula dance on Wall Street while
wearing a grass skirt. He did not realize that his colleagues had arranged
for worldwide television coverage and a troupe of professional hula dancers to embarrass him. With revenues of $5 billion, Sam was a long way
from fusing plastic knockoff hula hoops in his attic.

Sam was always looking for a tidbit of advice from a stock boy or a
shopper. A stock boy who worked in the sporting goods section had
come back from a fishing trip with a bandage on his thumb. He had
"caught" his finger with his fishhook while casting. From this accident
came the idea to sell bandages next to the fishing tackle, not just in the
health and beauty aid aisle. In another example, Wal-Mart wanted to
boost its sales to hunters who frequented the sporting goods department.
Executives at Wal-Mart phoned Hormel Foods, suggesting they come up
with a "snack that it could place alongside the rifles and fishing rods.
Within weeks 'Spamouflage'—Spam in camouflage cans—was blowing
out the doors of 760 rural Wal-Marts."[20]

Perhaps the most impressive aspect of Sam Walton's career was his
refusal to morph into someone else. Whenever a man or woman hits the
big time, there is a gravitational pull toward behaving like others in the
elite crowd. How often does a maverick, muckraking freshman congressman burst into Washington, D.C., only to be seduced by kind words from
the *Washington Post* or a cushy seat at the Kennedy Center? Before long
the rough edges are smoothed, the Spamouflage goes to the back of the

pantry, and the Georgetown cocktail circuiteers toast the roughneck for "growing" in the job. Not Sam. He could not be smoothed, seduced, or shaken from his focus on the bottom line. He grew angry when he walked through an employee parking lot and saw a Jaguar. When he noticed the owner of Gibson's Discount Stores speeding by in a Cadillac, Sam knew that Wal-Mart would triumph. When other companies wasted money on egos and paid big bucks to place their corporate names on stadiums, he sneered. Back in the late 1990s, during a single week, I found myself in Nashville and flew over Adelphia Stadium, then St. Louis and TWA Stadium, then Houston and Enron Field—all bankrupt companies that squandered their shareholders' money. When I traveled to Baltimore, I could find PSI Net Stadium, but I could no longer find the company's shares in the stock listings.

Sam Walton did not want a trophy building, a trophy car, or, for that matter, a trophy wife. He wanted only to fight for his customers. In 1982, at the age of sixty-four, Sam was starting feel run-down. For any other man who had worked nonstop, that might seem natural. But Sam's weather-beaten face looked excessively pale. He was diagnosed with hairy cell leukemia, a blood cancer that destroys white blood cells. It was time to fight for his life, not just his customers' wallets. He found the best doctors in Houston and opted to become an experimental interferon patient, administering shots to himself several times a week. The leukemia began to retreat, and he jumped back into the fray, building stores, cutting prices, and taking pride in the many workers who were able to turn their shares of Wal-Mart into retirement nest eggs. Alas, the leukemia returned seven years later, and in 1992, Sam passed away, just a few weeks after President George H. W. Bush and his wife, Barbara, flew to Bentonville to award him the Presidential Medal of Freedom. Sam declared it the best day of his life, but then reconsidered. The greatest days of his life, he said, were spent flying around the heartland, rummaging through stores, trading stories with his truckers, and chatting with his loyal customers. Among his final visitors at the Little Rock hospital was the manager of the local Wal-Mart. Sam wanted to know how the week was stacking up.

SHOPPING IS OUR NATIONAL SPORT: COSTCO

Sam Walton was not an arrogant egotist; he admitted that he "borrowed" lots of ideas. Milton Berle, who was known as the "thief of bad gags," once said, "I know a good joke when I steal one." Sam frequently mentioned Sol Price, whose Price Club later merged into Costco. Costco has transformed shopping into an adventure sport, packed with surprises and savings. I have to admit I am a card-carrying member of the Costco Club, along with forty-eight million others. Costco receives my annual "membership fee" and invests it, earning the float. In return, I believe their claim that they do not mark up any prices by more than 14 percent. Like Sam Walton, Costco CEO Jim Sinegal wants customers to leave his stores bragging about the bargains they pocketed. Like Sam Walton, Sinegal does not provide a lush setting or entrancing pianists. Harsh lights, cement floors, and high shelves greet shoppers. There are no changing rooms. I once saw a man sneak behind a tower of toilet-paper rolls to strip down to his boxer shorts and try on trousers. Costco offers no express lane, although if it did, it would have to be marked "100 items or less." Yet I and others keep coming back. Costco has improved on Sam's model, though, by pushing quality so high. Costco's own Kirkland brand often nabs top prizes from testers at *Consumer Reports*. Costco shoppers rave about the quality of meats and the size of the breasts of their rotisserie chickens. Owners of small restaurants will buy Costco's cheap rotisserie chickens and then resell them, serving them from their own kitchens. When I needed an optometrist, I asked myself, "Where do I get my veal chops?" Costco. Well, if I trust them with the meat I eat, I could trust them with my eyes. You can see how deep the enthusiasm runs. Sam would be envious and disappointed that his warehouse club, Sam's Club, lags behind Costco today in winning the "carts and minds of shoppers."

While just a few years ago, Wal-Mart seemed an unbeatable beast that had gobbled up and spat out Toys "R" Us, Caldor, and others, Costco proves a store can survive against Wal-Mart. So does Target, which offers "cheap chic," as well as sharp-elbowed specialty stores like Best Buy and Bed, Bath & Beyond. Wal-Mart stores do not necessarily have the resources or know-how to offer specialized advice on a wide range of products. Further, Sam's tricks and lessons have trickled down and up to more upscale stores. That's a tribute to Sam, even if it makes Wal-Mart shares less applauded on the New York Stock Exchange.

There's a corollary to Wal-Mart's newly noticed vulnerability. The scare stories and sheer hatred of Wal-Mart may recede. The nostalgic yearning for small-town storefront proprietors may not really jibe with reality. Did Horace Vandergelder from Thornton Wilder's *The Matchmaker* provide full health insurance to Cornelius Hack, his slow-witted skittish clerk? Did Cornelius Hack ever have a chance of rising to upper management or getting a retirement plan? How long did his customers have to wait for a popular newfangled appliance or vital medicine? Some years ago my brother was serving as legal counsel to a small town near the Jersey Shore. A bitter debate broke out at a planning board meeting among those for and against a new set of stores. Finally, an old man stood up and pleaded, "I just want to be able to buy a pair of socks here in Jackson."

NEW IDEAS ON CRUISING:
TED ARISON AND CARNIVAL

While Sam Walton was building a miracle money machine in the heartland, an ambitious man named Ted Arison was struggling to do the same at sea. Ted did not mind struggles. He was amiable, optimistic, and fearless as a businessman. He learned his fearlessness as a boy in Yugoslavia. The Nazis were on a rampage, rolling over the country in tanks while the Luftwaffe pounded Belgrade. With moments to spare, Ted and his family rushed to the airport and found seats on the last rusty plane out. It was headed to Haifa, in Palestine, where the Arisons had roots. After escaping the Nazis, young Ted was not willing to sit back and simply watch the war from a patio on the Mediterranean. After all, the Italians had already bombed Tel Aviv and Britain's naval base in Haifa. Ted lied about his age and at sixteen signed up for the British Army's Jewish Brigade. Churchill had sent a missive to Franklin Roosevelt arguing that "the Jews . . . of all races have the right to strike at the Germans as a recognizable body." Soon Ted was back in the deadly triangle of Italy, Yugoslavia, and Austria, attacking German posts and smuggling Holocaust escapees to safety in Palestine. After the Allies vanquished the Nazis, Ted joined the Israeli

Army, serving as a lieutenant colonel in the 1948 War of Independence. After surviving these bloody challenges, Ted probably thought civilian life would be easy. But that was before he tried to build the modern cruise line industry.

Ted Arison's vision and strategies often recall Sam Walton's, though their personal histories could not have been more different if one had come down from space on Sputnik. Ted was a courtly man, with large hands, who often said he wanted to be a concert pianist. His family never heard him play a piano (though he ultimately founded the New World Symphony). Ted was a good bluffer. Like Sam Walton, he got off to a rough start. By 1966, he had started and lost two air cargo businesses. When he heard that a Miami-based cruise operator was having trouble managing his business, Ted called the operator and offered to manage the ships. "He was basically bluffing," his son Micky said, "because he in fact knew nothing about the passenger cruise business." [21] Ted flew to Miami and began to operate the ships and obtain passenger bookings. Then the ships disappeared. They were repossessed. Ted had passengers, but no ships. All he needed was a vessel—which is like saying all I need to win a Cy Young Award is an arm that throws a baseball one hundred miles per hour. Except for that arm, I'm ready. In despair, Ted was flipping through travel magazines when he spied a photo of a brand-new ship called the *Sunward,* which was stranded in Norway. The owners had planned to use it to ferry Brits to a summer holiday in Gibraltar. Unfortunately, Generalissimo Franco, who wanted to "liberate" Gibraltar from the British, got in the way of the tourists. Ted called up the Norwegian owners and persuaded them to send the ship to Miami, where he could turn the *Sunward* into a cruise ship for Americans vacationing in the Bahamas. My family have been cruise line buffs since my grandparents cruised to Havana on their honeymoon in 1929. I remember seeing the *Sunward* when I was a little boy visiting Miami. At night, its lights shone like a circus tent, and by day, the sleek lines set it apart from the old tugs docked at the pier, like a Corvette among Ford Fairlanes.

Ted ran the *Sunward* and later its sister ships until 1971, when he fell into a bitter financial dispute with the Norwegians. They accused him of keeping the "float" on passenger tickets paid in advance; he accused them of sabotaging his profits by buying extra engine parts and deck chairs, and then hurling them into the bay. Nobody won the contract dispute. But like Sam Walton, who lost his first successful store because of a lease, Ted found himself lost at sea without a boat.

LET THE PEOPLE CRUISE

In the next decade, Ted would rise again, but this time with a coherent strategy that would turn him and his extraordinarily able son Micky into billionaires. First some background on the industry. As any viewer of *Titanic* knows, early-twentieth-century cruise liners were made for two types of people: the Cary Grant types cradling cognac upstairs in the salon, and the huddled, stinking refugees stuck in steerage. Like Sam Walton, Ted believed that there was a massive market to be served among the masses of middle-income Americans. People who earned average incomes were, to the traditional cruise line industry, the equivalent of "flyover country." To Ted, they were unserved and untapped. Let the other companies pursue the swells who owned tuxedos for formal night; Ted was happy to attract the guy who celebrated formal night by taking off his cap with the Caterpillar logo on it.

To capture this market, he announced to his family that he had bought "an incredible ship," which he called the *Mardi Gras,* to begin a new cruise line. Micky assessed the ship, which had sailed for eleven years as the *Empress of Canada:* "It was such a piece of crap. It was dirty, in horrendous shape. I thought my father had lost his mind." [22] Nonetheless, Ted poured millions of dollars into refurbishing it, all the while advertising it as the "Flagship of the Golden Fleet." Never mind that it was not gold and there was no fleet!

For its maiden voyage, Ted and Micky stood next to the captain. As is the custom, new ships (even rebadged ships) draw lots of attention from photographers, industry watchers, and enthusiasts. The *Mardi Gras* dwarfed the cruise ships docked nearby. Then the ship began to pull away from the pier, headed to San Juan, Puerto Rico. Ted felt proud that this ship could not be lost in a contract dispute. Then the ship turned toward the sea. It was a beautiful sight, floating on the turquoise water.

"Oh, my God!" A scream from the bridge as people started sliding and bumping into one another on deck.

The ship ran aground on a sandbar, and the propellers began spraying sand, seaweed, and water into the air. As the leviathan lay beached, onlookers showed up, including camera crews from television stations and a photographer from the *New York Times*. For twenty-eight hours, Ted endured the humiliating sight of the launch of Carnival Cruise Lines. Compared to this, Sam Walton was lucky; Sam's famous botched grand opening involved only burst watermelons and donkey dung. Ted's ship finally broke free when the tide rose and the crew had lightened the ship by unloading diesel oil onto a fuel freighter. When the ship arrived in San Juan and needed to refuel, the oil company would not extend Ted credit. It demanded cash. Where could he get cash to fill up the massive ship? He and his crew emptied the bar cash registers and the coins in the slot machines. As they dumped the coins in bags, they realized that the cruise ship had turned into a five-and-dime.

As pathetic as this escapade might sound, note, however, that the registers and slot machines were full! The *Mardi Gras*'s passengers enjoyed their voyage. The festive bartenders even created a new drink, "Mardi Gras on the Rocks." Carnival's younger crowd, paying less money for their voyage, were more forgiving than stodgy traditional dowager passengers would have been. Carnival's current CEO, Bob Dickinson, worked with Ted and Micky in 1973 to devise a new marketing approach. Traditional cruise companies created advertisements and posters highlighting destinations. Instead of emphasizing exotic ports of call, Carnival would emphasize its "fun ships." Because the *Mardi Gras* was 50 percent larger than other ships, it had more room for wacky activities like belly-flop contests, exercise classes, and beer pong.

Like Sam Walton at Wal-Mart, Ted began to exploit the virtues of bigness. He bought and then built from scratch even bigger ships, while growing profits at a 20 percent annual pace. The whole industry began to grow, with passengers rising from about 1 million in the mid-1970s to 2.5 million in the mid-1980s. Ted convinced Americans that bigger ships were more fun and more stable in foul weather. In the meantime, he began to persuade Wall Street that bigger ships achieved economies of scale.

An eighty-thousand-ton ship would hold four times as many passengers as a twenty-thousand-ton ship, but it would not need four times as many captains or engine rooms. Buoyed by surging revenues, in 1987, Ted raised $400 million in a public offering.

Ted's team was known, like Sam Walton's on land, as the toughest negotiators on the seven seas. Somehow they wrangled everything from pineapples to bedsheets at a cheaper price. When Richard Fain took the reins as CEO of archrival Royal Caribbean, he marveled at Carnival's provisioning skills, even as he wrestled with the Arisons in business disputes. (A smooth-mannered Wharton MBA, Fain has successfully captained Royal Caribbean and it's premium-service sister Celebrity Cruises so that his company and Carnival dominate virtually the entire industry.) By controlling costs, the Arisons showed that you could offer cheaper cruises while still earning larger profits than hoity-toity brands. By the 1990s, Carnival's strategy allowed then–CEO Micky to gobble up snobby brands that used to sneer at its perky advertisements starring Kathie Lee Gifford warbling, "Ain't We Got Fun." Micky also brought success to professional basketball, drawing marquee names like Pat Riley and Shaquille O'Neal to Miami, where they could capture the NBA championship. When Ted died in 1999 of a heart attack at age seventy-five, people mourned but did not worry about the company he had created and the industry he had helped to reinvent.

While serving in the White House under the first President Bush, I was asked to give a talk to the CEOs of the cruise industry, including Micky Arison, Richard Fain, the polished and perceptive Peter Ratcliffe from Princess, and others. Each ate at a separate table, and the host asked me to move to a different table for each course of the meal. Why? Did they not get along? Were they afraid of antitrust officials raiding the restaurant? Was each afraid he would get stuck with the whole bill? The host avoided my questions. That evening, moving from table to table, I did learn one thing: these CEOs were competing in a furious way, while creating better bargains *and* better products for their customers. I left before they served the midnight buffet.

People like Sam Walton, Jim Sinegal, and Ted Arison have created the scissors economy. Forget faddish-food diets—the entire world economy is on a low-fat diet, where any extra margin will get snipped. Shoppers

storm into a car dealer and slap invoice prices onto the desks of salesmen, then stride into an electronics store and demand that the company
honor the coupons of its archcompetitor. Ninety years ago, teenage vio-
lin virtuoso Jascha Heifetz was giving a breathtaking recital in New York.
The reigning violinist of the day loosened his collar, turned to his friend,
and said, "Isn't it hot in here?" "Not for pianists," came the reply. It's ex-
cruciatingly hot out there for any middle manager sitting behind his desk
with his legs up. Not for shoppers, thank Sam.

Conclusion: No Roads Ahead

I dare you. Search this book for the solitary secret that will guarantee riches while protecting you from being flung against a wall by competitors. You won't find it. Not because I failed to divulge the lives and lessons of great CEOs, but because I tried to reveal the simple truth about making it big: It does not take a village, a Harvard MBA, or even a rich uncle. It takes passion, an obsession with turning a small idea into a sweeping revolution. A person must bolt out of bed at three o'clock in the morning eager to plot his next move. It also takes some raw talent and a lucky break. Even an unlucky break might work, like David Sarnoff knocking on the wrong door or Akio Morita running out of change at a pay phone, cutting off bad advice from his board of directors.

"One machine can do the work of fifty ordinary men. No machine can do the work of one extraordinary man," Elbert Hubbard wrote. The CEOs in this book proved the point. But by choosing these CEOs, I do not nominate them for sainthood, nor would I call them the "Mozarts of capitalism." If you are looking for Mozart in a corporate boardroom or any other place, I would give up. In my career I have worked at Harvard, the White House, and the most prestigious addresses on Wall Street. Still, I have not found anyone worthy of nicknaming Wolfgang. At best, they are Salieris, just trying to bang out a hummable tune. That's not so bad.

The CEOs whose lives we have explored did have one thing in common. At some point they all tumbled into failure and heard trusted friends whisper, "Quit." Battle-weary Ray Kroc had heard it for thirty years before he found McDonald's. These CEOs knew to ignore pessimists. The son of a tomato picker in California imagined a bigger bank than J. P. Morgan's. A girl from Queens aspired to knock down the hallowed doors of Saks Fifth Avenue, which looked no less intimidating than the doors of Saks's next-door neighbor, St. Patrick's Cathedral. In despair, a Japanese soldier put down his sword just days after Hiroshima, but thought he could win friends in America. The CEOs profiled here ignored the accountants who sneered at their ideas and also the social pundits who sneered at their "American dreams." The twentieth century, for all its bloodshed and turmoil, also brought longer lives and bigger homes and gave even working-class people the chance to travel the world. In the 1890s, when Thomas Watson Sr. hopped on a wagon to escape his little town called Painted Post, life expectancy was just forty-six. Neighbors could not understand why anyone would risk crossing the county line. People knew that the world was not flat, yet they lived as if Columbus had been proved wrong. For the millions who sweated in factories that belched soot, descended into mines without much air, or toiled on farms that turned to dust bowls, life was risky, grievous, and short. Over the next one hundred years, these CEOs helped people become better informed, better paid, and, if you believe Estée Lauder and Mary Kay Ash, better looking, too.

What lies ahead in our young century? Tonight in some attic, garage, or high school laboratory, a midnight light flickers, and some naive young person tugs on her own hair, struggling to push a pet idea one more step ahead. Those who stay up till 3 a.m. might have the right stuff. If you traveled back in time to join Thomas Watson on his horse-drawn wagon ride out of Painted Post or young David Sarnoff on a crowded boat across the heaving Atlantic, you would not spot airplanes, automobiles, radios, televisions, computers, or antibiotics. What road will we take next? As a futuristic movie once put it, "Roads? Where we're going, we don't need roads." [1] We just need people made of the right stuff.

Acknowledgments

I would like to thank Johannes Gutenberg for making this possible. The founders of Google also helped with research. No one helped more than my beautiful and talented wife, Debby, and our remarkable daughters Victoria, Katherine, and Alexia, who kept me smiling while I tried to write two vastly different books at once (this book and the novel *The Castro Gene*), while also revising my first book, *New Ideas from Dead Economists*. All three works are hitting bookstores at the same time, and so that breeze you hear from California is not the Santa Ana wind blowing, but my exhaling a loud "Whew!"

My father, Alvin, taught me a great deal about business. He spent his career working for railroads, for many years in the Pan Am building above New York's Grand Central Station. When I was a kid that building (now bearing Met Life's name) was listed in the Guinness Book of World Records as the world's largest. My brother, Scott; sister, Jill; and I called it "Daddy's building," as if he owned the whole block. He owned our hearts instead. My mother, Joan, continues to inspire us with her wit and awesome energy.

I would also like to tip my metaphoric hat to my wife's grandparents, Maury and Helen, who teach our children so many lessons about life and the pursuit of happiness. Thanks also to my wise agent, Susan Ginsburg, the impeccable taste of David Hathaway from Barnes and Noble, and the team at HarperCollins, including Ethan Friedman, Marion Maneker, and Angie Lee.

To the many great CEOs who are disappointed not to be mentioned in this book, I wish you long life and the hope of a sequel.

Notes

CHAPTER 1. A. P. GIANNINI:
BANK OF AMERICA—THE GLADIATOR OF BANKING

1. Gerald D. Nash, *A. P. Giannini and the Bank of America* (Norman: University of Oklahoma Press, 1992), p. 10.
2. Giovanni Federico, "Heights, Calories, and Welfare: A New Perspective on Italian Industrialization, 1854–1913," *Journal of Economics and Human Biology* 1 (2003), p. 291.
3. Nash, p. 14.
4. Felice Bonadio, *A. P. Giannini: Banker of America* (Berkeley: University of California Press, 1994), pp. 9–14.
5. Nash, p. 13.
6. See Todd G. Buchholz, "Benefactors of Great Wealth," *New York Times Book Review,* October 2, 2005, p. 24.
7. *It's a Wonderful Life,* directed by Frank Capra (1946).
8. For a primer on monetary policy, see Todd G. Buchholz, *From Here to Economy* (New York: Dutton, 1995), pp. 54–56.
9. Marquis James and Bessie R. James, *Biography of a Bank: The Story of Bank of America NT & SA, 1904–1953* (San Francisco: BankAmerica Corporation, 1982), p. 310.
10. Len Benham, "The Effect of Advertising on the Price of Eyeglasses," *Journal of Law and Economics* 15 (October 1972), pp. 337–352.

11. You may also thank Charles Schwab. I would also give thanks to John Bogle of Vanguard for driving down mutual fund prices. See my review of his book in "Dollars and Damnation," *Wall Street Journal,* October 15, 2005.

12. Paul Rink, *A. P. Giannini: Building the Bank of America* (Chicago: Encyclopaedia Britannica Press, 1963), p. 48.

13. Ibid., p. 49.

14. See Alan Greenspan, "Consumer Credit and Financial Modernization," Federal Reserve Board, October 11, 1997. www.federalreserve.gov/boarddocs/speeches/1997/19971011.htm.

15. Nash, p. 43.

16. Quoted by William Haraf, "Democratizing Financial Institutions," Milken Institute, June 1–2, 1998, p. 11. www.milkeninstitute.org/pdf/dem_cap_round table3.pdf.

17. Nash, p. 70.

18. Ibid., p. 32.

19. Chapin Hill, "Daily Trade Talk," *Los Angeles Times,* November 28, 1922.

20. House of Representatives, Hearings before the Committee on Banking and Currency, 71st Congress vol. 2, part 2, 1930, p. 1341.

21. See ibid., pp. 1547, 1556; James and James; and Bonadio.

22. Mark Carlson and Kris James Mitchener, "Branch Banking and the Transformation of Banking in California," May 2005, table 5. www.e.u-tokyo.ac.jp/cemano/research/DRSS/documents/mitchener.pdf.

23. Ibid., pp. 4, 23.

24. Milton Friedman pointed to this in his classic *A Monetary History of the United States, 1867–1960,* written with Anna J. Schwartz (Princeton, N.J.: Princeton University Press, 1963); see also Kris Mitchener, "Bank Supervision, Regulation, and Instability During the Great Depression," *Journal of Economic History,* 65, no. 1 (2005).

25. Rink, p. 147.

26. Christopher Palmeri, "For Korean Banks, Truly a Golden State" *Business Week,* February 17, 2003.

27. E. Scott Reckard, "Crop of New Banks Takes Root in Niches," *Los Angeles Times,* November 29, 2006.

28. Quoted in "Financing California's Future," *State of the State,* Milken Institute, November 6, 2001, p. 25. Incidentally, I own some common shares in East West Bancorp, though I have never had any contact with management.

CHAPTER 2. THOMAS WATSON SR. AND JR.:
IBM—A TALE OF TWO WATSONS

1. Thomas J. Watson Jr. and Peter Petrie, *Father, Son & Co.: My Life at IBM and Beyond* (New York: Bantam, 1990), p. 213.

2. Thomas Graham Belden and Marva Robins Belden, *The Lengthening Shadow: The Life of Thomas J. Watson* (Boston: Little, Brown, 1962), pp. 5–11.

3. Watson and Petrie, p. 9.

4. See Walter A. Friedman, "John H. Patterson and the Sales Strategy of the National Cash Register Company, 1884 to 1922," *Business History Review* 72, no. 4 (Winter 1998), pp. 552–584; and Richard S. Tedlow's discussion of NCR's John Patterson in his insightful *Giants of Enterprise* (New York: HarperCollins, 2001), pp. 199–206.

5. Samuel Crowther, *John H. Patterson* (Garden City, NY: Garden City Publishing, 1926), p. 136.

6. William H. Rodgers, *Think: A Biography of the Watsons and IBM* (New York: Stein and Day, 1969), p. 38.

7. Richard S. Tedlow, *The Watson Dynasty* (New York: HarperBusiness, 2003), p. 25.

8. Belden and Belden, pp. 19–20.

9. Watson and Petrie, p. 79.

10. Jean Strouse, *Morgan* (New York: Random House, 1999), p. 5.

11. Video clips of the flood can be seen at www.ohiohistory.org/etcetera/exhibits/swio/pages/content/1913_flood.htm.

12. Belden and Belden, p. 93.

13. For data on how the century turned out, see Theodore Caplow, Louis Hicks, and Ben J. Wattenberg, *The First Measured Century* (Washington, D.C.: American Enterprise Institute, 2000).

14. Lou Mobley and Kate McKeown, *Beyond IBM* (New York: McGraw-Hill, 1989), p. 5.

15. Gerald Breckenridge, "Market-Marker: IBM's Watson Proves He's Still Salesman No. 1," *Saturday Evening Post,* May 31, 1941, p. 41.

16. Emerson W. Pugh, *Building IBM* (Cambridge, MA: MIT Press, 1995), p. 248.

17. Watson and Petrie, p. 33.

18. Rowena Olegario, "IBM and the Two Thomas J. Watsons," in Thomas K. McCraw, ed., *Creating Modern Capitalism* (Cambridge, MA: Harvard University Press, 1997), p. 372.

19. Ibid., table 10.4.

20. Watson and Petrie, p. 31.

21. Ibid., p. 7.

22. Ibid., p. 63.

23. Ibid., p. 96.

24. Richard P. Feynman, "Los Alamos from Below," First Annual Santa Barbara Lectures on Science and Society, given at the University of California at Santa Barbara in 1975. In 2001, author Edwin Black wrote a book called *IBM and the Holocaust,* which outlined how the Nazi regime used IBM equipment in its persecution of Jews and others. Though Thomas J. Watson Sr. had met Hitler before the war and even received a medal from him, Watson repudiated the award and any ties to the Nazis.

25. Michael Korda, *Power! How to Get It, How to Use It* (New York: Ballantine, 1975).

26. www.choiceartwork.com/shop/index.php?page=shop-flypage-10111467.

27. Watson and Petrie, p. 269.

28. Ibid., p. 273.

29. Pugh, p. 237.

30. See Malcolm Gladwell, "No Mercy," *New Yorker,* September 4, 2006, pp. 37–38.

31. See David Mercer, *The Global IBM* (New York: Dodd, Mead, 1988), p. 49.

32. T. A. Wise, "The $5,000,000,000 Gamble," *Fortune,* September 1966, p. 118.

33. See "The IBM 360: Giant as Entrepreneur," Harvard Business School case study 9-389-003 (April 1, 1998), p. 7.

34. The truest and ultimately most frustrating sign of success was an antitrust lawsuit leveled by the federal government on the last day of the Johnson administration and dropped in 1982. IBM's files included a lawyer's bill for a twenty-seven-hour day. The lawyer flew to the West Coast during the day and caught an additional three hours of time to charge to the company.

35. Olegario, p. 370.

MARY KAY ASH AND ESTÉE LAUDER:
THE MOST BEAUTIFUL BALANCE SHEET

1. Todd G. Buchholz, *Bringing the Jobs Home* (New York: Penguin, 2004), p. 57.

2. A'Lelia Perry Bundles, *Madam C. J. Walker: Entrepreneur* (New York: Chelsea House, 1991), p. 35.

3. "Wealthiest Negro Woman's Suburban Mansion: Estate at Irvington, Overlooking Hudson and Containing All the Attractions That a Big Fortune Commands," *New York Times Magazine,* November 4, 1917.

CHAPTER 3. MARY KAY ASH:
THE BILLION DOLLAR COFFEE KLATSCH

1. "Mary Kay Ash," *Journal of Business Leadership* 1, no. 1 (Spring 1988), p. 1.
2. Gilbert Vail, *A History of Cosmetics in America* (New York: Toilet Goods Association, 1947), p. 138.
3. U.S. Bureau of Labor Statistics, "100 Years of U.S. Consumer Spending," May 2006, p. 5; Todd G. Buchholz, "Burgers, Fries, and Lawyers," *Policy Review,* no. 123 (February–March 2004), p. 47.
4. Lola Montez, *The Arts of Beauty, or, Secrets of a Lady's Toilet with Hints to Gentlemen on the Art of Fascination* (1858), (New York: Ecco, 1982)
5. Buchholz, "Burgers, Fries, and Lawyers," p. 50.
6. Mary Kay Ash, *Miracles Happen* (New York: HarperCollins, 1994), p. 48.
7. Ibid., p. 17.
8. "Pink Cadillacs, Diamond Bumblebees, and the Golden Rule," *Positive Living Magazine,* November 1979, p. 5.
9. James Dyson and Robert Uhlig, eds, *A History of Great Inventions* (New York: Carroll-Graf, 2001), p. 163.
10. Mary Kay Ash, p. xi.
11. "Pink Cadillacs," p. 6.
12. Roul Tunley, "Mary Kay's Sweet Smell of Success," *Reader's Digest,* November 1978, p. 5.
13. *Journal of Business Leadership,* p. 8.
14. Anne Coughlan, "Mary Kay Inc.," Kellogg School of Management, KEL034 (2004), p. 6.
15. Max Weber, "The Nature of Charismatic Authority and Its Routinization," in *The Theory of Social and Economic Organization,* translated by A. M. Henderson and Talcot Parsons (1947). (New York: Oxford University Press, 1947).
16. Morton Walker, *The Power of Color* (New York: Avery, 1991), pp. 50–52.
17. Jim Underwood, *More Than a Pink Cadillac* (New York: McGraw-Hill, 2003), p. 93.
18. "Mary Kay Cosmetics, Inc.," Harvard Business School, case 9-481-126 (January 1, 1981), p. 3.
19. Howard N. Fullerton Jr., "Labor Force Participation: 75 Years of Change," *Monthly Labor Review* 22, no. 12 (December 1999), p. 4.
20. "AARP Announces 2006 Best Employers for Workers Over 50," *Aging Workforce News,* September 1, 2006.

CHAPTER 4. ESTÉE LAUDER: EVEN THE RICH LIKE FREEBIES

1. Estée Lauder, *Estée* (New York: Random House, 1985), p. 4.
2. Ibid., p. 7.
3. See Alan Deutscheman, "The Carp in the Bathtub," Salon.com, April 10, 2001. http://dir.salon.com/story/mwt/sust/2001/04/10/gefilte_fish/?pn=1.
4. See Nancy F. Koehn, "Estée Lauder and the Market for Prestige Cosmetics," Harvard Business School, case 9-801-362, p. 4, and Nancy F. Koehn, *Brand New: How Entrepreneurs Earned Consumers' Trust from Wedgwood to Dell* (Boston: Harvard Business School Press, 2001), p. 156.
5. Lee Israel, *Estée Lauder: Beyond the Magic* (New York: Macmillan, 1985), p. 14.
6. Lauder, p. 14.
7. Koehn, "Estée Lauder," p. 5.
8. Israel, p. 21.
9. Lauder, p. 39.
10. Linda M. Scott, *Fresh Lipstick* (New York: Palgrave Macmillan, 2004), p. 222.
11. "Is Beauty Worth Half a Billion?" *New York Times Magazine,* December 20, 1942, p. 25.
12. See Michael Spence, "Signaling in Retrospect and the Informational Structure of Markets," *American Economic Review* 92, no. 3, (2002), pp. 434–459.
13. Israel, p. 31.
14. Lauder, p. 50.
15. Ibid., p. 115.
16. "A Prune by Another Name Sells Better," *Nation's Restaurant News,* February 18, 2002. http://findarticles.com/p/articles/mi_m3190/is_7_36/ai_83247518.
17. The following link will take you to a study by the U.S. Department of Agriculture entitled "The U.S. and World Situation: Pistachios": www.fas.usda.gov/htp/Hort_Circular/2005/Charts%20Circluar/2005%20Pistachios.pdf.
18. Marian Burros, "The Fish That Swam Upstream," *New York Times,* May 16, 2001.
19. Shoinn Freeman, "The Rap on Detroit," *Wall Street Journal,* September 2004, http://wsjclassroom.com/archive/04sep/mktg_rap.htm.
20. Lisa Belkin, "The Makeover at Estée Lauder," *New York Times,* November 29, 1987.
21. Richard Severo, "Estée Lauder, Pursuer of Beauty and Cosmetics Titan, Dies at 97," *New York Times,* April 26, 2004.

CHAPTER 5. DAVID SARNOFF: THE ROAD TO 30 ROCK

1. George and Ira Gershwin, "They All Laughed" (1937).
2. Kenneth Bilby, *The General* (New York: Harper & Row, 1986), p. 12.
3. www.davidsarnoff.org/gallery-ds/Sarnoff_family.htm.
4. I saw Kandinsky's *Cossacks 1910–11* at London's Tate Modern Museum in 2006. The museum's curator skillfully traced Kandinsky's political trajectory from anticzarist to anticommunist.
5. Bilby, p. 15.
6. Henry J. Browne, *One Stop Above Hell's Kitchen: Sacred Heart Parish in Clinton* (New Brunswick: Rutgers University Press, 1977).
7. Bilby, p. 25.
8. Tom Lewis, *Empire of the Air* (New York: HarperCollins, 1991), p. 105.
9. Bilby, p. 33.
10. "Wireless for Railroad Trains," *Scientific American,* December 6, 1913.
11. Lewis, p. 113.
12. "I have in mind a plan of development which would make radio a 'household utility' in the same sense as the piano or phonograph. The idea is to bring music into the house by wireless.

    "While this has been tried in the past by wires, it has been a failure because wires do not lend themselves to this scheme. With radio, however, it would seem to be entirely feasible. For example—a radio telephone transmitter having a range of say 25 to 50 miles can be installed at a fixed point where instrumental or vocal music or both are produced. The problem of transmitting music has already been solved in principle and therefore all the receivers attuned to the transmitting wave length should be capable of receiving such music. The receiver can be designed in the form of a simple 'Radio Music Box' and arranged for several different wave lengths, which should be changeable with the throwing of a single switch or pressing of a single button.

    "The 'Radio Music Box' can be supplied with amplifying tubes and a loudspeaking telephone, all of which can be neatly mounted in one box. The box can be placed on a table in the parlor or living room, the switch set accordingly and the transmitted music received. There should be no difficulty in receiving music perfectly when transmitted within a radius of 25 to 50 miles. Within such a radius there reside hundreds of thousands of families; and as all can simultaneously receive from a single transmitter, there would be no question of obtaining sufficiently loud signals to make the performance enjoyable. The power of the transmitter can be made 5 k.w., if necessary, to cover even a short radius of 25 to 50 miles; thereby giving extra loud signals in the home if desired. The use of head telephones would be obviated by this method. The development of a small loop antenna to go with each 'Radio Music Box' would likewise solve the antennae problem.

"The same principle can be extended to numerous other fields as, for example, receiving lectures at home which can be made perfectly audible; also events of national importance can be simultaneously announced and received. Baseball scores can be transmitted in the air by the use of one set installed at the Polo Grounds. The same would be true of other cities. This proposition would be especially interesting to farmers and others living in outlying districts removed from cities. By the purchase of a 'Radio Music Box' they could enjoy concerts, lectures, music, recitals, etc., which may be going on in the nearest city within their radius. While I have indicated a few of the most probable fields of usefulness for such a device, yet there are numerous other fields to which the principle can be extended. . . .

"The manufacture of the 'Radio Music Box' including antenna, in large quantities, would make possible their sale at a moderate figure of perhaps $75.00 per outfit. The main revenue to be derived will be from the sale of 'Radio Music Boxes' which if manufactured in quantities of one hundred thousand or so could yield a handsome profit when sold at the price mentioned above. Secondary sources of revenue would be from the sale of transmitters and from increased advertising and circulation of the *Wireless Age*. The Company would have to undertake the arrangements, I am sure, for music recitals, lectures, etc., which arrangements can be satisfactorily worked out. It is not possible to estimate the total amount of business obtainable with this plan until it has been developed and actually tried out but there are about 15,000,000 families in the United States alone and if only one million or 7% of the total families thought well of the idea it would, at the figure mentioned, mean a gross business of about $75,000,000 which should yield considerable revenue.

"Aside from the profit to be derived from this proposition the possibilities for advertising for the Company are tremendous; for its name would ultimately be brought into the household and wireless would receive national and universal attention." (Gleason Archer, *History of Radio to 1926* [1936; repr., New York: American Historical Society, 1971]) pp. 110–113.

13. See Louise Benjamin, "In Search of the Sarnoff 'Radio Music Box' Memo: Nolly's Reply," *Journal of Radio Studies* 9, no. 1 (2002), pp. 97–106.

14. "CBS Q3 Down, but Dividends Near," *Hollywood Reporter*, November 3, 2006.

15. Woodrow Wilson, speech in Des Moines, Iowa, Coliseum, September 6, 1919.

16. Carly Fiorina's book is *Tough Choice* (New York: Portfolio, 2006). Also see Joe Nocera, "Carly Fiorina's Revisionist Chronicles," *New York Times,* October 14, 2006.

17. In fact, Dempsey received a domestic exemption in order to support his family. See Randy Roberts, *Jack Dempsey: The Manassa Mauler* (New York: Grove Press, 1979), pp. 103, 112.

18. Ibid., p. 115.

19. AT&T would not actually allow a direct line from the ring to the broadcast transmitter. RCA improvised by having the announcer's voice "jump" from one telephone to another that was placed next to it. By creating this loophole, RCA diluted the sound quality, but managed to confound AT&T. See J. Andrew White, "The First Big Broadcast," *Reader's Digest,* December 1955, pp. 81–85.

20. A photograph of the rolling chair can be seen at www.eht.com/oldradio/arrl/2002-06/Dempsey.htm.

21. Daniel Stashower, *The Boy Genius and the Mogul* (New York: Broadway Books, 2002), p. 79.

22. www.youtube.com/watch?v=zjsJnu63AQQ.

23. Bilby, p. 88.

24. www.pbs.org/speak/images/radio1940.jpg.

25. Although the sign was replaced by GE in 1988, many New Yorkers still point tourists to the "RCA Building."

26. See Peter N. Golder and Gerard J. Tellis, "Pioneer Advantage: Marketing Logic or Marketing Legend?" *Journal of Marketing Research* 30, no. 2 (May 1993), pp. 158–170.

27. Sorkin's play is consistent with Stashower's view in *The Boy Genius and the Mogul.*

28. Bilby, p. 118.

29. See footage at www.youtube.com/watch?v=fVLejeO707Q.

30. See Lewis, pp. 292–294.

31. David E. Fisher and Marshall Jon Fisher, "The Color War," *Invention and Technology Magazine,* Winter 1997, vol. 12, issue 3, p. 18.

32. www.time.com/time/magazine/article/0,9171,824531-1,00.html.

33. Bilby, p. 198.

34. Leslie Wayne, "Boeing Not Afraid to Say 'Sold Out,'" *New York Times,* November 28, 2006.

35. Max Kingsley-Jones, "Strong Airbus Sales for 2006 Belie 'Absolute Mess' Tou-

louse's Top Salesman Leahy Admits Company Is In," *Flight International,* November 28, 2006.

36. "A380 Superjumbo: The White Elephant" *Belfast Telegraph,* November 22, 2006.

37. Barbara S. Peterson, "Jumbo Trouble: The Airbus A380 Was Supposed to Be the Future of Aviation. Will It Ever Get Off the Ground?" *Popular Mechanics,* December 2006, www.popularmechanics.com/science/air_space/4201627.html.

CHAPTER 6. RAY KROC:
MCDONALD'S—KING OF THE ROAD

1. Saul Bellow, *The Adventures of Augie March* (New York: Penguin, 1953), p. 3.

2. Ray Kroc with Robert Anderson, *Grinding It Out* (New York: St. Martin's, 1977), p. 20.

3. Ibid., p. 19.

4. Amy Zuber, "McD-Disney Marketing Alliance Grows with Burger Invasion Concept's Debut," *Nation's Restaurant News,* January 22, 2001.

5. Kroc with Anderson, p. 34.

6. Ibid., p. 39.

7. Ibid., p. 43.

8. Marriott was inspired to sell cold root beer by the blistering humid heat of Washington, D.C., summers. See Robert O'Brien, *Marriott: The J. W. Marriott Story* (Salt Lake City: Deseret Book Company, 1977), p. 87.

9. For an entertaining look at cooking during wartime, see Joanne Lamb Hayes, *Grandma's Wartime Kitchen* (New York: St. Martin's, 2000).

10. See Andrew Schmitz and Douglas Christian, "The Economics and Politics of U.S. Sugar Policy," in Stephen V. Marks and Keith E. Maskus, *The Economics and Politics of World Sugar Policies* (Ann Arbor: University of Michigan Press, 1993), p. 49.

11. For a fun history of kitchen appliances, see Charles Panata, *Panati's Extraordinary Origins of Everyday Things* (New York: HarperCollins, 1989), p. 96.

12. Kroc with Anderson, p. 8.

13. John F. Love, *McDonalds: Behind the Arches* (New York: Bantam, 1986), p. 19.

14. Ibid., p. 40.

15. Ibid., p. 70.

16. Ibid., p. 118.

17. Roger D. Blair and Francine Lafontaine, *The Economics of Franchising* (New York: Cambridge University Press, 2005), pp. 126, 120, 175.

18. U.S. Department of Agriculture, Economic Research Service, "The Economics of Food, Farming, Natural Resources, and Rural America," 2004.

19. Cited in John Mariani, *America Eats Out* (Boston: William Morrow, 1991). A study also showed that more people in the U.S., Europe, India, and Japan recognized the Golden Arches than the Christian cross, by 88 percent to 54 percent: "Golden Arches More Familiar Than the Cross," *Cleveland Plain Dealer,* August 26, 1995.

20. Leva M. Augstums, "Sales Go Stale for Krispy Kreme," Association Press, November 3, 2006.

21. Kroc with Anderson, pp. 185–186.

CHAPTER 7. AKIO MORITA:
SONY—THE SOUND OF THE PEOPLE

1. See Albert Axell and Kase Hideaki, *Kamikze: Japan's Suicide Gods* (New York: Longman, 2002).

2. Robert J. C. Butow, *Japan's Decision to Surrender* (Stanford, CA: Stanford University Press, 1954), p. 176.

3. Donald Roden, "Baseball and the Quest for National Dignity in Meiji Japan," *American Historical Review* 85, no. 3 (June 1980), p. 511

4. Akio Morita with Edwin M. Reingold and Mitsuko Shimomura, *Made in Japan* (New York: Dutton, 1986), p. 17.

5. From the Mandarin Chinese *gonghe,* an abbreviation for a workers' cooperative.

6. Morita, et al., p. 26.

7. John Nathan, *Sony* (Boston: Houghton Mifflin, 1999), p. 36.

8. Ibid., p. 2.

9. See, for example, John W. Dower, *Embracing Defeat: Japan in the Wake of World War II* (New York: Norton, 1999).

10. Morita et al., p. 53.

11. See Austin Osueke, "J-Pop Is the Quiet Storm in American Culture," *Asian Week,* July 7, 2006; John Edward Hasse, ed., *Jazz: The First Century* (New York: William Morrow, 2000).

12. Ronald Gilson and Mark Roe, "Understanding the Japanese Keiretsu," *Yale Law Journal* 102 (1993), p. 884.

13. See Alfred Marshall, *Principles of Economics,* 9th ed. (1920; London: Macmillan, 1961), vol. 1, pp. 587–588.

14. Kenji Kawakami et al., *101 Useless Japanese Inventions: The Art of Chindōgu* (New York: Norton, 1995).

15. Morita et al., p. 65.
16. See John DeFrancis, "Politics and Phonetics," *Far Eastern Survey* 16, no. 19 (November 5, 1947), p. 220, and John DeFrancis, *The Chinese Language: Fact and Fantasy* (Honolulu: University of Hawai'i Press, 1984), p. 216.
17. For some amusing examples, see Danny Gregory, *Change Your Underwear Twice a Week: Lessons from the Golden Age of Classroom Filmstrip* (New York: Artisan Publishers, 1984).
18. Peter Ross Range, "Akio Morita Interview," *Playboy,* August 1982., p. 18.
19. *The Analects of Confucius,* book 7, chap. 1, trans. Arthur Waley (New York: Vintage; 1938); see also William Alford, *To Steal a Book Is an Elegant Offense* (Stanford; CA: Stanford University Press, 1997).
20. "World Leader in Patents Concentrates in Incremental Innovations," *Financial Times Special Report,* October 12, 2005.
21. Jennifer Saranow, "U.S. Cars Slip in Durability Study," *Wall Street Journal,* August 10, 2006.
22. Nathan, p. 31; Morita et al., p. 75.
23. Morita et al., p. 93.
24. Ibid., p. 101.
25. Nathan, p. 80.
26. Sea-Jin Chang and Philip M. Rosenzweig, "A Process Model for MNC Evolution: The Case of the Sony Corporation in the United States," Institute for Applied Studies in International Management, Working Paper 95–9 (1995).
27. Quoted in Naoyuki Agawa, "Akio Morita's American Dream," *Gaiko Forum: Journal of Japanese Perspectives on Diplomacy* (Tokyo: Toshi Shuppan, 2000).
28. See Robert Lutz, *Guts* (New York: John Wiley & Sons, 1998).
29. www.edmunds.com/40thanniversary/index.html.
30. Nancy Griffin and Kim Masters, *Hit and Run: How Jon Peters and Peter Guber Took Sony for a Ride in Hollywood* (New York: Simon & Schuster, 1996).
31. Loren Gary, "Where Does the Competitive Advantage Lie?" *Harvard Management Update* 7, no. 7 (July 2002).
32. Eric von Hippel, *Democratizing Innovation* (Boston: MIT Press, 2005); Chris Anderson, *The Long Tail* (New York: Hyperion, 2006), p. 79
33. David Pogue, "iPod's Law: The Impossible Is Possble," *New York Times,* September 15, 2005 at www.nytimes.com/2005/09/15/technology/circuits/15pogue.html?ex=1284436800&en=e0f5c2e60bdd20f2&ei=5090.

CHAPTER 8. WALT DISNEY:
DISNEY—THE IMAGINATION MACHINE

1. Quoted in Steven Watts, *The Magic Kingdom* (Columbia: University of Missouri Press, 1997), p. 18.
2. Ibid., p. 9.
3. Ibid., p. 20.
4. Marc Eliot, *Walt Disney* (New York: Birch Lane Press, 1993), p. 9.
5. Walt Disney, "I Have Always Loved Trains," *Railroad,* October 1965.
6. Watts, p. 15.
7. Bob Thomas, *Walt Disney: An American Original* (New York: Simon and Schuster, 1976), p. 71.
8. "Biographical Sketch of Walt Disney," released by RKO, 1937.
9. Quoted in Watts, p. 44.
10. In our chapter on Akio Morita, we see Sony's cofounder turning down a fast buck from the Bulova watch company because it would hinder Sony's independent growth.
11. Walt Disney, "The Cartoon's Contribution to Children," *Overland Monthly and Out West Magazine,* October 1933, p. 138.
12. Quoted in Watts, p. 253.
13. "The Walt Disney Family Museum," Walt Disney Online. http://disney.go.com/disneyatoz/familymuseum/collection/biography/sillysymphonies/index.html.
14. Michael G. Rukstad and David Collis, "The Walt Disney Company: The Entertainment King," Harvard Business School case study, 9-701-035, September 1, 2005.
15. David Smith and Steven B. Clark, Disney: The First 100 Years (New York: Disney, 1999). 101.
16. Frank Nugent, "That Million Dollar Mouse," *New York Times Magazine,* September 21, 1947, p. 61.
17. "Walt Disney Puts Soap in the Movies," *Soap,* December 1, 1937, p. 34.
18. A few years ago, I took my family to Pinocchio Park, in a village called Collodi, outside Florence. It's worth a visit with children to remind them of the European roots of so many Disney tales.
19. Lillian Disney, "I Live with a Genius," *McCall's,* February 1953, pp. 38–41.
20. Steve Jobs, "You've Got to Find What You Love, Jobs Says," *Stanford Report,* June 12, 2005.
21. "The Walt Disney Family Museum," Walt Disney Online. http://disney.go.com/disneyatoz/familymuseum/collection/insidestory/inside_1946c.html.

22. Quoted in Watts, p. 367.

23. Walt Disney, "The Storyteller and the Educator," *Television Quarterly,* Spring 1957, p. 5.

24. Quoted in "Growing Impact of the Disney Art," cover story of *Newsweek,* April 18, 1955, p. 62.

25. See Friedrich Nietzsche, *The Birth of Tragedy.*

26. Nina Munk, *Fools Rush In* (New York: HarperCollins, 2004).

27. Jim Hu, "Case Accepts Blame for AOL–Time Warner Debacle," CNETNews. com, January 12, 2005.

28. Of course, many Internet media companies saw their prices collapse, but remember that the AOL–Time Warner merger came together in early 2001, almost a year after the bubble started bursting.

CHAPTER 9. SAM WALTON: WAL-MART—A PENNY SAVED IS A BILLION EARNED

1. The robber baron myth has finally been revised so that Rockefeller and Carnegie look less dastardly. See my "Benefactors of Great Wealth," *New York Times,* October 2, 2005, p. 24.

2. Bob Ortega, *In Sam We Trust* (New York: Random House, 1998), p. 18.

3. Sam Walton with John Huey, *Sam Walton: Made in America* (New York: Bantam, 1993), p. 5.

4. Ibid., p. 86.

5. Michael Bergdahl, *What I Learned from Sam Walton* (New York: John Wiley & Sons, 2004), p. 63.

6. Ibid., p. 7.

7. Walton with Huey, p. 81.

8. Ibid., p. 39.

9. Don Soderquist, *The Wal-Mart Way* (Nashville: Nelson, 2005), p. 156.

10. See Mordechai E. Kreinin and Charles A. Lininger, "Ownership and Purchases of New Cars in the United States," *International Economic Review* 4, no. 3 (September 1963), pp. 310–324.

11. Walton with Huey, p. 102.

12. Sandra Stinger Vance and Roy V. Scott, *Wal-Mart* (Twayne, 1997), p. 43.

13. Adam Smith, *An Inquiry into the Nature and Causes of the Wealth of Nations,* R.H. Campbell, A. S. Skinner, and W. B. Todd, eds, 2 vols. (Oxford, UK: Clarendon Press, 1976 [1776]), vol. 1, p. 26–27.

14. John Huey, "Wal-Mart: Will It Take Over the World?" *Fortune,* January 30, 1989, p. 56.

15. Soderquist, p. 96.

16. Ibid., p. 167.

17. Lucas Conley, "De-Constructing Wal-Mart's Wonder Truck," *Fast Company,* May 2006, p. 32.

18. Matthew Boyle, "Why Costco Is So Damn Addictive," *Fortune,* October 30, 2006, p. 128.

19. Bradley C. Johnson, "Retail: The Wal-Mart Effect," *McKinsey Quarterly,* no. 1 (2002).

20. Kelly Baron, "Spamouflage and Cajun Crawtator," Forbes.com, October 29, 2001. www.forbes.com/forbes/2001/1029/085.html.

21. Bob Dickinson and Andy Vladimir, *Selling the Sea* (New York: John Wiley & Sons, 1997), p. 23.

22. Kristoffer A. Garrin, *Devils of the Deep Blue Sea* (New York: Viking, 2005), p. 71.

CONCLUSION: NO ROADS AHEAD

1. *Back to the Future,* directed by Robert Zemeckis (1985).

Index